The Mythic Indian

The Mythic Indian: The Native in French and Québécois Cultural Imaginaries charts a genealogy of French and Québécois visions of the Amerindian.

Tracing an evolution of paradigms from the sixteenth century to present, it examines how the myths of the Noble, Ignoble, and Ecological Savage as well as the Vanishing Indian and Going Native inform a variety of discourses and ways of thinking about Québécois culture. By analyzing mythic depictions of the Native Figure that originate at first contacts, this book demonstrates that an inextricable link exists between discourses as disparate as literature and science.

This book will be of interest to scholars in French Studies, Francophone Studies, Indigenous Studies, Hemispheric Studies, Social Sciences, and Literary Studies.

James Boucher is an Assistant Professor of French at Rutgers University-Camden, USA, where he also serves as Director of French and Global Studies. His research focuses on Indigenous peoples, ecocriticism, and globalization.

Routledge Research in Transnational Indigenous Perspectives
Series editors: Birgit Däwes, Karsten Fitz and Sabine N. Meyer

Routledge Research in Transnational Indigenous Perspectives features scholarly work exploring both indigenous perspectives that are explicitly transnational and transnational perspectives on indigenous topics. As such, it is committed to fostering and presenting high-quality research in the area of Indigenous Studies, addressing historical and contemporary political, social, economic, and cultural issues concerning the indigenous peoples of North and South America, Europe, Australasia, and the larger Pacific region. The series is thus not limited to one particular methodological approach, but looks at the highly dynamic and growing field of Indigenous Studies that is of central interest for a range of different disciplines.

Members of the series' advisory board include Chadwick Allen (Ohio State University); Philip J. Deloria (University of Michigan); Christian Feest (em., Johann-Wolfgang Goethe University Frankfurt); Hsinya Huang (National Sun Yat-Sen University).

The series considers contributions from a wide range of areas in the field of Indigenous Studies. These include but are not limited to:

- Indigenous literatures, film, performance, music and visual arts
- Indigenous peoples and the law, settler imperialism, rights and human rights
- Indigenous histories, politics, knowledges and religion
- Representations of indigenous peoples in non-indigenous cultural productions
- Indigenous peoples and the museum
- Indigenous languages
- Gender/*Queer* Indigenous Studies
- Transnational flows of indigenous ideas and cultures
- Methodological issues in Indigenous Studies

The Mythic Indian
The Native in French and Québécois Cultural Imaginaries
James Boucher

For more information on this series, please visit https://www.routledge.com/Routledge-Research-in-Transnational-Indigenous-Perspectives/book-series/RRTIP

The Mythic Indian
The Native in French and Québécois
Cultural Imaginaries

James Boucher

NEW YORK AND LONDON

First published 2024
by Routledge
605 Third Avenue, New York, NY 10158

and by Routledge
4 Park Square, Milton Park, Abingdon, Oxon, OX14 4RN

Routledge is an imprint of the Taylor & Francis Group, an informa business

© 2024 James Boucher

The right of James Boucher to be identified as author of this work has been asserted in accordance with sections 77 and 78 of the Copyright, Designs and Patents Act 1988.

All rights reserved. No part of this book may be reprinted or reproduced or utilised in any form or by any electronic, mechanical, or other means, now known or hereafter invented, including photocopying and recording, or in any information storage or retrieval system, without permission in writing from the publishers.

Trademark notice: Product or corporate names may be trademarks or registered trademarks, and are used only for identification and explanation without intent to infringe.

ISBN: 9781032625959 (hbk)
ISBN: 9781032638768 (pbk)
ISBN: 9781032638751 (ebk)

DOI: 10.4324/9781032638751

Typeset in Times New Roman
by codeMantra

Contents

	Introduction: Mythmaking: How the West (Was) "Won"?	1
1	Mythic Origins and the Origins of Myth	12
2	Voltaire, La Condamine, and Buffon: Fabricating Fact and (Science) Fiction	45
3	The Vanishing Indian: Manifest and Imperial Destinies	79
4	Going Native: The Myth of Being Indian	119
5	Voices in Francophone Indigenous Literature: A History and Future of Native American Literature	168
	Index	*219*

Introduction
Mythmaking: How the West (Was) "Won"?

Europeans came and what happened? How could this genocide have happened? Why does it continue to happen in the guise of settler-colonialism throughout the Western hemisphere in the twenty-first century? Although it may not seem like a likely place to go looking for answers to these complex questions concerning contact between the *Old* and the *New* Worlds, literature can tell us something significant about what happened and what continues to happen today. Texts that represent Native peoples inform European populations about what Amerindians and American geographies *signify*. For example, Europeans' territorial claims are based on Western mythic constructs such as *terra nullius*, which Glen Sean Coulthard (Yellowknife Dene) defines as a "racist legal fiction that declared Indigenous peoples too "primitive" to bear rights to land and sovereignty when they first encountered European powers on the continent" (212). These legal fictions are anteceded by mythic paradigms that position the Native as "primitive". These structures delineate how Europeans understand and interact with the Indigenous peoples of the Americas. Representations, and the epistemological choices inherent in narratives, greatly affect praxis.

Indigenous peoples reject these mythic definitions. They do not recognize the rationality behind the myth's skewed semantics. Resisting the logic of the mythic is nearly always related to land and sovereignty. Taiaiake Alfred (Mohawk) underscores the intricate symbiosis between culture, community, and the land in Amerindian interpretations of identity and governance. Alfred states that, "Land, culture, and government are inseparable in traditional philosophies; each depends on the others, and this means that the denial of one aspect precludes recovery for the whole" (25–6). Alfred situates his conception of a non-coopted Native sovereignty as "rooted in indigenous ground" (22). While myth, wielded as a narrative technology, participates in the atrocities of genocide and dispossession, it is through sovereignty and renewed connection to the land that "recovery" is possible for contemporary Indigenous peoples. Many Native authors articulate a uniquely "indigenous relationship to, appreciation for, awareness of, or understanding of the land that is significantly different from non-Indian relationships" (Schweninger, Introduction). These Indigenous

DOI: 10.4324/9781032638751-1

2   Introduction: Mythmaking: How the West (Was) "Won"?

writers pinpoint a clear epistemological clash between Western and Indigenous conceptions of land and its stewardship. While the Western perspective is informed by the mythic paradigms discussed throughout this book, culminating in the depredations of late liberal capitalism, the Native viewpoint is grounded in what Alfred distinguishes as common to Native attitudes toward the land, namely the ideals of "harmony, autonomy, and respect" (29). Mythic visions born from the period of early contacts abet deterritorialization.

The centrality of these early mythic images is one of the recurrent themes of this study. Representations of the Amerindian from the period of the earliest contacts persistently shape French thinking and writing about the Amerindian. By examining texts from this early and subsequent periods, shifts in visions of the Native that nevertheless remain genealogically connected to earlier perspectives emerge as identifiable myths. These forms operate as narrative technologies. By referring to myth as a narrative technology, a critical emphasis is proposed regarding the functioning of the mythic machine. Myth performs similar work in the business of conquest as military technologies do: they contribute to the genocide and dispossession inherent in the contact between Europeans and Amerindians. Philip J. Deloria (Standing Rock Sioux) reminds us that mythic visions of the Native are central to constructions of the Self in Euro-American settler-colonial societies. They also perform the same cultural work vis-à-vis the French and Québécois communities' apprehension of the Amerindian Other. Deloria locates the penchant for "extermination or inclusion" of the Amerindian squarely within the narrative technology of myth (4). *The Mythic Indian* traces the evolution of the French and Québécois visions of the Indigenous peoples of the Americas. This mythological genealogy informs the cultural imaginaries of the French(-Canadians) from the earliest periods of contact until the present day, marking the boundaries of sameness and difference in French and Québécois representations of the Amerindian. In *The Mythic Indian*, I elucidate intertextual and transdisciplinary mythologies in the genres of literature, travel writing, philosophy, and scientific discourses. Not only have these mythic paradigms determined literary representation, but they have also inordinately influenced the articulation of *scientific truth*, notably the reification of Native ontological difference from a Eurocentric perspective. The inextricable link between representation and praxis, confirmed by insights into the mythic origins of scientific discourses (Buffon, Durkheim, Lévi-Strauss, and others), underpin the analytical connection that *The Mythic Indian* makes between fiction and non-fiction. The original narrative technology in the mythic genealogy of the French and Québécois representations of Native can be considered as a duality, as a metaphorical form that mirrors Deloria's categories of "extermination or inclusion".

The mythic paradigms of the Noble and Ignoble Savage are the original binary that French writers and thinkers utilize to instrumentalize the mythic *idea* of the Native. The Ignoble Savage is a mode that casts the Amerindian as utterly Other, animalistic and dangerous, inhabiting at best a liminal or at worst a wholly

Introduction: Mythmaking: How the West (Was) "Won"?   3

alien space, outside of humanity and culture. It presents the Amerindian as non-human, animal, or monster, both morally and physically. At the opposite extreme of the spectrum is the Noble Savage. Seemingly in contrast to, but actually in convergence with the Ignoble Savage, it creates an image of the Amerindian as pure and innocent, a living Edenic model of universal human history. Texts written by the philosophers Michel de Montaigne and Jean-Jacques Rousseau are instrumental in the propagation of this mythic archetype. Noble Savage mythology excludes the Native from full belonging to civilization via paternalistic, infantilizing idealization rather than marginalizing vitriol. Both modes are appropriative, reductive, and dehumanizing voicings of the mythic machine. Both the Noble Savage myth's insistence on the positive connotations and the Ignoble Savage myth's portray of the Native as animalistic, lead to an epistemological shift that gives rise to a successive mythology: the nexus of Nature and Native, or the Ecological Savage.

Directly related to the Noble and Ignoble Savage paradigms, the narrative technology of the Ecological Savage (sometimes referred to in these pages as the nexus of Native and Nature) defines the Amerindian as part of Nature within the epistemology of the French and Québécois cultural imaginaries. At times valorizing, discourses of Amerindians living harmoniously with Nature must be problematized. The human reality and diversity of the Americas before and after contact is richer and more varied than this myth would suggest. Relegating the Native to the natural environment bolsters conceptions of authenticity that discredit non-traditional lifeways and perspectives within Amerindian communities, freezing them in time, hamstringing dynamism, a phenomenon reserved solely for European cultures. Relation to the animal *and* the human relegates the Native to a third, liminal space outside the fully human. Ironically, any absence of environmentally destructive tendencies in Native communities is often proffered as evidence of their lack of industriousness or collective development. The domination of nature inherent in the colonization of the Americas echoes the dispossession and conquest of the Amerindian. Native epistemological engagement with the natural world is often predicated on a spatial rather than a temporal plane. Vine Deloria Jr. (Standing Rock Sioux) made this well-known distinction in the fundamental text *God is Red*, stating that, "Space… is determinative of the way that we experience things. Time is subservient to it because to have time, there must be a measurable distance to travel during which time can pass" (xvii). The key to Deloria Jr.'s insight is one that delineates a profound difference between Western notions of nature and the immediate experiential understanding attributed to the Native. In many Indigenous philosophies sacredness only happens *in situ*. Western millenarianism, focusing on a temporal *end* of history, alongside *scientific* distanciation from the natural world built on a false Cartesian dichotomy, precludes a spatial understanding of the world. In Western thought systems, anywhere will do. When time puts an expiration date on all interaction with the natural environment, rather than the trite adage "there's no

4   *Introduction: Mythmaking: How the West (Was) "Won"?*

place like home", in settler ways of seeing, there's no place that *is* home. That is to say: objectification, commodification, and exploitation do not allow for a direct knowledge of the natural world. On these grounds, many Indigenous thinkers challenge the bases upon which Western knowledge systems claim universal understanding of the natural world. *The Mythic Indian* deconstructs non-Indigenous ways of knowing in *conversation* with Native philosophies of nature and humanity's place within it. The settler-colonial mindset is one that always relies on availing the land to despoliation. The *disappearance* of the buffalo, of the frontier, and, mythically, of the Indian are handmaidens to invasion. The mythologies of Noble, Ignoble, and Ecological Savage are not static; they evolve. In the nineteenth century, the myth of the Vanishing Indian becomes a lens through which French writers understand the Native.

The Vanishing Indian is genealogically linked to the preceding Noble and Ignoble Savage. The persistent influence of these two original paradigms does not wane; the Vanishing Indian myth constitutes a new articulation that further entrenches earlier perspectives. Fraught with collective, civilizational nostalgia and guilt, the myth of the Vanishing Indian perpetuates a teleological image of the Amerindian as (nearly) extinct. This narrative technology *disappears* the Native. The inevitability of this *disappearance* is a logic that informs the French Western novel (a genre in the French category of *roman d'aventure*, but also derivative of the American Western). The mythic machine in the Vanishing Indian mode textually precludes a viable future for the Indigenous within French and Québécois cultural imaginaries, an example of what Gerald Vizenor refers to as "tragic victimry", paradoxically erasing Amerindian presence on the land, opening the metaphoric, textual space for its appropriation by Europeans (*Survivance: Native Narratives of Presence* Chapter 1). The French Western, a mirror genre of the American prototype, presaging the final evolution of the mythic genealogy framework, the mythology of Going Native, greatly influences the French and Québécois cultural imaginaries. Despite its supposed simplicity, the French Western novel is a space wherein cultural difference and conflict are resolved (if only apparently) through representations that are accessible to a mass audience and contribute to articulations of French nationalism in the age of empire. Jodi Byrd (Chickasaw) suggests that "reading mnemonically" can elucidate the "transit" of Indianness onto diverse populations in what she terms the "continual reiterations of pioneer logics" (*The Transit of Empire*, Preface). In a period when France is expanding its imperial presence, frontier fables do the cultural work of reinforcing nationalist ideologies while simultaneously insisting on the racial hierarchies that underpin them. The last mythic paradigm to examine is Going Native.

Primarily prevalent in the twentieth and twenty-first centuries, a new archetype emerges: the myth of Going Native. The myth of Going Native is genealogically connected to the Vanishing Indian myth, which continues to operate, informing the creation of meaning around the *idea* of the Amerindian.

Introduction: Mythmaking: How the West (Was) "Won"? 5

Following metaphorical *disappearance*, Going Native mythologies (re)present the Amerindian as catalyst for the transformation or self-actualization of characters of non-Native origins. French and Québécois fantasies of Going Native reiterate the same appropriative epistemological techniques as earlier mythologies. Taking the American context as her object of study, Shari M. Huhndorf (Yup'ik) posits that, "In its various forms, going native articulates and attempts to resolve widespread ambivalence about modernity as well as anxieties about the terrible violence marking the nation's origins" (*Going Native*, Introduction). Discussions of Going Native have nearly universally been analyzed in a settler-colonial context, yet there are varying *reasons* beyond the American story for Going Native. In contemporary French fiction, the Native serves as a site of resistance to late liberal capitalism. Through rewritings of conquest, French authors critique globalized capitalism. Furthermore, narratives of Going Native are often centered on representations of Native sexuality as a source of *truth* and liberation. A *queer* critique can open specific elements of the Going Native mythology to a more profound analysis. For example, the taboo *and* fascination around Amerindian sexuality is emblematic of the mythic machine and the limits it places on epistemology and praxis. Via mythologized knowledge of the Amerindian, non-Native characters are transformed into *truer* versions of themselves, completing their narrative arc as mythic Indians in their own right. Participating in and conversing with the Going Native exemplar, the *disappearance* of the Amerindian motivates a nostalgic rewriting of histories of the conquest of the Americas. Quintessentially American motifs, such as the cross-country road trip, as well as more traditional literary tropes, such as the Bildungsroman, are structures that inform Québécois fictional representations of the Native. Instrumentalizing the Native as a site of veridiction wherein Québécois characters locate the *truth* about their (sexual) identity, Going Native has persistent purchase in the French-Canadian literary world and cultural imaginary. The mythology of Going Native is evidence of the continued preeminence of the mythic machine, as well as the lack of evolution in non-Native comprehension of the Amerindian Other.

In addition to literary texts, *The Mythic Indian* focuses on how myths of the Native are presented in French scientific writing as bases for *scientific truth*. In the eighteenth century, the field of natural history (Buffon) utilizes images of the Native derived directly from the Ignoble Savage tradition. In the nineteenth century, one of the foundational texts of the discipline of sociology (Durkheim's *The Division of Labor in Society*) utilizes images of Amerindian gender ambiguity to formulate a distinction between *primitive* and *modern* peoples. In the twentieth and twenty-first centuries, French anthropological writing (Lévi-Strauss) demonstrates how myth inspires ethnographers to seek solutions for European problems via journeys of Going Native. The work of Georges E. Sioui (Wendat) is a contrapuntal message from an Indigenous perspective. Sioui's work debunks the myth of cultural evolutionism that situates Indigenous peoples in a position

6   *Introduction: Mythmaking: How the West (Was) "Won"?*

of inferiority vis-à-vis linear, positivistic Eurocentric epistemological structures. Proposing the wisdom of a circular vision of time and a universally connected view of the environment and (non-human) Others (7). Furthermore, my discussion of *scientific truth* from a French perspective will also give voice to Indigenous ways of knowing, attempting to right the imbalance of science's claims to *the* truth. As Laurelyn Whitt (Mississippi Choctaw) reminds us, "The existence and value of indigenous knowledge systems have... been systematically denied. In the origin stories of the dominant culture, indigenous peoples have superstitions, myths, or belief systems based on ignorance. They do not have knowledge systems" (31). Following a discussion of scientific literature, the penultimate chapter of *The Mythic Indian* explores how French and Québécois writers of the twentieth and twenty-first centuries engage with, interrogate, and restate the myths of the Ignoble Savage, Noble Savage, Ecological Savage, Vanishing Indian, and Going Native. A comparative analysis of the Québécois cultural imaginary underscores the similarities between French-Canadian and continental French representational traditions.

To better comprehend the import of the mythic genealogy in European discourses it is crucial to consider the scholarly work of one of the most significant voices in Indigenous Studies, Gerald Vizenor. Central to Vizenor's (Chippewa) thinking is the concept of the "indian". The "indian" refers directly to the suite of mythic visions that I have identified above. An "indian" is merely the aggregate of these "simulations", or mythic paradigms. The use of these narrative technologies to reduce the Amerindian to the "indian" is an essential element of "the literature of domination". Vizenor insists that these, "Simulations are new burdens in the absence of the real" ("The Ruins of Representation", 7). For Vizenor then, the mythic machine produces consumable simulacra of the Native, or "indians". In keeping with my theoretical framework of narrative technology, simulations empty the signifier of Amerindian of any content and participate in the (settler-)colonial campaign of "domination". Speaking back to this paradigm is Vizenor's key concept of survivance, which offers a "tribal counterpoise to the literature of dominance" ("The Ruins of Representation", 21). This "tribal counterpoise" will be discussed in the final chapter on First Nations authors writing in French. This section maps the landscape of Francophone First Nations literature, too often ignored by the academy and Native American and Indigenous Studies. Emphasizing the ways in which Amerindian voices navigate contact and settler-colonialism, my analysis engages with the Indigenous stories that contest the hegemony of the mythic machine.

The Mythic Indian demystifies myths of the Amerindian in the Francophone sphere (France and Québec), integrating Native and Indigenous Studies into the domains of French and Québécois literary scholarship through Indigenous, settler-colonial, postcolonial, *queer*, and ecocritical perspectives. My research brings to light the influence of myth in the representation of the Amerindian outside of the Anglosphere and the Hispanosphere, the primary focus of much academic attention. Interdisciplinary, transhistorical, and transindigenous, my analyses reveal a connection between the mythic in fiction and how fiction claims the authority to present itself in scientific discourse as objective *truth*. The transnational vision of the Amerindian from both a French and Québécois cultural context dovetails with the interdisciplinary theoretical methodology taken up in this volume to create a unique examination of Francophone (mis) understandings and (mis)representations of the Native.

1 Chapter 1: Mythic Origins and the Origins of Myth

In this chapter, the mythic origins of man in the philosophical theory of Jean-Jacques Rousseau's state of nature begin an exploration of the fundamental ambiguity of the Amerindian in European epistemology. Vacillating between the Ignoble and Noble Savage poles, the abstract presents itself as fact in representations of the Native. Chronologically preceding Rousseau, two explorers and prolific authors' writings on the Amerindian emphasize the penchant for the mythic in French letters. In the sixteenth century, the royal cosmographer André Thevet's proto-ethnographic observations of the Tupinamba of South America are prefaced by the tall tale of the Patagonian Giants, an episode from Magellan's planetary circumnavigation. The distortion of the Amerindian body via the Ignoble Savage, serves as a guide for all that follows in the description of the Americas in the author's *Cosmographie universelle*. In the seventeenth century, Samuel de Champlain's depictions of the Armouchiquois typify the *transferability* and ambiguity of myth. Having first heard reports on the Armouchiquois from an inimical group in the region, Champlain creates an image in the Ignoble Savage mode, wherein the Amerindian body is deformed into simian grotesqueness. First-hand experience with the Armouchiquois, however, inspires the explorer to revise the portrait using a Noble Savage brush, idealizing corporeal *and* cultural aspects of Armouchiquois society. To conclude the analysis of the origins of the mythic Indian in the French cultural imaginary, the paradoxes of Michel de Montaigne's foundational *Bon Sauvage* are decorticated, revealing the Eurocentric instrumentalization behind the cultural relativism often associated with the High Renaissance essayist's œuvre. The works under discussion in this preliminary chapter lay the groundwork for subsequent centuries of mythic (mis)understandings of the Amerindian in the French and Québécois cultural imaginaries.

2 Chapter 2: Voltaire, La Condamine, and Buffon: Fabricating Fact and (Science) Fiction

This chapter focuses on three authors in disparate domains of the Enlightenment. The ages of Reason and Revolution, those forefathers of modern liberal democracy and *laïcité* (France's vision of secularism) are linked to

8 *Introduction: Mythmaking: How the West (Was) "Won"?*

Voltaire's oeuvre. Voltaire's legacy is difficult to pin down with precision, yet he remains an iconic figure of French *esprit*. Considered by some to be the "first modern intellectual" and arguably the most well-known European writer of the eighteenth century, Voltaire makes an indelible mark on the French cultural imaginary, specifically how the French comprehend the category of Amerindian in fictional and non-fictional texts. The discussion concentrates on three mythic representations of the Amerindian taken from Voltaire's well-known *Candide* (1759): the Oreillons (another example of the deformation of the Native body), supposed Amerindian bestiality, and Candide and Cacambo's adventure in Eldorado. In addition to highlighting the prevalence of the Ignoble and Noble Savage, another function of the mythic is introduced: *transferability*. *Transferability* points to the slipping of the mythic message from distinct epistemological frameworks, from philosophy to fiction, for instance, and thence to science. *Transferability* is a defining characteristic of myth. The history of the scientific expeditions of French explorer La Condamine is illustrative in this context. La Condamine's *scientific* accounts of his expedition's encounters with the Oreillons inform Voltaire's mythic representation of the group in his novel, *Candide*. This indistinguishability of fact and fiction is not restricted to science informing fiction, but also of mythic models informing science. The second section of the chapter explores mythic representations of the Amerindian in scientific discourses, which are then naturalized as *truth*. Science, in contemporary society, has a narrower meaning than during the Enlightenment. However, in the evolution of the sciences, the Enlightenment is a formative period wherein the transformation from the broader all-inclusive conceptualization of *sciences* begins to resemble our modern notion more closely. The truth value that will increasingly be attributed to scientific discourse in favor of other ways of knowing requires examination at this relatively early stage, because the vision of the Amerindian espoused by science will have a profound effect on (settler)-colonial praxis. Examining the scientific reveals how the same mythic paradigms that characterize previous discourses are constitutive of scientific discourse's treatment of the image of the Native. In the discursive field of science, one major shift that takes place in the representation of Amerindians is the attempt to expand the moral sphere into the biological, an ideological turn that inspires, among other things, modern notions of race. In short, the moral judgments made by previous generations of writers become more firmly anchored in the biological being of the Amerindian. This embodiment serves as a bridge whereby the mythic is transferred into *truth*. My analysis demonstrates this phenomenon through a reading of the *Histoire naturelle* by the father of natural history, the Comte de Buffon. The mythic origin of scientific discourses is a key feature of the evolution and genealogy of the representation of the Amerindian.

Introduction: Mythmaking: How the West (Was) "Won"? 9

3 Chapter 3: The Vanishing Indian: Manifest and Imperial Destinies

This chapter examines the myth of the Vanishing Indian in the nineteenth century, in a genre that is often ignored, the French Western novel. A popular form with wide-reaching influence, the French Western is largely responsible for the *crystallization* of mythic visions of the Amerindian in the French cultural imaginary. These mythic *truths*, speak to identity-based discourses of nationalism and race during the age of empire. The second section presents a close reading of one of the foundational texts of sociology in Émile Durkheim's *De la division du travail social*. My interpretation of the text focuses on the articulation of the central research question of the monograph and how the author instrumentalizes mythic representations of Native sexuality to naturalize European superiority, both biologically and morally. Supporting his argument with evidence taken from the *hard science* of biological racism of the late nineteenth century, Durkheim situates ontological difference in *primitive* "sexual resemblance". I examine the role of Native sexuality in Durkheim's philosophy by theorizing gender ambiguity via Scott Lauria Morgensen's insights into berdache and the role of sexuality in modern European identity formation. While Durkheim does not directly reference berdache as a specially revered Native identity, the author's articulation of Native sexuality utilizes the same narrative technologies as the more modern discourses targeted by Morgensen's *queer* and settler-colonial critique. In particular, the "uniformity of sex, gender, sexuality, and indigeneity" that the construction of berdache allows Westerners to claim, mimics how Durkheim employs Native sexualities to "represent principles of human nature and culture" (Morgensen 55). Not only does Durkheim locate ontological difference in what he interprets as androgyny, but he utilizes that distinction to naturalize European superiority over Indigenous peoples. I disentangle the rhetorical turns in *De la division du travail social* to reveal how the author's discourse of *scientific truth* originates in the logics of the mythic paradigms of the Ignoble Savage and the Vanishing Indian through a theoretical point of view that incorporates Indigenous scholars' critiques of science as a narrative technology.

4 Chapter 4: Going Native: The Myth of Being Indian

This chapter explores the twentieth- and twenty-first-century myth of Going Native in French literature, Québécois literature, and French anthropology (Lévi-Strauss). Going Native appropriates Noble Savage mythologies, instrumentalizing contact with Indigenous peoples as catalyst for a transformative journey of self-actualization for non-Native characters. Theoretically buffeted by postcolonial theories (Pratt, Bhabha) and Indigenous scholars articulations of the Going Native narrative (Vizenor, Veloria, Huhndorf), my analyses

10 *Introduction: Mythmaking: How the West (Was) "Won"?*

delineate how Going Native functions as a narrative technology to reinforce racial hierarchies that situate the Native as inferior to the European. First, I interpret rewritings of earlier mythic imaginations of the Native in Michel Tournier's *Vendredi, ou les limbes du Pacifique*, a reboot of Defoe's classic *Robinson Crusoe*, and Jean-Christophe Rufin's *Rouge Brésil*, a historical novel that rethinks the *France antarctique* colonial expedition to coastal Brazil in the sixteenth century. Through the dual lens of an ecocritical and *queer* critique, these texts reveal the underlying structures of the Going Native model. In the second section of the chapter, I widen the scope of this study by chronicling the history of Québécois representation of First Nations peoples from the nineteenth century until the present day. In the following section, I analyze the Québécois texts *Volkswagen Blues* by Jacques Poulin and *Le dernier été des Indiens* by Robert Lalonde in greater detail, situating them in *conversation* with contemporary French fictional models. In both novels, mythic Native sexualities characterize Amerindian characters as agents of change for the French-Canadian protagonists. This sexualizing of the mythic literary *identity* of First Nations peoples is coupled with an iteration of the Going Native myth wherein Amerindians act as guides permitting the Euro-Canadian characters' *discovery* of their own *true* identities. Section three examines how anthropological writing engages directly with the mythic genealogy discussed in *The Mythic Indian*. The discursive field of anthropology performs the mythic journey of Going Native, envisioning the Amerindian as a site of veridiction, offering solutions to the ills of modernity. In examining French anthropology's engagement with the Going Native mythological framework, I examine the discursive regime of science via the lens of Laurelyn Whitt's (Mississippi Choctaw) critique of Western knowledge systems' limitations. Additionally, Pierre Bourdieu's critical discourse analysis with a focus on symbolic power is an appropriate theoretical tool for elucidating the mechanisms of the narrative technology of Going Native. Putting these critical voices in *conversation* with Indigenous voices and postcolonial perspectives provides a unique methodological take on the narratology of Going Native.

5 Chapter 5: Voices in Francophone Indigenous Literature: A History and Future of Native American Literature

In the final chapter, I examine the rich history of French language contributions to Indigenous literatures. Focusing on Native contestation of the mythic paradigms traced in the initial four chapters of the book, this chapter seeks to introduce the Anglophone-dominated field of Indigenous Studies to First Nations Francophone authors. Having long been neglected by the academy, *The Mythic Indian* takes an initial step toward remedying the paucity of research in this subfield of Native American Literature. One of the first recognized authors of Amerindian descent in Québec, Yvès Thériault has an extensive œuvre that directly addresses the violence and cooperation associated with contact between

Introduction: Mythmaking: How the West (Was) "Won"? 11

Inuit, First Nations, and Euro-Canadians. An Antane Kapesh's *Je suis une maudite Sauvagesse* is the first text published in Canada in an Indigenous language (Innu-aimun) and represents a seminal moment in the history of Francophone Indigenous Literature. Finally, the acclaimed novelist Naomi Fontaine's novels *Kuessipan* (inspiration for the eponymous 2019 film), *Manikanetish*, and the essay *Shuni* have squarely placed Indigenous literature at the center of contemporary conversations on Québécois literature writ large. Her unique vision of Innu identity and her practice of a pedagogy of generosity that acts as an invitation to non-Indigenous to understand Native culture, but also as a counterweight to mythic misunderstanding, will conclude our investigation of Indigenous authors and their voices.

Works Cited

Alfred, Taiaiake. *Peace, Power, Righteousness: An Indigenous Manifesto*. New York: Oxford UP, 2009.

Byrd, Jodi A. *Transit of Empire: Indigenous Critiques of Colonialism*. Kindle version. Minneapolis: University of Minnesota Press, 2011.

Coulthard, Glen Sean. *Red Skin White Masks: Rejecting the Colonial Politics of Recognition*. Kindle version. Minneapolis: University of Minnesota Press, 2014.

Deloria, Philip J. *Playing Indian*. New Haven, CT: Yale UP, 1998.

Deloria, Vine Jr. *God Is Red: A Native View of Religion, 30th Anniversary Edition*. Golden: Fulcrum Publishing, 2003.

Huhndorf, Shari M. *Going Native: Indians in the American Cultural Imagination*. Kindle version. Ithaca, NY: Cornell University Press, 2015.

Morgensen, Scott Lauria. *Spaces between Us: Queer Settler Colonialism and Indigenous Decolonization*. Minneapolis: University of Minnesota Press, 2011.

Schweninger, Lee. *Listening to the Land: Native American Literary Responses to the Landscape*. Kindle version. Athens: The University of Georgia Press, 2008.

Sioui, Georges. *Les Wendats: une civilisation méconnue*. Sainte-Foy: Les Presses de l'Université Laval, 1994.

Vizenor, Gerald. "Aesthetics of Survivance: Literary Theory and Practice." *Survivance: Narratives of Native Presence*. Edited by Gerald Vizenor. Kindle version. Lincoln: University of Nebraska Press, 2008.

———. "The Ruins of Representation: Shadow Survivance and the Literature of Dominance." *American Indian Quarterly*, vol. 17, no. 1, 1993, pp. 7–30.

Whitt, Laurelyn. *Science, Colonialism, and Indigenous Peoples: The Cultural Politics of Law and Knowledge*. Cambridge: Cambridge UP, 2009.

1 Mythic Origins and the Origins of Myth

1 Introduction

From first contact between the Old World and the *New* World, myth has informed representation of the Native. The lens through which Europeans view the Indigenous is influenced by a tradition of fantasy regarding the Other. History reveals Western culture as mythological in apprehending and interpreting the known and the unknown. The West structures the world through myth, as anthropology has long argued. During the early modern period and beyond, Europeans utilize myths to understand Others that they encounter as Europe expands geographically, culturally, and economically. In this context, myth is *the* foundation of representations of the Amerindian. In French texts in a wide variety of genres, the Native is systematically mythologized. The unreality of the "indian" has been a part of Western depictions of the Native from the beginning according to Gerald Vizenor (Chippewa), "The American Indian has come to mean *Indianness*, the conditions that indicate the once-despised tribes and, at the same time, the extreme notions of an exotic outsider" (*Native American Literature* 1). Here Vizenor locates the dichotomous framework of myth at the genealogical origin of contact, the Noble and Ignoble Savage mythologies, rightly surmising the West's use of myth as a tool of conquest.

In this preliminary chapter, I trace the origins and evolution of the mythologies that the French construct as a conceptual framework in describing the Amerindian Other in philosophical essays, travel writing, fiction, and more. A clear grasp of the original mythic paradigms will allow for assessing the continuities and shifts that occur in the modern period. First, I identify key mythic models employed by early French authors to describe the Native, illustrating how these seminal mythic archetypes are structured. The valence of the mythic models that the French use to describe the Native resides in its iterability. It is for this special reason that I have elected to evaluate some of the most iconic and transformational works of the early modern period as my starting point. Iterability is a pivotal concept in the representation of the Amerindian. The repetition over the last five centuries of the same mythic models points to the adaptability and

DOI: 10.4324/9781032638751-2

Mythic Origins and the Origins of Myth 13

resiliency of these primary mythic patterns within the evolving movements of thought that characterize the High Renaissance, Enlightenment, Modernity, and Post-Modernity.

In this chapter, the mythic origins of man in the philosophical theory of Jean-Jacques Rousseau's state of nature will underscore the fundamental ambiguity of the Amerindian in European epistemology. Vacillating between the Ignoble and Noble Savage, the abstract presents itself as fact in Rousseau's writing. Stepping back chronologically from Rousseau, the royal cosmographer André Thevet's proto-ethnographic observations of the Tupinamba are prefaced by the reiteration of the tall tale of the Patagonian Giants, an incident in Magellan's circumnavigation. This distortion of the body, as monstrous Ignoble Savage, serves as a guide for the interpretation of the author's *Cosmographie universelle*'s depiction of the Americas and their inhabitants. In the seventeenth century, Canadian founding father Samuel de Champlain's textual depictions of the Armouchiquois (Abenaki) typify the *transferability* and ambiguity of myth. Initially receiving reports on the Armouchiquois from enemies, Champlain describes them in the Ignoble Savage mode, deforming the Amerindian body into simian grotesqueness. Later personal experience with the Armouchiquois inspires repainting their portrait with a Noble Savage brush, romanticizing corporeal and cultural features. To conclude the analysis of the origins of the mythic Indian in the French cultural imaginary, the paradoxes of Michel de Montaigne's foundational *Bon Sauvage* are deciphered, highlighting the Eurocentrism of cultural relativism often associated the philosopher's essays. The texts analyzed in the preliminary chapter lay the groundwork for subsequent centuries of mythic (mis)understandings and (mis)representations of the Amerindian Other in the French and Québécois cultural imaginaries. Comprehending how these mythic models morph and inhabit such disparate epistemological spaces as philosophy, fiction, and science is not possible without making sense of the origins of the mythic Indian.

2   Mythic Ambiguity in the Philosophy of Jean-Jacques Rousseau: The Ignoble and Noble Savages

The myth of the Noble Savage is perhaps the most essential mythological schema that Europe employs when representing and/or imagining the Amerindian. The perseverance *and* adaptability of the Noble Savage mythology in ever-changing historical contexts is a characteristic feature of myth. The Noble Savage dehumanizes through the idealization of the Amerindian in specific ways. It situates the Native outside of Western history, culture, and civilization. The Noble Savage functions as a double discursive narrative technology. In short, the Noble Savage myth iterates two discourses simultaneously. First, on the surface, it attempts to describe the living, breathing Native in the language of myth to qualify the Amerindian as original, associated with parentage/paternalism, and a universal

14 *Mythic Origins and the Origins of Myth*

human origin. The very *discovery* of the Americas leads to a questioning of the genealogy of the human species. The former philosophical security of the Biblical explanation is shaken by the discovery of a previously unknown hemisphere. The attribution of primordiality imputes a higher degree of authenticity or purity to the Native. Antediluvian and, a priori, sinless, the Edenic status of the Noble Savage speaks to the childhood of the human species. Infantilization becomes one of the recurrent methods of depicting the Native. The universalist ancestor element of the Noble Savage mythic lens is perhaps most recognizable in French letters in Jean-Jacques Rousseau's vision of the origins of humanity in his *Discours sur l'origine et les fondements de l'inégalité parmi les hommes (Discourse on the Origin and Basis of Inequality Among Men)* (1755). Therefore, Rousseau is a logical springboard for the exploration of the intellectual and literary history of this prominent imaginary paradigm, what Vizenor refers to as a "cold simulation" in the "literature of dominance" ("The Ruins of Representation" 7).

The New World and its Indigenous peoples constitute a formative element of the philosophy of Jean-Jacques Rousseau throughout his lifetime. The *idea* of the Americas and its original inhabitants holds a particular fascination for Rousseau from an early point in his writing career. One of the very first creative works completed by the author is the tragedy, *La découverte du Nouveau Monde (The Discovery of the New World)* (1740). *La découverte du Nouveau Monde* serves as a reflection on the missed opportunity of the New World, made even more poignant because the Old World had fully acknowledged long before 1740 that the population of the Americas had largely been destroyed as a direct result of their contact with Europeans. The play is fundamental for understanding the centrality of the New World and the Amerindian in Rousseau's philosophy. The New World and the violence engendered by contact is a thought experiment that informs the *philosophe*'s thinking about human nature and society. Fourteen years before *Discours sur l'inégalité*, Rousseau discusses the Native as a privileged site for *imagining* and *reimagining* our collective human past. The Amerindian is the primary source for Rousseau's philosophical state of nature. They function as a contemporaneous case study of what Rousseau posits as the initial stage in his conception of a universal human history (Duchet 335). One of the fundamental features of the Noble Savage mythology is becoming apparent: the Amerindian present equals the European past. This temporal relegation of the Native to the past has far-reaching ideological consequences in how Europeans apprehend and behave toward Amerindians.

Within the *Discours sur l'inégalité*, Rousseau explicitly associates the state of nature with the Native. A paradoxical philosophical proposition at best, it is built on an amalgamation of conjecture *and* truth. Nevertheless, the state of nature is a pillar in Rousseau's legacy as the father of a certain direction of political thinking that many believe leads directly to the French Revolution. Whatever knowledge Rousseau has of the Native is acquired through reading, however. Rousseau has no personal experience with Amerindians. This is indicative of a common

Mythic Origins and the Origins of Myth   15

feature of the mythologizing of the Native in French letters: second-hand written accounts or witnesses. As in earlier periods, the textual carries a weight that today seems overreaching. The often-odd mixture of abstraction and fantasy that one encounters in _Discours sur l'inégalité_ does not preclude what would have been considered legitimate claims to _truth_. Authorial authority is textually and intertextually established despite little or no direct experience with the subject at hand. This is typical of the early modern period, when little separates fact from fiction, myth from reality. In French sociologist Pierre Bourdieu's analysis of the power dynamics of discourse, the author enjoys a symbolic power based on a pre-supposed recognition of the inherent structures and rules of the narrative technology of myth. Bourdieu argues that the recognition of the coded messages of discourse, what I am referring to as myth, is essential to the (symbolic) violence inherent in the mythic machine's othering function (266). The authority with which the author speaks is based on a linguistic, cultural recognition that permits an attribution of _truth_ to Rousseau's speculative fiction about the Native. The acceptance of the blurring between the boundaries of fact and fiction is typical of the pre-modern epistemological history of the West. Furthermore, this fluidity does not incite the same anxiety that it might in today's empirical world.

For Rousseau, extant Amerindian populations provide a unique opportunity: a window into the past. The contemporaneous Native is a "living artefact", providing information about universal human origins. Along with scientific theorists like the Comte de Buffon, Georges Cuvier, and Charles Darwin, Rousseau considers traits as indicative of a position on a temporal linear plane that is defined as ineluctably progressive. Evolutionism and perfectibility undergird the conceptualization of both the state of nature and state of civil society for Rousseau. Yet, there is a duality at the heart of Rousseau's Noble Savage wherein the Amerindian is represented as radically dehumanized. A brief discussion of specific elements of the state of nature will demonstrate how Rousseau envisions the Native, and by extension the history of humanity. One key feature of the human condition in the state of nature is a much-reduced cognitive capacity when compared to Rousseau's own Europeanness. Representation is often a barely veiled form of cultural domination and violence. Edward Saïd laments the paucity of studies that interrogate the connections between cultural productions of the West and its imperial propensities in _Culture and Imperialism_, stating that "Few full-scale critical studies have focused on the relationship between modern Western imperialism and its culture" (Chapter 4). Saïd indicates the mythic bent of Western discourses concerning the non-Western Other, indicating its structural centrality as "deeply symbiotic" with the violence wrought by Europe outside of the Old World, echoing Bourdieu's insight about the violence inherent to mythic discourses. Rousseau's _Discours sur l'inégalité_ is part of that imperialist cultural tradition, consciously or unconsciously. When Rousseau writes about the Native as a representative of the state of nature, the agency of writing that the _philosophe_ embodies is exclusively French (European) and functions as a

16 *Mythic Origins and the Origins of Myth*

narrative technology. By narrative technology, I refer to the instrumentalization of writing as an element of the *technos* of imperium. Writing is a technology associated with memory and intellectual superiority, cultural accomplishments systematically denied to the Indigenous peoples of the Americas.

Rousseau's vision of the Native's inability to comprehend the world with the same cognitive powers that the lowliest of Europeans would naturally possess is evident in the following passage:

> But who does not see, without recurring to the uncertain testimony of history, that everything seems to remove from savage man both the temptation and the means of changing his condition? His imagination paints no pictures; his heart makes no demands on him. His few wants are so readily supplied, and he is so far from having the knowledge which is needful to make him want more, that he can have neither foresight nor curiosity. The face of nature becomes indifferent to him as it grows familiar. He sees in it always the same order, the same successions: he has not understanding enough to wonder at the greatest miracles; nor is it in his mind that we can expect to find that philosophy man needs, if he is to know how to notice for once what he sees every day. His soul, which nothing disturbs, is wholly wrapped up in the feeling of its present existence, without any idea of the future, however near at hand; while his projects, as limited as his views, hardly extend to the close of day. Such, even at present, is the extent of the native Caribean's [sic] foresight: he will improvidently sell you his cotton-bed in the morning and come crying in the evening to buy it again, not having foreseen he would want it again the next night. The more we reflect on this subject, the greater appears the distance between pure sensation and the most simple knowledge: it is impossible indeed to conceive how a man, by his own powers alone, without the aid of communication and the spur of necessity, could have bridged so great a gap. (Cole, Discourse on Inequality, The First Part)

In this passage Rousseau advances contemporary Natives as evidence for the state of nature. On one hand, Rousseau establishes the Amerindian as a tableau vivant of his theoretical abstraction. Contemporaneous Natives are enfolded into a common human genealogy, an extant ancestor of modern humanity. Through allusion to radical elements of alterity in the realm of cognitive abilities, Rousseau simultaneously relegates the Native to the non-human, to the natural world. Berkhofer Jr. identifies that this bias "first popularized by Rousseau, to internalize the relation between nature and man and to combine the wildness of men in other places with the wildness within all men" is a leitmotiv in the French representation of the Amerindian (134). However, Rousseau's identification *with* nature does not go as far as his attribution of the Native *as* nature. This is one of many tensions, or aporias, present in Rousseau's *Discours sur l'inégalité*. The passage begins with an incredulous question meant to persuade through the inclusion of the reader, through what Bourdieu calls "recognition". After all, "who does not see?" exactly as I, Rousseau sees. The author then proceeds to see for his readership. While the question, "who does not see?", focuses expressly on the author's assertion that contemporary Natives are perfect examples of his theory of the state of nature, this question also opens the door for the creation of two opposing camps. The rhetoric of self-evidence is one of Rousseau's signature techniques. This question explicitly tells the reader that they risk being out of the norm, if they subscribe to an alternative to his assertion that that current Amerindians illustrate the abstract concept of the state of nature. Inclusion and exclusion are at the heart of Rousseau's articulation of the state of nature as a comprehensive, universal framework of human nature and evolution. By extension, they are central to the mythology of the Noble Savage as a narrative technology circumscribing how the Native should be understood. The inclusion of the reader in the author's logic goes well beyond mere *captatio benevolentiae*, however. The inclusion of the reader serves as a jumping-off point for the violent exclusion of the Native that is effectuated precisely as the author posits that group as an illustration of the origin of man. Rousseau is laying out a line of tolerance of the Amerindian Other that is immediately crossed. The boundary between the acceptable and abhorrent is that which divides the state of nature and the state of civil society, despite Rousseau's insistence that it is precisely within the former that the purity and innocence of man truly lies. This demarcation is what Elizabeth Povinelli terms "the limits of recognition" (*The Cunning of Recognition* 3). Simultaneously inclusive and exclusive, idealizing and condemning, Rousseau's Noble Savage is a double discursive narrative technology that mythologizes the Amerindian as superior *and* inferior. This is the work of the mythic machine within the French and Québécois cultural imaginaries. In its exclusionary vein, the description of the Caribs is not one likely to inspire identification on the part of Rousseau's French readers. Why spend so much time and energy discussing this distinction between inclusion and exclusion? Because not only is it a defining feature of both Rousseau's theory of the state of nature and of the myth of the Noble Savage, but also, as such, this tension between inclusion and exclusion typifies many representational strategies employed by the West to attempt to incorporate the peoples of the Americas into a universalized understanding of humanity (or of human history) from the early contact period to the present day. The West's existential questionings following the *discovery* of the Western hemisphere play out time and again in the mythic paradigms it attaches to the original inhabitants of that *New* World.

The most obvious way in which Rousseau dehumanizes the Native is through privative mode: what is supposedly absent in the Amerindian constructs a *negative* definition of the *primitive* Other. Key elements of what Rousseau would consider to be integral to his own identity are imagination, foresight, and curiosity. All three are cognitive. Therefore, the Native is framed as lacking these basic cognitive features that historically have been the dividing line between human

18 *Mythic Origins and the Origins of Myth*

and animal ontologies. It is difficult to imagine a fully *human* being without imagination, foresight, or basic inquisitiveness. Of course, this intellectual inferiority does not preclude a certain nostalgia and idealization of the Native from emerging in Rousseau's writing.

Two aspects of the *negative* definition of the Native merit further scrutiny. The lack of foresight of the original inhabitants of the Caribbean is particularly poignant in regard to both the dehumanization of the Native more generally, as well as the establishment of a connection in Rousseau's thinking between the contemporary Amerindian and the theoretical state of nature. The details of the Carib who sells a hammock in the morning only to bemoan not having it when bedtime comes around would likely have been quite shocking to Rousseau's readers. Europeans who write back to the Old World about the original inhabitants of the New repeat throughout the centuries this image of the Native as lacking the basic cognitive skill of foresight. This characterization of the Amerindian poses some fundamental problems. If it were true that the Native is lacking the essential human cognitive ability to anticipate needs, how could it be that the same Native would be able to supply his needs, i.e. survive at all? The answer put forth by Rousseau is a relatively simple one: natural abundance. It is the surfeit of resources in the environment that maintains the Native in the *infancy* of the state of nature. Infantilizing and paternalizing function complementarily in mythic discourses about the Amerindian. Glaring facts refute Rousseau's claims. The Native is not lacking in any abilities of foresight in comparison with the European. Many Amerindian groups' capacity to procure resources in difficult environmental circumstances is remarkable. The theory that natural abundance forgives the cognitive deficit of the Amerindian by providing easy subsistence is easily disproven. Many Natives thrived for centuries in areas that in today's age of technological advancement do not sustain large human populations. The fact that Amerindians cover the entire Western hemisphere at the arrival of the Europeans is evidence of their adaptability. These suppositions about the nature of man (i.e. of the Native) in Rousseau's theories are highly influential in the articulation of later social science definitions of the Amerindian. Authors that follow in Rousseau's philosophical footsteps notably include Émile Durkheim and Claude Lévi-Strauss. The hammock narrative is a clear example of misunderstanding. When the Carib *sells* the hammock, this is an interpretation from a Eurocentric perspective that may not fully encompass how the Carib understands the exchange. The Carib returning later requesting the return of the hammock and expressing regret at the European's refusal points to the Carib's interpretation of the exchange in an entirely different manner than a commodity exchange. The capitalistic perspective that undergirds Rousseau's misunderstanding is especially ironic given that the essay focuses on private property as the source of Western society's ills. Lack of foresight is significant within the broader context of Rousseau's vision of the Native. Because it indicates a lack of cognitive abilities that one might consider essentially human. Indeed,

Mythic Origins and the Origins of Myth 19

it is through such examples as the Carib's hammock that Rousseau justifies his theorizing about the Amerindian as lacking other cognitive abilities. The *truth* of the original proposition is immaterial in relation to the theoretical abstractions that it inspires. Thus, Rousseau's Native and his theory of the state of nature is more creative than empirical, relying on imagination rather than fact, what Frantz Fanon calls a "construction du Blanc", a White construction (11). The mythic structures that characterize the Native from contact to the present day resonate with this early nod to the abstract. As such, it is a cornerstone of propositions about the Amerindian in various discursive registers such as literary, philosophical, and scientific discourses. Lack of humanity in Rousseau's state of nature is perhaps nowhere more striking than in the domain of sexuality and the family. Rousseau's theory of reason and intellectual superiority in the state of civil society hinges on the passions. Passions are not merely desires; they are desires that are developed because of the promiscuity and competition of society itself. Sexual desire is one of the most important passions, a linchpin in the demarcation of civilized and savage. While desires developed into passions are the impetus of the evolution of human intellect, there is a nefarious side. The very thing that allows man to reach the heights of rationality is criticized as anathema to civility itself. In the realm of sexual passion, violent crimes linked to jealousy represent the negative consequences of passions in the state of civil society. Passion does not exist within the Native, as equated to the state of nature. It is critical to look more carefully at what it means to be deemed passionless when the West (mis)represents the Amerindian. An early stereotype of the Native man purports a marked lack of sexual enthusiasm. The French see the Amerindian man as having a deficit of masculine virility. Having read some of the earlier sources cited above, Rousseau makes claims that echo that literary tradition of representing the Native as passionless.

> [I]t is more absurd to represent savages as continually cutting one another's throats to indulge their brutality [reference to sexual desire or lust], because this opinion is directly contrary to experience; the Caribeans [sic], who have as yet least of all deviated from the state of nature, being in fact the most peaceable of people in their amours, and the least subject to jealousy, though they live in a hot climate which seems always to inflame the passions. (Cole, Discourse on Inequality, The First Part)

This passage indicates the concrete link that Rousseau himself makes between contemporary Amerindians and the state of nature. After having established passions as the necessary ingredient for the development of human intellectual capacity, Rousseau discusses the negative pole of the passions in the context of violence associated with jealousy. It is at this moment that Rousseau points to the Amerindian's lack of sexual passion. The ambiguity of the lack of passion in this passage appears simple and points to the nostalgia often attributed to

20   *Mythic Origins and the Origins of Myth*

Rousseau's descriptions of the state of nature. The sympathetic portrayal of the biological Native as a representation of the theoretical Native is a foundational perspective in what becomes known as the myth of the *Bon Sauvage*, the Noble Savage. After all, isn't it a positive thing to be lacking the type of passion that leads to 'continually cutting one another's throats'? Yes, of course, but the Amerindian's lack of passion is comprehensive and connotes an inability to reason. For Rousseau, the lack of sexual passion suggests a lack of intellect and even the inability to transmit knowledge through even the simplest of human institutions, the family.

Rousseau regards the family as the model for civil society, stating that, "The most ancient of all societies, and the only one that is natural, is the family" (Cole, The Social Contract, Chapter 2). After describing the Carib as the closest living relative to the savage in the state of nature, Rousseau provides an explanation of interpersonal relations in that state. However, Rousseau's depiction of humanity in the pure state of nature is a radical departure from what many would recognize as human.

> Let us conclude then that man in a state of nature, wandering up and down the forests, without industry, without speech, and without home, an equal stranger to war and to all ties, neither standing in need of his fellow-creatures nor having any desire to hurt them, and perhaps even not distinguishing them one from another; let us conclude that, being self-sufficient and subject to so few passions, he could have no feelings or knowledge but such as befitted his situation; that he felt only his actual necessities, and disregarded everything he did not think himself immediately concerned to notice, and that his understanding made no greater progress than his vanity. If by accident he made any discovery, he was the less able to communicate it to others, as he did not know even his own children. Every art would necessarily perish with its inventor, where there was no kind of education among men, and generations succeeded generations without the least advance; when, all setting out from the same point, centuries must have elapsed in the barbarism of the first ages; when the race was already old, and man remained a child. (Cole, Discourse on Inequality, The First Part)

One of the most salient elements of Rousseau's description of the pure state of nature is radical solitude, situating *primitive* humanity in a non-social state that lacks many of the quintessential components of *culture*. On the nature/culture divide, the Amerindian falls squarely in the camp of nature. The lack of ability to recognize other humans is one of the most sensational of Rousseau's claims. As mentioned above, the family is the original unit of culture, but man in the state of nature "did not know even his own children". In this passage, Rousseau insists on a radical separation between what is commonly understood as human in the West and the Native. One of the most glaring paradoxes in Rousseau's

Mythic Origins and the Origins of Myth 21

thinking involves the contiguous expression of a nostalgia for the simplicity and (a)morality of the state of nature and the decadence and immorality of the state of civil society. On one hand, Rousseau idealizes the European *past* (i.e. the Amerindian *present*). On the other hand, there is a progressivism in Rousseau's philosophy that does not cohere well with his disparaging view of the state of civil society. Rousseau views contemporary society as a *devolution* of morality and overall happiness, however, he promotes the notion of the perfectibility of man. Rousseau firmly asserts that the Native lacks the *philosophy* that humanity *needs*. This assertion clearly shows that Rousseau's essay does not seek to merely elucidate the development of the practice of 'private property' in the *past*, but is turned resolutely toward the *future*. That future can be nothing but a continued *evolution* (not *devolution*) of the material and intellectual superiority of the state of civil society and *not* a return to an idealized state of nature. Within the *Discours sur l'inégalité*, Rousseau insists on the advantages of the state of civil society and his own culture's accomplishments and future prospects. While Rousseau needs a pure origin for humanity for his philosophical façade to stand, his thought is wholly progressive, offering no concession to the lifeways of contemporary Natives. This is the Noble Savage mythology as double discursive narrative technology. In a double voice, Rousseau at once pronounces the Amerindian as superior *and* inferior, as *primitive yet* pure. However, the Noble Savage myth is never wholly positive. There is always a negative element. Another way of looking at the aporia in Rousseau's articulation of the evolution of humankind is through the prism of his own statements in the text. The author admits that any *scientific* verification of his propositions would be impossible, but then proceeds to assert that even though certainty cannot be attained, it *had to happen more or less in the way that he describes*:

> I confess that, as the events I am going to describe might have happened in various ways, I have nothing to determine my choice but conjectures: but such conjectures become reasons, when they are the most probable that can be drawn from the nature of things, and the only means of discovering the truth. The consequences, however, which I mean to deduce will not be barely conjectural; as, on the principles just laid down, it would be impossible to form any other theory that would not furnish the same results, and from which I could not draw the same conclusions. (Cole, Discourse on Inequality, The First Part)

Thus, mythically inflected conjecture becomes not only the basis of theoretical abstraction, but for a sole and unique *truth*. This pattern repeats itself throughout the history of the representation of the Amerindian. Rousseau sets the stage for the entrenchment of the mythological in the epistemological handling of the category of Amerindian in the West. Informed by previous iterations of the Noble Savage, it is Rousseau and his vision of the Amerindian that is

22   *Mythic Origins and the Origins of Myth*

destined to have a profound, lasting influence on the French cultural imaginary. Rousseau's reach expands transhistorically. Perhaps most famously, the founder of structuralism in anthropology, Claude Lévi-Strauss, will harken back wistfully to the theories and writings of Jean-Jacques when he encounters Amerindians nearly two centuries later. In *Tristes tropiques* (1955), Lévi-Strauss is directly influenced by Rousseau in his own theorizing about the Amerindian populations of Brazil that he writes about. Early mythological visions of the Native are transformed into other discursive formations, such as the social sciences. This *transferability* is definitive of the mythic modalities utilized to represent the Native in French and Québécois contexts and beyond. The plasticity of mythic imaginings of the Native makes fictional, hypothetical abstractions take on *truth* value. This is a foundational reality about how the French represent the Amerindian.

Rousseau's rhetorical project in *Discours sur l'inégalité* is to elucidate how the rampant inequalities of the *Ancien Régime* came to be the accepted norm. It is with wistful nostalgia that Rousseau turns his gaze laterally toward the contemporary Native to see the European past. Rousseau compares the states of nature and civil society in the following passage:

> [As] I understand the word *miserable*, it either has no meaning at all, or else signifies only a painful privation of something, or a state of suffering either in body or soul. I should be glad to have explained to me, what kind of misery a free being, whose heart is at ease and whose body is in health, can possibly suffer. I would ask also, whether a social or a natural life is most likely to become insupportable to those who enjoy it. We see around us hardly a creature in civil society, who does not lament his existence: we even see many deprive themselves of as much of it as they can, and laws human and divine together can hardly put a stop to the disorder. I ask, if it was ever known that a savage took it into his head, when at liberty, to complain of life or to make away with himself. Let us therefore judge, with less vanity, on which side the real misery is found. On the other hand, nothing could be more unhappy than savage man, dazzled by science, tormented by his passions, and reasoning about a state different from his own. It appears that Providence most wisely determined that the faculties, which he potentially possessed, should develop themselves only as occasion offered to exercise them, in order that they might not be superfluous or perplexing to him, by appearing before their time, nor slow and useless when the need for them arose. In instinct alone, he had all he required for living in the state of nature; and with a developed understanding he has only just enough to support life in society. (Cole, Discourse on Inequality, The First Part)

In comparing the two states, Rousseau concludes that misery resides in civil society. Suicide in Western cultures and the lack thereof in Amerindian societies bolsters that conclusion. Citing this extreme form of self-destruction, Rousseau schematizes a complex set of data into a digestible duality. This rhetorical choice allows the author to set up the two pillars of his philosophy of man as a reductive binary, positioning the Amerindian at the antipodes of the corruption *and* complexity of Western society. Lacking complexity is not wholly positive, however. Barely hidden within Rousseau's articulation is the presumed superiority of the author himself and by extension that of Europe. This hierarchy is an integral part of the mythic paradigms that characterize mythic representations of the Native. Despite gestures toward relativism, nostalgic guilt, or even supposed assimilation of Amerindian lifeways as remedy for the ails of decadent European society, the instrumentalization of the Native is ensconced in an ideological framework that never questions the naturalized and naturalizing superiority of Western epistemologies. Throughout *Discours sur l'inégalité*, Rousseau is unable to eradicate the trace of European superiority that underpins his discourse, despite the rhetorical objective of the text being predicated on the opposite being true, namely that the state of nature is happier than that of civil society. From the perspective of Philip Deloria (Standing Rock Sioux), the ambiguity at the heart of the *Discours sur l'inégalité* is symptomatic of the French "wanting to savor both civilized order and savage freedom at the same time" (3). This fundamental ambiguity in Rousseau's enunciation of the mythology of the Noble Savage exists because the Ignoble Savage is never completely absent.

Many features of the state of nature are articulated in contradistinction to the European civilization of Rousseau's time. Rhetorically, the Native serves as a contrapuntal figure that permits the philosopher to address matters of concern to his uniquely French audience. The equation of contemporary Indigenous experiences with ancient European history is characteristic of mythologies of the Noble Savage. While Rousseau constructs mythic forms based on the object of the Amerindian, his project is a wholly European one. When French and Québécois authors write the Native, they are writing for and about themselves with the Amerindian playing the dichotomous roles of Same and Other at turns to further advance the rhetorical project's message. Coupled with the temporality employed by Rousseau in the *Discours sur l'inégalité*, this externalized vision of the Amerindian is an act of archiving, a narrative technology that echoes imperialist aims of subjugation. Gerald Vizenor, in *Native Liberty: Natural Reason and Cultural Survivance*, states that:

> The simulation of the *indian* is the "archive fever" of preservation, simplification, and the cause of narrative dominance. Natives are evermore the other, actually twice the other in the transethnic sentiments of *indian* victimry. The *indian* is an archive: the simulations, discoveries, treaties, documents of ancestry, comparative traditions in translation, museum remains, and the aesthetics of victimry. Cultural studies are common cues to the *indian* archive, but not to an actual native presence, or native stories, that unnamable sense of

24 *Mythic Origins and the Origins of Myth*

cultural distinctions. The *indian* archive is *institutive* and, at the same time, the conservation and deconstruction of an elusive native presence in literature and history. (Chapter 1)

Although, Vizenor references modern museological practices of archiving, he does so within a context of 'the simulation of the *indian*', or mythologizing that is redolent of the mythic vision of the Amerindian. Vizenor visualizes the diminished and distorted vision of the Amerindian inherent to Western representational strategies through the use of "indian" with a lower-case letter, echoing the conclusion reached by Saïd that there is something 'deeply symbiotic' that converges within imperialist projects in the periphery and the cultural productions of the center. For Vizenor, simulation points to the Indian, but never evokes the presence of the Native, rather only a caricature of the "indian" that abets the cultural dominance it performs. Rousseau's state of nature is an equally appropriative and subjugating narrative technology. By engaging with the "elusive" Indian, Rousseau only manages to miss the point by repeating the refrain of victimry modeled in the mythic structures of the Western cast of mind. While the text excludes the *real* Amerindian, a surface reading might suggest that the Native is the primary object. The Native's expulsion from civil society adheres whether the mythic category of Indigenous is cast as pure human origin or *primitive* beast, as noble hero or savage villain. There is a third space of bare life left to the Amerindian after the violence of the genocide and conquest, after the representational violence of myth wrought through narrative technologies and structures of the Noble Savage and subsequent mythic evolutions, it is a space outside the ineluctably progressive march onward of history. Expelling the Amerindian permanently and definitively from the Edenic metaphorical ground associated with origins and innocence, the Noble Savage is always already chained to another mythic vision, one of a humanity that inhabits a categorical geography somewhere between the animal and the fallen: the Ignoble Savage.

3 André Thevet's Patagonian Giants and Mythic Circumscription

The Ignoble Savage or simply the Savage *tout court* has a long history in the representation of the Native. One of the earliest French examples can be found in the works of André Thevet. Thevet's *Cosmographie universelle (Universal Cosmology)*, published in 1575, intends to convey the most accurate knowledge available of the known world at the time. Thevet repeatedly insists on the value of his eye-witness expertise of the marvels that he recounts. Paradoxically, much of what Thevet describes was never actually seen by the author. It is in the fourth and final section of the text that the Americas are discussed. It is this section of the *Cosmographie universelle* that is pertinent to the mythic origins of representations of the Amerindian in French. Thevet's writings are at the root of mythic French visions of the Amerindian. Thevet's two principal texts, *Les singularitez de la France antarctique (Singularities of Antarctic France)* (1557) and the *Cosmographie universelle* are some of the earliest examples of French textual representations of the Native. As such, Thevet's depictions of the Amerindian are fundamental in the framing of what the Amerindian signifies in French and Québécois cultural imaginaries. Thevet's texts are in *conversation* and competition with other French writers. In the *Cosmographie universelle*, Thevet never hesitates to inveigh against the ignorance of earlier writers, especially the *cosmographes de cabinet* (armchair cosmographers), who never suffer the difficulties of long, dangerous sea voyages, so vital in his own expert first-hand experience. Therefore, it is striking that the self-appointed French authority on the planet's geographies and peoples begins his discussion of the Americas with a tall tale that he borrows from the Portuguese: a description of the Patagonian giants.

Thevet begins with the description of an alien race of giants and monsters (who are actually quite civil and hospitable until mistreated by the Portuguese sailors). However, as the narrative continues to cover the areas of modern Brazil that Thevet does see, a completely different image of the humanity of the Tupinamba in contradistinction to the Patagonians emerges. This oscillation of mythic poles is ubiquitous in the literature of the early modern period. Copying and plagiarizing descriptions of far-flung peoples that read like bigoted science-fiction in the twenty-first century is just one of many topoi that define the genre of European travel writing that begins the literary representation of the Native in the French tradition. Europe's vision of the Amerindian, as it appears in both travel writing and fiction, engages in the same narrative practices and technologies employed to depict other non-European groups. In *Conquest of America: The Question of the Other* (1982), Tzvetan Todorov draws a connection between this type of mixed methodology predicated on myth as a *sine qua non* of knowledge and genocide:

> At the beginning of the sixteenth century, the Indians of America are certainly present, but nothing is known about them, even if, as we might expect, certain images and ideas concerning other remote populations were projected upon these newly discovered beings. The encounter will never again achieve such an intensity, if indeed that is the word to use the sixteenth century perpetrated the greatest genocide in human history. (Howard 5)

Todorov parallels the mythic at the center of Europeans' attempts to better understand the newly discovered inhabitants of the Americas with genocidal violence. The mythic in representation, especially in literary contexts, is often accompanied by or emerges in the wake of extreme violence. It is crucial for gaining a deeper comprehension of the particularity of the representation of the Native to recognize the centrality of the mythical apparatus. During the early

26 *Mythic Origins and the Origins of Myth*

contact period, comparisons with and reiterations of mythic paradigms utilized in written accounts of other peoples regularly appear. Even after great shifts such as the Enlightenment and the evolution of thought that would become what we now call *science* over subsequent centuries, the mythological origins of the representation of the Amerindian have never been wholly eradicated by rationalism. The mythic is omnipresent in the history of the representation of the Amerindian in French and Québécois cultural imaginaries.

The authorial claims of eye-witness accounts and first-hand experience painstakingly attached to meticulously described locales were anything but anodyne. For, as Thevet explains at the beginning of the tall tale about the Patagonians, his mission is to write about,

> the whole of animals, birds, fishes, grasses, trees, fruits, roots and other particularities that I have been able to gain knowledge of, as well as everything that has been produced for the sole use of man in accordance with God's will: these all being subject to the power of God, in order to omit none of the benefits of nature, together with the order of heaven, the movements of the stars and signs that allow us to know the location of places and the positioning of the time to come. (*Cosmographie universelle* 903, my translation)

Thevet's project mirrors the colonial enterprise: both are extractive. Thevet's extraction happens textually, as opposed, for example, to the material extraction of Brazil wood from the coastal forests and islands that Nicolas Durand de Villegagnon, the leader of the expedition that took Thevet to the New World, oversees. However, both acts of removal (of knowledge and of resources) are complicit, reinforcing one another systematically in the colonial endeavor, much in the same sinister symbiosis signaled by Todorov involving mythic representation and genocide. In the tale of the Patagonian giants, an early form of the Ignoble Savage casts the subsequent discussions of the Amerindian as monstrous *mythic* beings. Additionally, it is worth noting the listing involved in Thevet's description of his project. The list above addresses the natural world and its resources. Understanding and inventorying the non-human animals, natural *productions*, and peoples of the Americas structure many texts of exploration during the sixteenth century. Thevet's text is exemplary in the way that he dissects elements of the environment, separating them textually by subdividing them into distinct chapters. Compartmentalization is an important feature of Western civilization. Wole Soyinka describes this feature of the Western bent for myth as a,

> recognisable Western cast of mind, a compartmentalising habit of thought which periodically selects aspects of human emotion, phenomenal observations, metaphysical intuitions and even scientific deductions and turns them into separatist myths (or 'truths') sustained by a proliferating super-structure of presentation idioms, analogies and analytical modes. (Soyinka 37)

Mythic Origins and the Origins of Myth 27

Soyinka pinpoints how an original object appropriated through observation is transformed by the systematic culturally determined and naturalized mythic apparatus, thereby generating *truth*. The choice of the term 'separatist' is a fortuitous one. Soyinka emphasizes the divisiveness of the mythic mode by locating its nexus in the use of analogy and allegory that function as a categorical line severing any possible connection with the European subject and the non-European object or Other. This mental super-structure and cultural imaginary paves the way for rhetorical appropriation and representation and its practical extensions: exploitation and violence. Disconnecting shared humanity, mythological formations dichotomize, serving as a hinge between Same and Other that inevitably hierarchizes, thereby reinforcing notions of European superiority. Crucially, the epistemological influence of this mythic mode of thinking within the Western mind resonates *textually*. The construction of paradigmatic mythological genealogies, what Soyinka refers to as 'presentation idioms', creates a lexicon of Otherness whereby the West subordinates the non-Western. This allows for the textual to function as an avant-garde for imperialism. By making a monster of the Amerindian, the mythology of the Ignoble Savage facilitates deterritorialization, a necessary first ideological step in the project of empire.

The New World and its inhabitants are transformed through writing. They are wrested from the chaos of the unknown and reconfigured to fit within a defined categorical space. They are assigned a specific position in the ordering of the world. That assignation is always mythic. Written compartmentalization reinforces the ordering of the newly found lands and peoples. Michel Foucault elucidates this concept of order as it relates to the visual and the written:

> Order is at one and the same time, that which is given in things as their inner law, the hidden network that determines the way they confront one another, and also that which has no existence except in the grid created by a glance, an examination, a language; and it is only in the blank spaces of this grid that order manifests itself in depth as though already there, waiting in silence for the moment of its expression. (Sheridan, *Order of Things*, Preface)

For Foucault, the Western propensity toward a compartmentalizing vision of world order, that is then conjured linguistically, represents an innate reality, one that was always 'already there'. It is the 'waiting in silence' of that order, however that speaks most directly to the matter at hand: mythological paradigms of representation of the Other. Simultaneously silencing and naturalizing, the West's speaking and evoking the Native is an act of scripturally performative violence based on the narrative technology of the mythic mode. Foucault's formulation touches on the core of the West's experience of the external. When the Old and New World 'confront one another', it is the *mythic* and not the 'inner law' of reality and truth itself that has finally arrived at its long-anticipated 'moment of expression'. The naturalizing of the defining gaze of categorization

28 *Mythic Origins and the Origins of Myth*

that Foucault painstakingly deconstructs in 1969's *Order of Things* is one of the fundamental features of the mythological. It is the cornerstone upon which the ontological difference between the Same and the (Amerindian) Other emerges from the context of Western mythic paradigms. What position, then, does the Amerindian occupy in the grid of the Western ordering of the world, in the French cultural imaginary in one of the first instances of the confrontation of the Old and New Worlds being committed to writing? At the moment of scriptural revelation of that intrinsic truth that was always 'already there, waiting in silence for its moment of expression', how do the French apprehend, interpret, and represent the Native? In short, the answer is: as a monster. The Ignoble Savage myth dehumanizes through deformation and exaggeration, employing what Soyinka calls Europeans' 'metaphysical intuitions' to portray the Amerindian as non-human animal.

Returning to Thevet's *Cosmographie universelle*, how does Thevet categorize the Native in the grid of the naturalized order of the world as defined by the mythic lens of Western culture? What introduction does the royal cosmographer make between his French readership and the Amerindian? The initial vision of the Native in the *Cosmographie universelle* is a retelling of the mythically inflected account of Magellan's exploration of Cape Horn in Patagonia.

First, it is the Patagonian giant that usurps the Amerindian Other through metonymic legerdemain, thereby substituting real Natives for the Ignoble Savage. Thevet's recounting of the legend of the Patagonian giants is a seminal moment in the representation of the Amerindian in the French cultural imaginary. Thevet could well have begun his discussion of the Americas by reporting on the coastal groups in the region of modern-day Rio de Janeiro with whom he had direct experience. Yet, he chooses to begin with the mythic and the monstrous. In the sixteenth century, this juxtaposition of mythical and proto-ethnographical elements is in no way problematic. It is conventional. The mythical coexists with(in) the real and the objective infiltrates the realm of fantasy. *Truth* emerges from the fictionalizing and naturalizing lens of analogic mythologies and their inherent narrative technologies. Second, as in Thevet's list above: the Native is categorized as part of Nature. The Amerindian is implicitly equated with that all-encompassing totality which includes the birds, fishes, trees, etc. This is evident to the reader of the *Cosmographie universelle*, because immediately after having constructed the list of what it is in his purview to describe, the author begins that encyclopedic inventory by telling the tale of the Patagonian giants. The Native's position in the ordering of the world occupies a liminal space of monstrosity, on the same level as natural resources. The equation of the Amerindian with Nature is a fundamental aspect of mythic (mis)understandings of the Amerindian Other. The imbrication of Nature and Native is a central component of the genealogy of mythic representation of the Amerindian in French and Québécois cultural imaginaries. Thevet begins his discussion of the Americas with the tale of the Patagonian giants. It is critical to comprehend how the

Patagonian tale functions in the broader history of the mythic representation of the Native in the French cultural imaginary. This framing of the Amerindian through the mythic lens of the Ignoble Savage precludes other possible visions of the Native. The dual system of Ignoble Savage and Noble Savage is a mythological system that resists any conclusive definition of the Native. This double discursive narrative technology locks the signification of the Amerindian into a mythic space. However, it is essential to recognize that the mythic machine inevitably categorizes the Amerindian as inferior. One of the principal consequences of this form of mythological representation is that the Native, whether Ignoble or Noble is forever condemned as Savage. The Savage is non-human. Whether Patagonian giant or symbol of a primordial innocence associated philosophically with the Edenic, identification between the European and the Amerindian Other is thwarted by the 'separatist myths' that pass themselves off as *truth*. The Ignoble Savage myth posits the Amerindian as *subhuman*. The Noble Savage myth defines the Amerindian as *superhuman*. The Amerindian is never wholly *human* in the same way that the European is, due to the categorization of the Native via the mythological mode. In Thevet's introduction to the Americas in his *Cosmographie universelle*, the depiction of the Native that emerges from the tall tale of the Patagonian giants is one of dehumanized, mythologized monsters. The Patagonian episode conditions the possibilities available to the French in their attempts to apprehend and incorporate the Amerindian into their worldview. In this way, when the early modern French writer mythically represents the Amerindian, it is an act of circumscription. It is not merely descriptive, but also prescriptive.

Myth goes beyond description; it calls for belief, or what Bourdieu calls "recognition", in a different way than a realistic portrayal does. Much ink has been spilt discussing the appropriative acts of writing or gazing at the Other in deconstructionist and postcolonial theoretical discourses. However, mythic representation has not been adequately analyzed with regard to the epistemological grappling with human difference that is the textual representation of the Other. The history of the evolution of the mythic representation of the Amerindian Other offers an ideal example of the mythologizing tendency as it is expressed in Western cultures. The Indigenous is the spectral unknown. The unknown carries along with it the seeds of curiosity and panic. It is through myth that French writers imbue the Amerindian with this capacity to conjure wonder or anxiety, consequences that emerge from Thevet's reiteration of the tale of the Patagonian giants. The specific mythic mode that Thevet engages with is one of the most prevalent images of the Native to emerge in Western representations: the Ignoble Savage. Throughout the history of French representations of the Amerindian, the Ignoble Savage trope is a ubiquitous narrative technology employed by authors in many disparate genres. Another historically significant travel writer from the early period of contact between the Old and New Worlds is Samuel de Champlain.

30 *Mythic Origins and the Origins of Myth*

4 The Inimical and Idealized: Champlain's Mythic Armouchiquois

Often in parallel with Jacques Cartier, Champlain is deemed a founding father of not only New France, but of Canada more generally. Champlain writes extensively about both the geographies and peoples of the Americas. Through his years of colony building and exploration he acquires vast experience with the Amerindians living in the St. Lawrence River Valley and beyond. There are, nonetheless, many examples of the mythic modes of both the Noble and Ignoble Savage in Champlain's oeuvre. It is the explorer's writings on the Armouchiquois that are particularly enlightening given the focus of this study, because they demonstrate the centrality of the mythic in early modern French and Québécois depictions of the Native. Champlain occupies a liminal space of convergence between French and Québécois paradigms. Founding the colony of New France, Champlain is an initial voice in the tradition of Québécois representations of the Native. Comparatively, the Québécois cultural imaginary is characterized by more direct experience with Natives. This proximity with the Amerindian does not preclude the mythic distortions typical of French representations, however.

Two specific passages are of special significance: Champlain's initial portrayal of the Armouchiquois, based on second-hand reports, employs the Ignoble Savage, and a second description of the Armouchiquois, based on Champlain's own eye-witnessing, evokes the Noble Savage. These examples are informative because they indicate a continuity in the use of mythological discourses. The connection between Thevet's giants and Champlain's monstrous Armouchiquois is in the mythology of the Ignoble Savage as articulated in the French and Québécois cultural imaginaries.

The Ignoble Savage presents the Native as animalized object, rather than human subject. It is a discourse of subordination, placing the Native in the position of inferior, as *subhuman* in the grid of the 'ordering of the world'. The tendency to represent the Amerindian as Ignoble Savage is a nearly omnipresent feature of European constructions concerning Others, while the Noble Savage motif is more limited in its reiteration (Dickason xv). Representations of the Native as Ignoble Savage are not merely philosophical, scientific, or literary forays into the world of myth; this narrative technology effects praxis. Olive Dickason states that:

> The fact that such views had little to do with reality did not mitigate their fundamental importance in colonization. By classifying the Amerindians as savages, Europeans were able to create the ideology that helped to make it possible to launch one of the great movements in the history of western civilization: the colonization of overseas empires. (xiii)

Mythic Origins and the Origins of Myth 31

Dickason associates written representation with political violence, dispossession, and genocide. Champlain's writings on the Armouchiquois are an illustrative example of the Ignoble Savage trope. This example is pertinent because of the revisionist turn taken by Champlain after meeting the Armouchiquois in person. Champlain's representations of the Armouchiquois constitute an informative case-study in the history of the monstrous Native, but also of the ambiguity of the mythic Amerindian in the French and Québécois cultural imaginaries.

The Armouchiquois occupied parts of what is now coastal Maine in the United States. A French name for the Abenaki, they are a prominent group in the region at the time of Champlain's first voyages in the area (Dickason and McNab 88). Champlain pens his first account according to the report of an associate named Prévert. Prévert undertakes a reconnoitering expedition to scout for deposits of copper. It is unknown whether or not Prévert ever lays eyes on the Armouchiquois, or if he simply relies on the descriptions of his Souriquois guides. One thing is certain: the Souriquois (Micmac) and the Armouchiquois (Abenaki) are not on amical terms. The Souriquois fear the Armouchiquois as formidable adversaries in a struggle for local strategic advantage. To understand the image of the Armouchiquois in Champlain's first account, a brief explanation of the French system of Amerindian alliances and how that system effects the representation of Indigenous groups is useful. The French-Amerindian system of alliances is influential in the discourses created about Amerindian groups in French texts. Alliances are not based on identifiable cultural elements; the French do not create alliances with groups because they are 'less savage' than other groups. Financial interests are pivotal, whereas moral and cultural considerations are secondary. The practical necessities of the extraction of resources and the subsistence of the colony's population determine which Native groups are French allies and which are not, ultimately being cast as enemies in the Ignoble Savage mode. The most glaring example of the arbitrary nature of the French-Amerindian alliance system is the French engagement with the Iroquoian group that occupies the St. Lawrence River valley during Jacques Cartier's voyages of exploration in the 1530s and 1540s. Though Cartier is not ultimately a very successful diplomat, the French seek alliance with the Iroquoians that they first encounter, because Cartier's expedition faces threats from scurvy to starvation. Upon Champlain's return at the beginning of the seventeenth century, the Iroquoians met by Cartier have been replaced by Algonquin peoples. The Iroquois are the enemies of the French in the seventeenth century, and remain so throughout much of the remainder of the colonial history of New France. Thus, there is little but expediency that influences French decisions regarding who will be included as allies or who will be excluded as enemies.

Representations of allies are typically more positive and romanticized (Noble Savage), whereas representations of enemies are often negatively inflected (Ignoble Savage). In the portrayal of the Armouchiquois, Prévert is guided by

32 *Mythic Origins and the Origins of Myth*

Souriquois (Micmac) who are antagonistic with the Armouchiquois. The desire to extract copper motivates the French to seek out guides. They first meet the Souriquois (Micmac) who take them to locations where they believe copper deposits exist, an area occupied by the Armouchiquois (Abenaki). This contextualization can inform a critical reading of Champlain's representation of the Armouchiquois by highlighting how the desires of the groups involved in the creation of this mythic representation intersect. The convergence of the French desire for copper and the Souriqouis desire for the defeat of the Armouchiquois are essential factors in the creation of the Ignoble Savage myth of the Armouchiquois as subhuman monster. Had the geographical positions of the Souriquois and the Armouchiquois been reversed, and Prévert had instead initially encountered the Armouchiquois, the Souriquois as mythic monster would likely be the topic presently being discussed. Intrinsic, identifiable qualities are external and not integral to the mythic machine's deformations.

Champlain's initial description of the Armouchiquois is based on Prévert's report:

> [The] Armouchiquois, are savages that are wholly monstrous in their bodily form; because their heads are small and their bodies short, with tiny arms and thighs like those of a skeleton, with long, fat legs that are quite straight; and when they are sitting crouched on their heals, their knees stick out half a foot higher than the tops of their heads, which is strange and seems to be outside the natural order. They are nevertheless fit and determined, and they live on the best lands of the entire Acadian coast: it is for these reasons that the Souriquois fear them very much. (Champlain 122, my translation)

As in Thevet's tale of the Patagonian giants, Champlain situates the Native in the realm of the monstrous. The Armouchiquois body is deformed by the mythology of the Ignoble Savage. The focus on physical abnormalities concretizes ontological divergence. Excluding the Armouchiquois from the categorization of human and Same, the mythic contortions in Champlain's text render them as non-human Other. As in a funhouse mirror, some features are grotesquely shortened whereas others are exaggeratedly elongated. The trunk undergoes shrinkage just as the legs are stretched. Through his insistence on inhumanly long lower limbs, Champlain paints the Armouchiquois body in a simian posture, evoking a bizarre visualization with the knees towering impossibly over the head of the squatting figure. The accumulative effect disqualifies the Armouchiquois, dehumanizing and mythologizing the Amerindian body in the vernacular of the Ignoble Savage. Champlain's initial description of the Armouchiquois implies a sliding scale or spectrum of savagery or humanity that is reiterated in much European discourse regarding the Indigenous of the Americas. Although the Armouchiquois body may be portrayed in this way due to contextual motivations of both their Souriquois and French enemies, there is no clear demarcation

Mythic Origins and the Origins of Myth 33

between the Armouchiquois and the Souriquois, or any other Amerindian group. In depicting the Armouchiquois through the distorting lens of the Ignoble Savage, Champlain presents a discourse that inherently stains all Amerindian bodies with at least a trace of Armouchiquois monstrousness. Irrevocably banished from the Same, the Native is categorized as inhuman Other in the ordering of the world which evokes the deformed Armouchiquois body as if it were always "already there, waiting in silence for its moment of expression". One of the insidious aspects of the Ignoble Savage myth is its *transferability*, its slippery attribution to the entire category of Amerindian in a generalized fashion, allowing it to be applied in infinite frames of reference, despite clear contextual disparities. Within the most Noble of Savages exists a monster. Myths within this genealogy are intrinsically sticky, attaching themselves to multiple sites of meaning, semantic and syntactic shapeshifters that glob onto the Amerindian in various discursive registers transgeographically, transhistorically, and interdisciplinarily emerging as *truth*.

The geolocation of the Armouchiquois speaks to the motivations behind this specific representation in the Ignoble Savage mode. The Armouchiquois occupy the most beautiful areas of coastal Acadia; the obvious implication being that, as monsters, they do not deserve to occupy such geographies. Champlain employs the mythic language of the Ignoble Savage in conjunction with the Western ideology of *terra nullius* to narratively deterritorialize the Armouchiquois. As Glen Sean Coulthard (Yellowknife Dene) notes in *Red Skin, White Masks: Rejecting the Colonial Politics of Recognition*:

> Because Indigenous societies were so low on the natural scale of social and cultural evolution, settler authorities felt justified in claiming North America legally vacant, or *terra nullius*, and sovereignty was acquired by the mere act of settlement itself. (Chapter 3)

Terra nullius is an ideology in *conversation* and synergy with the mythic representational paradigms discussed in this volume. From the animalizing of the Ignoble Savage, to the Ecological Savage's more clement, but nonetheless dehumanizing situating of the Amerindian as part of the natural rather than the cultural, to the extinction narrative of the Vanishing Indian paradigm, to the act of Going Native whereby non-Indigenous attempt to culturally usurp Natives and (re)present themselves as superior examples of the mythic model, the connection between the Native and physical, as well as metaphysical, geographies is deemed one of vacancy rather than occupancy, thus clearing the path for invasion. Settler-colonialism is not merely a physical act of severing, it is accompanied by narrative technologies that abet more obvious forms of violence. Indeed, the mutual desire of the French and their Micmac allies is to dispossess the Armouchiquois. The Micmac seek to leverage their newfound French allies militarily against their old enemy in the region. The French value copper ore

34   *Mythic Origins and the Origins of Myth*

more than objective observation; therefore, the narrative technology of the myth of the Ignoble Savage functions to advance both the Micmac and French designs through the mythologizing of the Armouchiquois. Mythologizing discourses represent Amerindian bodies in exaggerated forms to expel those bodies outside of humanity. This expulsion opens the door, via the Western ideology of *terra nullius*, to the physical expulsion of the Amerindian from the land, revealing the vacancy that was "already there".

In the case of the Armouchiquois, another French writer in the region at the time, Marc Lescarbot, in his *Histoire de la Nouvelle-France* (1609) explains how Champlain is misled by Prévert *and* by extension by the Micmac. Lescarbot tells how Champlain eventually recognizes the inaccuracy of the Armouchiquois monster depiction:

> Thus, Champlain having trusted the account of Sir Prévert of Saint-Malo, wrote what we just reported concerning the Armouchiquois and the *Gougou*, as well as the glint of their copper mine. All of which Champlain has since recognized as being imaginary fabrications. (Book 3, ch. 29, my translation)

Speaking of the deformative description of the Armouchiquois, in addition to a legendary beast, the *Gougou*, Lescarbot recounts how Champlain later realizes that Prévert's account is fantastical. Lescarbot states that the glimmer of copper drives Prévert to present the Armouchiquois in such a grotesque light. Furthermore, Lescarbot turns the mythologized portrait on its head by insisting on the beauty of the Armouchiquois, "As for the Armouchiquois, they are as beautiful a people (with this term I also include the women) as we are, well put together and fit" (Book 3, Chapter 29, my translation). The reversal of the monster image emerges in Lescarbot's writings about the Armouchiquois, as it eventually does in Champlain's writing. In mythological discourses on the Native there is a fundamental capacity for accruing additional, often opposite mythological images and applying them to the same Amerindian group. During Champlain's exploration of coastal Maine, he gains extensive knowledge of the Armouchiquois. The representation of the Armouchiquois as monster is recanted. What impression do real Armouchiquois make? One element that Champlain remarks upon is their physical appearance. In his first description, deformed bodies of the Armouchiquois are central to the Ignoble Savage myth. Closer to animal than human, the Armouchiquois body evokes potential violence and excludes the Native from the cultural. The image that arises in Champlain's eye-witness account is strikingly different:

> [The Armouchiquois] appear to be very happy: their chief was in good shape, young and very fit: we sent some items onto land to trade with them, but they had nothing but their clothes, which they exchanged, because they don't stockpile any furs except the ones they use to wear. Sir de Mons had some

Mythic Origins and the Origins of Myth 35

merchandise taken to their chief, with which the chief was quite satisfied, he came on board our vessel several times to see us. These savages shave the hair off the tops of their heads and wear the rest of it quite long, which they dye and knot very neatly at the back in several different fashions, with feathers attached to their heads. They paint their faces in black and red like the other savages we have seen. These peoples' bodies are fit and well put together: their weaponry are pikes, clubs, bows and arrows, at the end of which some put the tail of a fish named Signoc, others affix bones, others are made entirely out of wood. They plow and cultivate the land, which we hadn't seen yet. Instead of ploughs, they have a very hard wooden implement, shaped like a spade. (Champlain 200–1) (my translation)

The first individual Armouchiquois depicted by Champlain is their young chief. His portrait is diametrically opposed to the earlier account. The Armouchiquois are endowed with positive physical and moral attributes. Civility and hospitality characterize the young Armouchiquois chief. The initial exchanges recounted by Champlain would have likely been understood as a ritualized reciprocal gift-giving ceremony from the Armouchiquois perspective, rather than a market transaction. A relationship between the Armouchiquois is quickly established, including regular visits to the French vessel. There is no evidence of conflict, only exchange and social calls aboard the ship. One feature that anchors the physical description is the hair style of the Armouchiquois. Champlain explains how they tie up their long locks neatly. Such care taken in outward appearance would be something a Frenchman of Champlain's status would have certainly appreciated, an evident sign of culture. Champlain quickly passes over the facial paint, the red and black typical of the Amerindian tribes he has already encountered on his many travels in the region, yet facial painting is also an undeniable sign of meaning and culture. Champlain insists that the Armouchiquois are healthy and well-proportioned. It is clear in the second portrait of the Armouchiquois that they are physically likened to a human model that resembles the category of which Champlain himself identifies, not the simian model of the previous description. However, the author has yet to pass over into the mode of the Noble Savage. It is only when Champlain discusses agricultural practices that idealization occurs. Agriculture serves as a marker of civility to the French exploring North America. Agriculture is the culmination of the idealized, Noble Savage image. While often related to warrior culture, there is equally an agrarian Nobel Savage that foreshadows idealizing sedentarism in subsequent periods. The cumulative effect of physical well-being, civility and hospitality in social relations, a finely equipped warrior class, and the practice of agriculture creates an iteration of the Noble Savage mythic mode. In contrast to more philosophical inflections of the Noble Savage myth (Montaigne, Rousseau), Champlain's Noble Savage appears organic and is based on observation.

36 *Mythic Origins and the Origins of Myth*

The Noble Savage in philosophical discourse of is a rhetorical tool. The philosopher weaponizes the myth of the Native. In the hands of Champlain, a colonizer with commercial and military objectives, the Noble Savage is a much more practical. Demonstrating the close relationship between the narrative technology of the mythic mode and settler-colonial praxis, the characterization of the Armouchiquois as pure and simple farmers and warriors inhabiting a beautiful, resource-rich region suspected of harboring copper ore materializes in the exploitative machinations formulated by Champlain, specifically plans to build a French fortress in the zone. The shifting perspectives on the Armouchiquois in Champlain's writings are significant. Both examples of Champlain's representations of the Armouchiquois are equally driven, motivated depictions. They say more about their author's shifting points of view or immediate objectives than about the Armouchiquois as real people. In the following section, the philosophical representations by famed essayist Michel de Montaigne are examined as a foundational moment in the evolution of the mythic vision of the Amerindian in French and Québécois cultural imaginaries.

5 Montaigne's *Bon Sauvage*

Having examined an Enlightenment articulation of the Noble Savage mythology in the writings of Jean-Jacques Rousseau, it is critical to contextualize that philosophical framework in its historical lineage derived from and in intertextual *conversation* with preceding authors' interpretations of the *bon sauvage*. The Noble Savage myth is a fundamental mythic vision of the Native in the French and Québécois cultural imaginaries that emerges during the period of first contacts and persists to the present day. Berkhofer Jr. describes the trope's ubiquity, stating that:

> As information about the inhabitants of the New World became better known in the Old, Native Americans entered the literary and imaginative works of European writers, particularly the French. In this way the American Indian became part of the *bon sauvage* or Noble Savage tradition so long an accompaniment of the Golden Age or paradisiacal mythology of Western civilization. (73)

In this section, I investigate the most famous example of the *bon sauvage* tradition in the French High Renaissance: Michel de Montaigne. The two essays he devotes to the New World, "Des cannibales" and "Des coches", illustrate the evolving rhetorical treatment that the Native would receive in the *Essais*. Efforts to define the relative importance of the Amerindian within the *Essais* have led many critics to conclude that they merely constitute a thought experiment, a random terrain upon which Montaigne's *essaying* of reason is played out. Todorov posits that "the other is *only* an instrument of self-knowledge"

("L'Etre et l'Autre", 127, my emphasis) in the *Essais*. The arbitrariness of the Native is apparent, because, "the other is…never known" (Todorov, "L'Etre et l'Autre", 125). Todorov insists on the author's inability to understand or represent the Amerindian. Montaigne's instrumentalization of the Native within the narrative technology of myth circumscribes the category of Amerindian. The Amerindian depictions are a *means* to construct a textual space that allows Montaigne's philosophical *ends* to become visible through form, but decidedly divorced from any real, tangible entanglement with the content they examine (De Lutri, "Montaigne on the Noble Savage: A Shift in Perspective," 207–8). Echoing Todorov, Duval places Montaigne's two chapters on the New World in the greater context of pedagogy, claiming that the essays that address the topic of the Amerindian play a specific role, "as working exercises, as kinetic tests of the reader's judgment", in Montaigne's Book of the World (112). Duval suggests that other non-European would have served just as well. A tradition of the indiscriminate confounding of *primitive* groups to support an author's suppositions becomes widespread in French literary and academic discourse in the centuries following Montaigne's *random* discussion of the Native. The father of natural history, Comte de Buffon, draws similar parallels according to his climate theory of evolution. As social sciences develop in the nineteenth, twentieth, and twenty-first centuries, this practice becomes endemic to much of anthropological and sociological discourse, especially in the work of Lucien Lévy-Bruhl, Émile Durkheim, and Claude Lévi-Strauss. Returning to Montaigne's instrumentalization of the Amerindian in a broader intellectual exercise, this mythical distortion of the real Native into the superhuman form of the Noble Savage sets a precedent of exploitive narrative technologies of representation of the Amerindian. Employing the pure, naïve Amerindian as counterpoint to the corrupt, decadent European, after all, is central to a critical understanding of Rousseau's *Discours sur l'inégalité* discussed in the first section. The *hypothetical* nature of the *bon sauvage* in Montaigne's has a profound impact on French and Québécois cultural imaginaries. Whether one considers the Amerindian to be an interchangeable pawn in Montaigne's game of rhetoric or not, the paradigm of the *bon sauvage* shapes Francophone understandings of the Native. "Des cannibales" is the more influential of the two essays, spurring "the sociological revolution [that] became a distinctive feature of French intellectual life" (Richman, 27). "Des coches" may be considered less influential, yet it is in this essay that Montaigne makes his most convincing points about a truly reciprocal, humanitarian vision of the Amerindian. Additionally, "Des coches" shows the evolution of Montaigne's philosophy of the Native. The second essay highlights examples of Amerindian culture and society that aim at a more material exposition of their equality, such as artisanal skills and architectural achievements. Therefore, "Des coches" can be seen as demonstrating in a much clearer way the importance of the Amerindian as philosophical object, rather than contemplative abstraction. As a point of departure, examining the articulation of the *bon sauvage* via the key concept of

38 *Mythic Origins and the Origins of Myth*

Native purity vis-à-vis European perversion permits a recognition of one of the primary features of the *bon sauvage*. In "Des cannibales", Montaigne illustrates the privative mode to highlight Amerindian virtue:

> It irritates me that Lycurgus nor Plato had any knowledge of them, for it seems to me that what experience has taught us about those peoples surpasses not only all the descriptions with which poetry has beautifully painted the Age of Gold and all its ingenious fictions about Man's blessed early state, but also the very conceptions and yearnings of philosophy. They could not even imagine a state of nature so simple and so pure as the one we have learned about from experience; they could not even believe that societies of men could be maintained with so little artifice, so little in the way of human solder. I would tell Plato that those people have no trade of any kind, no acquaintance with writing, no knowledge of numbers, no terms for governor or political superior, no practice of subordination or of riches or poverty, no contracts, no inheritances, no divided estates, no occupation but leisure, no concern for kinship-except such as is common to them all -no clothing, no agriculture, no metals, no use of wine or corn. Among them you hear no words for treachery, lying, cheating, avarice, envy, backbiting or forgiveness. How remote from such perfection would Plate find that Republic which he thought up. (Screech 98)

While the privative mode is typically wholly negative in its evaluation of the societal attributes of Native groups, deeming the Indian incapable of the achievements of civilization, Montaigne's privative description is innovative. De Lutri recounts that "Des cannibales" has traditionally been read as a manifestation of the device of inversion ("Montaigne's "Des cannibales": Invention/Experience," 77). This technique is at play in Montaigne's iteration of the privative mode, wherein the very things the Amerindians lack are coded as negative, turning the unfavorable into an advantage. In keeping with the linguistic bent of the essay in general, the semantics of the terms *barbare* and *sauvage* largely shape Montaigne's argument, the privileged site of the Tupinamba's lexicon is where the inversion is most radical. The Amerindians lack terms for "treachery, lying, cheating, avarice, envy, backbiting, or forgiveness". Of course, these lacunae are coded as positive. Not having recourse to words to describe vices, the lexical privative mode establishes the Amerindian as virtuous. The Noble Savage myth is polyphonic, speaking simultaneously about the Amerindian and the European, saying more about the latter than the former. It is polysemous, equally presenting an elegiac discourse regarding the Tupinamba and a derisory one vis-à-vis European. The *bon sauvage* is a comparative model that permits criticism of the author's own society while deflecting some of the consequences of an outright critique by the transference of the message onto the Amerindian Other, all in the guise of objectivity.

Semantics are central to Montaigne's argument. Starting with Pyrrhus' observation regarding the Roman army (notably the allusion to the Greek etymology of barbarian), Montaigne links the Amerindian to the Roman by concluding that

> there is nothing savage or barbarous about those peoples, but that every man calls barbarous anything he is not accustomed to; it is indeed the case that we have no other criterion of truth or right-reason than the example and form of the opinions and customs of our own country. (Screech 97)

Montaigne signals the cultural structures of myth in his designation of *truth* as contingent. The 'forms' of opinions and representations are the mythic structures of the Noble and Ignoble Savage. Despite the gestures toward relativism within the author's two essays dealing with the Amerindian, Montaigne recognizes the strictures of the categorizing cast of the Western mind, reiterating mythic discourses while he interrogates their validity philosophically. In the Renaissance, when an historical understanding of what we now refer to as the Dark Ages began to emerge, Antiquity is associated with the Golden Age as alluded to in Berkhofer Jr.'s quote at the beginning of this section, relegating the Native to a space governed by the "paradisiacal mythology of Western civilization". Purity is linked to Antiquity in the Renaissance mind. Despite the virulent sectarian religious strife that characterizes the period, many scholars share a reverence for the pagan thinkers of the Greco-Roman tradition. Identification of the Amerindian with Antiquity bolsters the Noble Savage myth in Montaigne's writings. Some critics have cast doubt, however, on Montaigne's sincerity in "Des cannibales" with regard to his lavish praise of the Tupinamba. This is most clearly evidenced by the final quip of the essay, the Rouen meeting. It is here that Montaigne comically signals the fact that the Tupinamba with whom he converses are not wearing pants. The Native-Roman comparison claims equality between the two groups in a specific way. The nostalgic vision of Rome and its now defunct greatness forever lost in the annals of history is the opposite number of the Tupinamba barbarian-Roman barbarian juxtaposition. The Tupinamba object is frozen in a past that never measures up to or reaches the plenitude of the present moment that the European subject occupies. Montaigne does make efforts to present architectural prowess on par with Antiquity in "Des coches", specifically in his discussion of the sculptural garden of the Peruvian king and the impressive Inca royal road between Quito and Cuzco, however the temporality remains fixed in the past (1424, 1431). The Inca examples are predicated on the fact that the Inca will no longer be able to create anything of this order ever again. Much in the same way that Ancient Egyptian civilization is treated in the orientalist mode in Western discourses, the assumption being that contemporaneous populations of the Nile Delta will never again build pyramids. The Amerindian as creator, as agentive actor is lost

40   *Mythic Origins and the Origins of Myth*

to history, as well. It is important to note the emergence of a certain temporality attached to the Amerindian: the relegation to the past.

In "Des coches" Montaigne clearly explains how the temporal dimension functions in his philosophical understanding of the two cultural groups. The author's discourse takes the metaphorical shape of a description of an individual's life cycle. In keeping with the Edenic associations of the mythology of the Noble Savage, the New World is coded as child:

> Our world has just discovered another one: and who will answer for its being the last of its brothers, since up till now its existence was unknown to the daemons, to the Sibyls, and to ourselves? It is no less big and full and solid than our own; its limbs are as well developed: yet it is so new, such a child, that we are still teaching it its ABC; a mere fifty years ago it knew nothing of writing, weights and measures, clothing, any sort of corn or vine. It was still naked at the breast, living only by what its nursing Mother provided. If we are right to conclude that our end is nigh, and that poet is right that his world is young, then that other world will only be emerging into light when ours is leaving it. The world will be struck with the palsy: one of its limbs will be paralysed while the other is fully vigorous, yet I fear we shall have considerably hastened the decline and collapse of that young world by our contagion and that we shall have sold it dear our opinions and our skills. (Screech 376–7)

The infantilization of the Amerindian takes a different direction, in contradistinction to Montaigne's overall portrayal of the innocence of the Native. The privative mode makes another appearance, yet what the Amerindian lacks are precisely the negative components of European civilization. Here, the privative mode takes its original form and is truly negative. The negative is most readily evident in the culinary examples of wheat and wine. French readers would, after all, find it difficult to admire a breadless, wineless world. One of the most ubiquitous representational models employed in descriptions of the Amerindian is the conflation of Nature and the Native. The form that the Native-Nature nexus takes in this example is the suckling infant (Amerindian) and the nurturing Mother (Nature). In conjunction with the rudimentary level of development that the privative mode of the passage suggests, a specific relationship with Nature is privileged in the imagery Montaigne chooses to employ. Far from more modern conceptions of the idealized, deeply knowledgeable symbiosis associated with the Indigenous in relation to the environment, Montaigne proposes a hierarchical relationship of dependence. The defenseless newborn is the analogy. Agency and understanding are precluded. Rousseau's state of nature, wherein the Amerindian does not recognize fellow humans and lacks the rudimentary social structure of the family, is another example of the dehumanizing that accompanies the purity of the mythic *bon sauvage*. Mythic infantilization is reductive and simplistic. The intimate store of information about the plants and animals that the Amerindian possesses about the world they inhabit is silenced. Epistemologically, Montaigne defines civilization as inherently capable of manipulating Nature. Couched within the author's praise of Native *innocence* is a naturalization of French agricultural and economic praxis. Within the apparently positive portrayal of the Noble Savage is a hierarchy that inevitably situates the Amerindian as inferior, as incapable of acting on/in the world as the European does. If the Amerindian is circumscribed via the device of infantilization, it is to put the decrepit, decadent European metaphor into starker relief. In another passage from "Des cannibales" Montaigne develops a portrait of the Native as lacking agency:

> They are not striving to conquer new lands, since without toil or travail they still enjoy that bounteous Nature who furnishes them abundantly with all they need, so that they have no concern to push back their frontiers. They are still in that blessed state of desiring nothing beyond what is ordained by their natural necessities: for them anything further is merely superfluous The generic term which they use for men of the same age is 'brother'; younger men they call 'sons'. As for the old men, they are the 'fathers' of everyone else: they bequeath all their goods, indivisibly to all these heirs in common, there being no other entitlement than that with which Nature purely and simply endows all her creatures by bringing them into this world. (Screech 87)

Rejecting Rousseau's radical notion of the Native as not existing in family units, Montaigne places the family at the center of social interaction, albeit in a narrowly masculine linguistic context. The abundance of natural productions implies an elementary level of interaction with the natural world, and, by extension, an elementary, infantile level of cultural achievement, which is implicitly linked via the privative mode to the genocidal conquest that Montaigne's condemnation of the Black Legend seemingly would abhor. Montaigne's Noble Savage resembles the gatherer of anthropology's hunter-gatherer categorizations. With everything that one could possibly need being there for the taking, the Native becomes fixed temporally and developmentally in the stage of infancy. Silenced, however, in such glaring generalizations, are the elaborate systems of knowledge gained and transmitted over generations that the Indigenous employ to successfully navigate their environments and thrive therein. Rather than constituting a humanistic vision of the Native, Montaigne's mythic mode privileges Western socioeconomic archetypes. Surface-level nostalgia concerning an 'earlier stage of development' that does not entail the same necessary desires does not imply that Montaigne has any intention to return to Nature, or that he espouses Going Native. If one unwittingly obfuscates the extensive know-how required as to what, where, and when to *gather* resources and how to process plant materials after having acquired them, an even larger, more significant omission (that Montaigne mentions obliquely later when discussing Tupinamba versions of bread and beer,

42   *Mythic Origins and the Origins of Myth*

derived from manioc root) is the existence of agriculture. The depiction of Nature as superabundant and facile and the representation of the Amerindian as living in a state of childlike dependency on this bounty are reductive. Denying the history of the independent development of agriculture in the Americas is one way that the Noble Savage myth supports epistemological, evolutionary hierarchies that mark the Amerindian as inferior.

The naturalized superiority of the European and the ineluctable exploitation of the natural resources of the Americas is an intrinsic part of the discursive formation wherein the trope of the Noble Savage is most influentially articulated in French literature in the sixteenth century, in the essays "Des cannibales" and "Des coches" by Michel de Montaigne. The identity of the Amerindian in these texts is coterminous with the natural environment. According to Montaigne's mythology, exploitation of Nature erodes purity, the defining characteristic of the *bon sauvage*. Military conquest and representation are reciprocal. The narrative technologies of the mythic mode echo the violence of conquest epistemologically, providing a cultural framework for understanding and subjugating the Amerindian Other. In the history of the invasions of the Americas, the innocence and simplicity of the Native incites the violent excesses that make up that difficult chronicle. This corruption or destruction of the Amerindian is not merely a historical fact, but also a defining feature of the *bon sauvage* representational technique that will become such an important epistemological strategy for categorizing and conceiving of the Indigenous of the Americas in the centuries to come. The Noble Savage myth is a starting point in the history of the representation of the Amerindian in French and Québécois cultural imaginaries. Originating at first contact, the foundational trope of the *bon sauvage* evolves, morphing into new forms. In the coming chapters, I trace the genealogy of the primary legend of the Noble Savage myth as it transforms into the myths of the Vanishing Indian, the Ecological Indian, and Going Native.

6   Conclusion

The mythic origins of the Amerindian and the origins of the mythological paradigms devised by the French to apprehend and assign meaning to the category of Amerindian have been explored in a variety of generic contexts in this chapter. The archetypes of the Ignoble and Noble savages in the philosophical conjectures of Jean-Jacques Rousseau, one of the most influential creators of the mythic Native in the French cultural imaginary, demonstrate the abstract, and often aporic logic of the origins of man and their close association in the *philosophe*'s thinking with contemporaneous Indigenous peoples. Monstrous and idealized iterations of the Amerindian are cornerstones of the legacies of the royal cosmographer André Thevet and the explorer and Canadian founding father Samuel Champlain. Situating the tall tale of the Patagonian Giants as prolegomenon to his discussion of the Americas, Thevet instructs his French readership to understand the Native though the lens of myth, insisting on a radical divide between the quotidian human experiences of his readership in Europe and those buttressed by authorial claims of eye-witness expertise that would cast the Amerindian as monster. In subsequent chapters of the *Cosmographie universelle* admittedly more ethnographic observations must be interpreted through the author's mythic overture in the Ignoble Savage mode. In Champlain's descriptions of the Armouchiquois, the *transferability* of myth is evident. An initial representation of the Armouchiquois in the Ignoble Savage mode traces its origins to a report given by an inimical group in the region. However, the explorer's first-hand experiences speak the lie to those initial portrayals and fall into the opposing mythological trap of the Noble Savage, idealizing both the corporeal and cultural traits of the Armouchiquois. The shifting sands of French understanding of the Amerindian correspond with the mythologized bases of that understanding. Champlain's Armouchiquois passages are an illustrative example of that prevalent tendency. In concluding this preliminary chapter, the *Bon Sauvage* as it emerges in the writing of another influential philosopher of the High Renaissance, Michel de Montaigne is necessary to have the historical background of the architecture of the Noble Savage mythology in French letters as we move forward. In the next chapter, we will examine Enlightenment discourses of philosophy and fiction and their close ties to a discourse that is attempting to upend religious understandings and carve out a place for itself in the pantheon of *truth*: scientific discourses. The *transferability* of mythic paradigms from fiction to fact and back again in the opposite direction will be a central theme of the exploration of the evolution of the mythic Indian in the French and Québécois cultural imaginaries.

Works Cited

Berkhofer, Robert F. Jr. *The White Man's Indian: Images of the American Indian from Columbus to the Present.* New York: Vintage, 1979.

Bourdieu, Pierre. *Langage et pouvoir symbolique.* Paris: Éditions du Seuil, 2001.

Cole, G.D.H., translator. *The Basic Political Writings.* By Jean-Jacques Rousseau, Kindle version, Kindle Edition, 2014.

Coulthard, Glen Sean. *Red Skin White Masks: Rejecting the Colonial Politics of Recognition.* Kindle version. Minneapolis: University of Minnesota Press, 2014.

Deloria, Philip J. *Playing Indian.* New Haven, CT: Yale UP, 1998.

De Lutri, Joseph R. "Montaigne's "Des Cannibales": Invention/Experience." *Bibliothèque d'Humanisme et Renaissance,* vol. 38, no. 1, 1976, pp. 77–82.

———. "Montaigne on the Noble Savage: A Shift in Perspective." *The French Review,* vol. 49, no. 2, 1975, pp. 206–211.

Dickason, Olive P. *The Myth of the Savage: and the beginnings of French Colonialism in the Americas.* Edmonton: The University of Alberta Press, 1984.

Dickason, Olive P. and David T. McNab. *Canada's First Nations: A History of Founding Peoples from Earliest Times.* 4th ed. New York: Oxford University Press, 2008.

Duchet, Michèle. *Anthropologie et histoire au siècle des Lumières.* Paris: Albin Michel, 1971.

44   *Mythic Origins and the Origins of Myth*

Fanon, Frantz. *Peau noire masques blancs*. Paris: Éditions du Seuil, 1952.

Howard, Richard, translator. *The Conquest of America: The Question of the Other*. By Tzvetan Todorov. Norman: University of Oklahoma Press, 1999.

Lescarbot, Marc. *Histoire de la Nouvelle France*. Kindle version, Chez Jean Millot, 1609.

Povinelli, Elizabeth. *The Cunning of Recognition: Indigenous Alterities and the Making of Australian Multiculturalism*. Kindle version. Durham, NC: Duke UP, 2002.

Richman, Michèle. "The French Sociological Revolution from Montaigne to Mauss." *SubStance*, vol. 31, no. 1, 2002, pp. 27–35.

Saïd, Edward. *Culture and Imperialism*. Kindle version, Vintage, 1994.

Screech, M.A., translator. *The Essays*. By Michel de Montaigne. Kindle version, Penguin Press, 2004.

Sheridan, Alan, translator. *The Order of Things: An Archaeology of the Human Sciences*. By Michel Foucault. Kindle version, Taylor-Francis, 2005.

Soyinka, Wole. *Myth, Literature, and the African World*. New York: Canto, 1990.

Thevet, André. *Cosmographie universelle*. Paris: Chaudière, 1575. *Gallica*. https://gallica. bnf.fr/ark:/12148/btv1b8626691v.image. 26 April 2023.

Vizenor, Gerald. *Native American Literature: A Brief Introduction and Anthology*. New York: HarperCollins College Publishers, 1998.

———. *Native Liberty: Natural Reason and Cultural Survivance*. Kindle version. Lincoln: University of Nebraska Press, 2009.

———. "The Ruins of Representation: Shadow Survivance and the Literature of Dominance." *American Indian Quarterly*, vol. 17, no. 1, 1993, pp. 7–30.

2 Voltaire, La Condamine, and Buffon
Fabricating Fact and (Science) Fiction

1 Introduction

The mythic origins of French and Québécois conceptions of Amerindian, namely the archetypes of the Ignoble and Noble Savage, are persistent paragons. The mythic machine holds the epistemological possibilities for apprehending the category of Native in thrall from first contacts until the present. While the binary of Noble and Ignoble Savage continue to influence and inform representational narrative technologies for depicting the Amerindian unabated, the *transferability* of myth to other discursive regimes is a significant development during the eighteenth century. The circumscription of the Amerindian continues to refer to these initial paradigms, while expanding its claims, proposing the mythic model as a site of veridiction, an authoritative version of *truth*. Building upon the mythological framework set down in the preceding chapter, this chapter centers on disparate aspects of the Enlightenment and its iterations of the mythic vision of the Native in the French cultural imaginary. Voltaire anchors a discussion of the Age of Reason and its problematic relationship with the Amerindian Other. Specifically, his novel *Candide* provides a case study for the various morphs that the mythological assumes in the writings of one of the most notorious authors of the period. Additionally, the sourcing of the fictional episodes of *Candide* points to the *transferability* of myth. La Condamine, a prominent scientist, provides Voltaire with information about the Oreillons, an Amerindian group that looms large in the Ignoble Savage mode in the plot that leads Candide and Cacambo out of the civilized spaces of colonial American geographies and into a mythical nature inhabited by the *monstrous* Native. Presenting bestiality as a practice of the Oreillons, Voltaire entrenches the same mythic modes discussed in the first chapter (Thevet's giants and Champlain's Armouchiquois). However, here fiction is formed from *fact*. The scientist La Condamine translates the Oreillons to the novelist Voltaire in the register of *truth* that increasingly characterizes the role of the discursive regime of the scientific in Western epistemologies. This naturalizing conversation between fact and fiction is illustrative of the *transferability* of myth in the genealogy of descriptive frameworks traced in this volume.

DOI: 10.4324/9781032638751-3

46   *Voltaire, La Condamine, and Buffon*

Demonstrating the conflation of the Ignoble and Noble Savage ideologies within a single author's thinking within a single text, Voltaire's *Candide* embraces both sides of the mythic binary. With the legendary space of Eldorado, Voltaire upholds the tradition of the idealization of the Amerindian, with an inflated utopic Enlightenment bent, by sending Cacambo and the protagonist into a geography shaped by the ideals of the Noble Savage framework. The pervasiveness of the mythic machine is exemplified by the dual narrative technologies of Ignoble and Noble Savage, of fact and fiction which converge in *Candide*. The Enlightenment does not primarily focus on the fictional, however.

The second section of the chapter explores the mythic origins of representations of the Amerindian in scientific discourses that transform mythic paradigms of the Native and concretize them as scientific *truth*. In the evolution of the sciences, the Enlightenment is a formative period wherein the transformation from the broader all-inclusive conceptualization of sciences begins to resemble our modern notion of this knowledge system. The truth value increasingly attributed to scientific discourse requires examination at this stage, because the scientific vision of the Amerindian will greatly affect (settler)-colonial praxis. The same mythic paradigms that characterize previous genera permeate science's representation of the Amerindian. Myth informs *truth* in scientific discourses that expand the moral sphere into the biological, galvanizing modern notions of race. Moral judgments in the mythic mode are embedded in Native bodies. This embodiment serves as a bridge whereby the mythic is transferred, fabricating *truth*. An examination of the *Histoire naturelle* (1749–1804) by the father of natural history, Comte de Buffon, reveals how science employs myth in its categorization of human diversity. The mythic origin of scientific representations of the Amerindian is a key feature of the genealogy of myth that will continue to evolve.

2   Science (and) Fiction: The Amerindian in Voltaire's *Candide*, The Oreillons and the Myth of Eldorado

Voltaire is a central figure in the French Enlightenment. The eighteenth century has often been referred to in France as the *age of Voltaire*. Victor Hugo writes that,

> Until Voltaire heads of state are the ones [that have ages named for them]; Voltaire is more than a head of state, he is a head of ideas. With Voltaire a new cycle begins. It is as though from now on the all-mighty governing principle for the human species shall be thought. Civilization obeyed brute force, but it will now obey ideals... That is the meaning of the expression "the age of Voltaire", and that is the meaning of that illustrious event, the French Revolution. (Actes et Paroles IV: Depuis l'exil 1876–1885, Chapter 2, Le centenaire de Voltaire, my translation)

The author and activist Hugo identifies the transformational nature of what Voltaire signifies within the French cultural imaginary. Considered by some to be the "first modern intellectual", Voltaire makes an indelible mark, specifically on how the French comprehend the category of Amerindian in fictional works such as *Candide* (1759) and *L'Ingénu* (1767), in non-fiction texts such as the *L'histoire universelle depuis Charlemagne* (1754) and *Essai sur les mœurs et l'esprit des nations* (1756–1778). I begin my discussion of the mythic representation of the Amerindian in the novel *Candide*. The Native group described by Voltaire are the Oreillons, a pejorative term. *Orejones* in Spanish, Oreillons and *Orejones* translate to "big ears". The name is reflective of a long Peruvian tradition of wearing ear plugs as a sign of social status (Rowe 236, 261). Voltaire's depiction echoes the Ignoble Savage framework engaged in Thevet's Patagonian Giant and in Champlain's Armouchiquois episodes. Voltaire's choice to portray the Oreillons indicates the purchase the Ignoble Savage myth already garners in the French cultural imaginary. Voltaire may be playing to expectations by including a mythic representation of the Amerindian within the peripatetic adventures of his protagonist. Native sexuality rather than the Native body exemplifies radical difference in *Candide*. In Thevet and Champlain, the body is altered. It is the inner nature of the Amerindian that undergoes deformation in Voltaire. As in depictions of cannibalism, the taboo of bestiality reveals the inner *monster*. By choosing the Oreillons who are also renowned for the physical difference of their elongated ears, Voltaire makes an implicit connection between monstrosity visible on the exterior and that which only is observable through behavior. The connection of physical traits and moral failings is a pillar of racist ideologies in the West. In keeping with Voltaire's polygenism (the belief that each race has a separate origin), the author apprehends physical attributes as emblematic of specific variation. In *Foreign Bodies* (2008), Bronwen Douglas signals

> a major discursive shift associated with the altered meaning of race: the metamorphosis of prevailing Enlightenment ideas about externally induced variation within an essentially similar humanity into a science of race that reified human difference as permanent, hereditary, and innately somatic. (33)

"Externally induced variation" refers to climate theory, the notion that climatological differences account for biological attributes coded as race. Racial violence against non-Europeans cannot be understood uniquely through the lens of climate theory, however. Voltaire rejects climate theory, favoring polygenism. The mythic machine is a harbinger of and collaborator in the articulation of racist ideologies in the European cultural imaginary and the disciplines of science. One of the objectives of this volume is to demonstrate how the mythic representations of the early modern period are transferred into scientific discourses and transformed into *truth* within the (il)logic of race. Voltaire's *Candide* is an instructive example in mythic *transferability* because the author

48   *Voltaire, La Condamine, and Buffon*

derives his *fictional* accounts of the Oreillons from *scientific* sources. Voltaire consults the writings of the French scientist La Condamine who traveled to South America and shared his findings directly with the author. A prominent scientist, La Condamine's contribution to Voltaire's mythology is significant because it effectuates a mythic transfer from the scientific to the literary. Although Voltaire does not reference La Condamine, the author's representation of the Oreillons appropriates a veneer of *truth* by associating itself with the renowned scientist's *findings*, an intertextuality that would have been recognized by educated readers.

Charles-Marie de la Condamine is a respected man of science throughout European intellectual circles of the period. He is named chemist to the Académie des sciences in 1730, granted membership to the Académie française in 1760. In 1735, he embarks on a scientific expedition to Martinique, Saint-Domingue, other locales in New Spain, including Ecuador and Peru. In addition to measuring the Equator, the expedition is charged with testing Newton's geodesic theories concerning the spheroidal shape of the planet. Next, he descends the Amazon River. From there, he makes a stop in French Guyane before returning to Paris in 1745. Back in France, La Condamine publishes reports to the Académie des sciences and two publications meant for a broader audience: *Relation abrégée d'un voyage fait dans l'intérieur de l'Amérique méridionale* (1745) and *Journal du voyage à l'Équateur* (1751). Voltaire and La Condamine's relationship predates these publications, however. After having inherited his share of his father's fortune, Voltaire turns to La Condamine and his mathematical prowess. The two devise, "a scheme to win enormous pay-offs in the national lottery by studying the rules and exploiting loopholes that they discovered in the system... He and La Condamine were soon pulling in from 5 to 6 million livres a month, startling amounts" (Turnovsky 24). They maintain correspondence thereafter. Voltaire certainly reads his friend publications. Scientific texts become a critical source for a European intelligentsia wishing to inform itself about the Americas, "[La Condamine's] reports make the Oreillons and Amazons a popular topic, as well as bringing Father Ramon's discoveries on the Orinoco and Amazon rivers to a European audience" (Duchet 44, my translation). La Condamine's texts create buzz with sensationalized mythic representations of the Oreillons and the Amazons. It is hardly surprising then that Voltaire employs La Condamine to embellish his novel with some *couleur locale*. As part of their correspondence, La Condamine sends Voltaire his travel writings in 1752, seven years before the publication of *Candide* (Duchet 44). Voltaire is one of the leading authors to write about the Amerindian in the eighteenth century. He pens the tragedy *Alzire, ou les Américains* (1736) and the novella *L'Ingénu* (1767) on the subject. Next, I explore what an Amerindian signifies in Voltaire's thinking and in the evolution of the mythology of the Native in the French cultural imaginary.

Pierre Bourdieu argues that social structures and contexts imprint discourses with varying levels of acceptance and *authority*, or *le langage autorisé* (authorized language) (167). *Author* in is etymologically affiliated with *authority*.

Voltaire, La Condamine, and Buffon 49

Despite criticisms, scientific discourse is generally sanctioned as *truth*. Within the field of discourses, scientific discourse is a site of veridiction near the apex of authoritative performance of language. During the eighteenth century, scientific discourse was establishing itself as a dominant discursive field. La Condamine and Voltaire, along with Buffon, are at the cusp of this tectonic move away site of veridiction of the past and new discourses of *reason*. The eighteenth century is a moment of great enthusiasm and momentous change in how the French, and other Europeans, make important, lasting decisions on the parameters and locations of *truth*. Scientific discourse becomes the mouthpiece of Enlightenment ideologies. What, then, is the general picture of the Amerindian that emerges in La Condamine's writing?

One of the most material aspects of the relation between La Condamine and the Amerindians he encounters is that of Master and Servant, redolent of the Hegelian framework of Master and Slave. Reading La Condamine one salient feature that emerges regarding is the liminal status of the Native. Amerindians are often shown as beasts of burden, helping the Frenchman carry his instruments and papers. The subservient position of the Native is hardly anodyne. It is a conventional aspect of many travel narratives, positioning the Other outside the intellectual work of science, a hierarchy echoed in the social sciences positioning of Investigator-Subject vis-à-vis Native-Object. The Amerindian is a subaltern object of inquiry not agentive subject. Vine Deloria Jr. (Standing Rock Sioux) argues that "[t]he development of Western science was based on the idea that human beings could abstract themselves from the observational and experimental situation. They could then devise objective principles that would be applicable at any time or place" (Ethnoscience and Indian Realities 64). La Condamine's South American expedition was just such a project. Deloria Jr. contends that knowledge is co-constructed with the place where that knowledge is obtained, denying the abstract, objectifying gaze at the core of Western scientific epistemologies (God is Red xvii). Place does become increasingly significant in Europe, however.

It is precisely during the eighteenth century that notions of nationality and distinctions between French and Spanish, or European and Amerindian, Asian, and African reify. Benedict Anderson claims that:

> What, in a positive sense, made the new communities [nations] imaginable was a half-fortuitous, but explosive, interaction between a system of production and productive relations (capitalism), a technology of communications (print), and the fatality of human linguistic diversity. (44)

For Anderson, the development of capitalism and print lead to a consciousness of national belonging, what Anderson deconstructs as an *imagined community*, a concurrent development with the emergence of the category of race in Western thought. The articulation of the Master/Slave relation that haunts La Condamine's

50 *Voltaire, La Condamine, and Buffon*

writing is a demonstration of what Anderson argues is one of the particularities of the emergence or convergence of print and capitalism as vectors of hegemony. Anderson claims that "print-capitalism created languages-of-power" (47). The intertextuality in texts such as *Candide* illustrates the beginnings of a condensation of nationalist and racist ideologies in the West, born of imperial expansion and scientific discourses. Bronwen Douglas contends that:

> The biological notion of race emerged and gained potency in a complex historical conjuncture. Intellectually, the information about non-white people pouring into Europe from around the globe both enabled and seemed to require the demarcation of new scientific disciplines—notably biology and anthropology—which classed human beings as natural objects. Publicly, the escalation of European encounters with non-Europeans provoked fear and revulsion about supposed 'savages.' (43–4)

Europe's movement outward and its textual avatars are a critical source of the naturalized notion of race that emerges with the mythic regimes of representation of the non-European Other, in particular the mythologies of the Amerindian. In *conversation* with Andersen, the nationalist and the biological turn toward race as a justificatory discourse for the worst excesses of colonialism in the type of transdisciplinary mythic discourses in Voltaire's *Candide* through intertextuality with La Condamine. Standardized vernaculars associated with unifying discourses of national identification permit intertextuality and iterability. Through the mythic mode, iterability establishes the Amerindian as mythic being. In addition, the *transferability* of myth reinforces the *truth* of mythic semantics in the French cultural imaginary. For Anderson, iterability and *transferability* are interchangeability. Anderson states that, "Documentary interchangeability, which reinforced human interchangeability, was fostered by the development of a standardized language-of-state" (58). On the one hand, 'documentary interchangeability' indicates capacity of the written word to reinforce the affiliation of the linguistic community. Frenchness is bolstered through reading French, shared linguistic competencies. However, identification is not uniquely linguistic; there are cultural components that shape the (imaginary) identification. Print-capitalism creates *imagined communities* that allow for identification with the nation-state on the geopolitical stage via an inclusive message of identification that strengthens affiliation through cultural and linguistic commonalities. Print-capitalism is also exclusive, banishing all other communities that do not share the same linguistic, cultural, and racial affinities. Mythic messages entrench an increasingly radical difference between the European and the Amerindian that culminates in the racist discourses of comparative human biology and eugenics. The mythic mode reinforces Frenchness *and* Indianness. Mythic discourses of alterity parallel mythic nationalist discourses. The mythic machine creates a symbiotic relationship whereby Frenchness requires Indianness

Voltaire, La Condamine, and Buffon   51

(Otherness) for its own reification. Frenchness is linguistically and culturally constructed. Mythic discourses such as the Noble and Ignoble Savage are constructed in obverse relation to the articulation of Frenchness that Anderson labels *imagined communities*. Frenchness is not possible without the mirror effect of its binary opposite, the (Amerindian) Other. Europeanness as a general category and Frenchness as a specific national character gains its truth value in obverse relation to the truth value of the mythologies of the Native. Fiction functions as fact to feed the obligatory mythic machine's articulation of right and might in the shared vernacular, the "language-of-state".

La Condamine's voyage is a typical example of the nationalistic. The *national* scientific expedition experiences a boom during the eighteenth century. Ordained by the French monarch Louis XV, La Condamine's is an imperial French mission into New Spain. La Condamine is threatened with imprisonment and suspected as a spy (*Journal du voyage à l'Équateur* 25–30). Distrust of foreigners in the Spanish colonies is well-known. The colonies are virtually closed to foreigners for two centuries when La Condamine is granted permission to perform scientific experiments in the region (Pratt 16). Furthermore, the 1735 expedition seeks to settle a nationalistic dispute: Is the Earth a sphere (a French Cartesian theory) or spheroid with flattened poles (an English Newtonian hypothesis)? (Pratt 16). Marie Louise Pratt claims that science in its transnational iteration demonstrates:

> [The] ambiguous interplay of national and continental aspirations that had been a constant in European expansion… was to remain so in the age of science. On the one hand, dominant ideologies made a clear distinction between the (interested) pursuit of wealth and the (disinterested) pursuit of knowledge; on the other hand, competition among nations continued to be the fuel for European expansion abroad. (18)

Despite the unifying potential of Science, the legal entanglements and violent end of some of the French participants in the expedition go some way toward belying this rosy view. In La Condamine's narratives one encounters a terrain upon which the concurrent articulations of Europeanness/Indianness and Frenchness/Spanishness/Englishness, etc. are couched in the greater articulation of a universal European *truth* in the authoritative voice of the scientific. Paradoxically, given their status as dutiful servants throughout much of the text, La Condamine repeatedly references the indolence of the Amerindian. In a passage that resonates with Pratt's theory of the capitalist avant-garde, indolence is directly related to potential profit as seen from La Condamine's scientific and capitalistic perspectives.

> Between these points, the river is joined by several streams originating in the North that, in the rainy season, transport sand mixed with gold flakes and

52 *Voltaire, La Condamine, and Buffon*

nuggets. The Indians collect only enough to pay their tribute and only when they are heavily pressured to do so. The rest of the time, they trample the gold underfoot rather than go to the trouble to pick it up and pan it. In this whole district, both banks of the river are also covered in wild cacao, equal in quality to the cultivated variety, that the Indians show as little interest in as they do in the gold. (30–1, my translation)

In the context of the expansion of science and capitalism, *progress* often pits the material interests of the European against the cultural and economic interests of the Native, naturalizing the legitimacy of Western practices and demonizing alternatives. Within scientific mythic discourse, primitivizing the Amerindian serves to favor the global capitalist ambitions of the West to the detriment of Native self-determination. In this context, binaries of indolence versus industry take on a sinister tone, as in this excerpt from La Condamine. Glen Sean Coulthard (Yellowknife Dene) situates the capitalist-colonialist turn in European expansion as a parallel to Karl Marx's *primitive accumulation*. Relating to the land and Native lifeways, a means to increase production and profit through altering the way in which land is inhabited is associated with brutality. Coulthard explains that,

these formative acts of violent *dispossession* set the stage for the emergence of capitalist accumulation and the reproduction of capitalist relations of production by tearing Indigenous societies, peasants, and other small-scale, self-sufficient agricultural producers from the source of their livelihood— *the land.* …The historical process of *primitive* accumulation thus refers to the violent transformation of noncapitalist forms of life into capitalist ones. (16–7, emphasis in original)

Echoing Deloria Jr.'s insight on the supreme relevance of place, Coulthard's reading of Marx helps us to better read La Condamine. La Condamine's *scientific* observations of Natives with no interest in gold or cacao is an example of the utilization of the narrative technology of scientific authority to *capitalize* the Amerindian. The non-objective gaze of La Condamine is prescriptive, relating how things should be in the guise of detailing realities that brook no other viable interpretation. Valuable goods left lying around offend La Condamine's vision of reality, which imbricates and naturalizes reason and capitalism as sites of veridiction. This imbrication of capital and science is labeled by Pratt as the "capitalist vanguard". In the passage from La Condamine, the Native's indolence signifies cultural inferiority. Pratt posits that, "Neglect became the touchstone of a negative esthetic that legitimated European interventionism" (149). For La Condamine, the Native's *failure* to recognize the imperatives of capitalism justifies the negative portrayal of the Amerindian. Amerindian non-participation in the scientific/capitalist project warrants the mythic label of Ignoble Savage. La Condamine's negative esthetic is also inspired by how Europeans imagine

American geographies. A central myth of the Americas derives from Western fascination with natural abundance. Rousseau links natural abundance and Native indolence in *Discours sur l'inégalité*. The copiousness of natural resources is often presented as an obstacle for Amerindian cultural development due to a lack of resource pressure which tests ingenuity and innovation. Successful inhabitation of every environmental niche from the Arctic to the southern tip of Tierra del Fuego speaks the lie to this mythic interpretation, however. When La Condamine speaks reprovingly of gold lying about, he engages intertextually with a mythic tradition born at first contact. Within Voltaire's *Candide*, informed by La Condamine, the mythic representation of the Oreillons is voiced in the Ignoble Savage mode. The Oreillons are a South American Amerindian group that becomes sensationalized in *Candide* in relation to aberrant sexual behavior. During his travels, La Condamine encounters the Oreillons and consecrates into writing the legend that Native Oreillons women copulate with monkeys. La Condamine sends Voltaire a copy of the relation of his voyage to Amazonia (Duchet 44). La Condamine's account serves as the source for Voltaire's scene that includes two Oreillons women engaging in sexual activity with primates. This sourcing of the Oreillons scene is a rare example of a specific reference being made to specific Amerindian groups in European writings of the period. Generalities are the rule to which Voltaire's specificity is the exception. Images of the Native typically lack specific referentiality. The Native in French texts often serves as blank canvas whereupon theoretical ideologies are grafted onto Amerindian bodies/cultures in the mythic mode. Within the structure of *Candide*, the specificity of the name Oreillons does not constitute ethnographic rigor. Rather, Voltaire chooses extreme examples that engage with the mythology of the Ignoble Savage (Oreillons *bestiality*) and the Noble Savage (the Eldorado myth). Voltaire instrumentalizes the coded messages in these mythologies vehicle his philosophical and comedic narrative. The representation of the Oreillons in the mode of the mythic Ignoble Savage is perhaps the most shocking of the portrayals of the Amerindian in the author's oeuvre.

Candide and Cacambo's arrival in Oreillons territory represents a spatial shift in the novel's geography. The protagonists move from a *civilized* space to a *savage* one. From the moment they disembark at Buenos Aires, they are confronted with European corruption (the Governor who kidnaps Cunégonde, the Jesuit slave colony in Paraguay). To escape being framed for the murder of Cunégonde's brother, Candide dons a Jesuit's costume and flees with Cacambo. The distinction between *civilized* and *savage* space is explicit. The two travelers carry all necessary ingredients to eat in a *civilized* way (bread, chocolate [ironically, chocolate originates in South America], ham, fruit, and wine). The Frenchness of the food they bring functions in implicit juxtaposition with the potential anthropophagy practiced by the Oreillons. The capacity for cannibalism haunts the European imaginary in relation to the Amerindian. This is a defining feature of the mythic machine which creates *truth* from the extreme psychic spaces

54   *Voltaire, La Condamine, and Buffon*

of fear and fantasy. The refinement of the *French* food is metonymically and ontologically associated with the superiority of French culture. Entering the territory of the Oreillons, Voltaire explains that "They penetrated with their Andalusian horses into a strange country, where they could discover no beaten path" (Smollett Chapter 16). The emptiness and ahistoricity implied in this description codes the Native as non-entity, nearer to animality than humanity, echoing the dogma of *terra nullius*. The absence of roads denotes an absence of civilization. What Voltaire's narrative elides are the Amerindian knowledge systems and lifeways present in that space. It is critical to examine how Voltaire represents the land in his representations of the Amerindian because of the author's belief in polygenesis. In Voltaire's cosmogony, Native and Nature are inseparable. The Native emerges from the specific geography where the European *discovers* him. Having located the (land of the) Oreillons outside *civilization*, Voltaire turns to the Oreillons themselves. The Oreillons are associated with anthropophagy and bestiality, two tropes that typify the Ignoble Savage. In keeping with the characterization of the land they inhabit as outside *civilization*, Voltaire describes practices that exclude the Oreillons as non-human. A common technique that European writers utilize when describing cannibalism focuses on the violence of anthropophagy without contextualizing the practice. Rather than including the highly ritualized, cultural, and spiritual meanings of cannibalism, Voltaire situates cannibalism within a humoristic register. The Oreillons are eager to cook Candide, because of the Jesuit outfit he wears, crying out "A Jesuit! A Jesuit!" (Smollett Chapter 16). Rather than welcoming the proselytizers as agents of the *mission civilisatrice*, their reputation in the region, due in no small part to their colonial and missionary experiments in Paraguay has envenomed the Indigenous population against them. Voltaire instrumentalizes Amerindian ritual cannibalism to sneer at the Jesuits, a common target of ridicule in his oeuvre. In addition, their reputation as well-fed may inspire the Oreillons to look favorably upon the possibility of such a copious meal. Contextualization of cannibalism does exist in the French literary tradition, however. The French (and other Europeans) often seek to diffuse the alterity of anthropophagy by linking it to vengeance and an Amerindian code of honor associated with warrior culture. Warrior culture is often equated with European nobility, thus the Noble Savage as a mythic lens. By disassociating anthropophagy from simple nourishment and revealing its ritual aspects, authors more accurately convey the practice's cultural significance. Groups that the French view as enemies are often described as eating people merely for sustenance or eating uncooked human flesh (Lestringant 69). To return to Voltaire and the Oreillons, using cannibalism, easily the most shocking aspect of Amerindian culture from a European perspective, as comedy is a novel technique. What consequences does the comic cannibal entail?

   Does Voltaire appropriate the Amerindian to poke fun at the Society of Jesus? In that reading, the Oreillons are a tool with which Voltaire can critique the Jesuits. Fundamentally, Voltaire's technique operates via a correlation between

Voltaire, La Condamine, and Buffon   55

the author and the Amerindian on one hand, while simultaneously insisting on insurmountable difference. The Amerindian is similar *and* fundamentally different. Homi Bhabha's theory of mimicry can aid our reading of Voltaire here. Bhabha explains that,

> colonial mimicry is the desire for a reformed, recognizable Other, *as a subject of a difference that is almost the same but not quite…* …mimicry emerges as the representation of a difference that is itself a process of disavowal. Mimicry is, thus the sign of a double articulation; a complex strategy of reform, regulation and discipline, which 'appropriates' the Other as it visualizes power… …[it] coheres the dominant strategic function of colonial power, intensifies surveillance, and poses an imminent threat to both 'normalized' knowledges and disciplinary powers. (Chapter 4)

According to Bhabha, the Author-Subject appropriates the Colonized-Object in order to represent him as similar to the European (in this case, the Oreillons share Voltaire's opinion of the Jesuits) in a particular, limited fashion. However, the merger of the colonized object with the colonizing subject is never complete. In the Oreillons example, the merger occurs on the level of the sarcastic or comedic, simultaneously rendering the sacred act of cannibalism ridiculous and comic while ironizing the corruption of the Society of Jesus. The author's French identity and *superiority* is incarnated in the written word. The Amerindian has no voice. While the Natives get the pots boiling, it is only Voltaire who cries out "A Jesuit! A Jesuit!" Through appropriation, the author erases the Amerindian's capacity for complete humanity, subjectivity, or Frenchness. This is the representative gap that cannot be overcome. The *inferior* status of Amerindian languages based on their lack of any recognized written forms excludes Native language for the scriptural. Appropriation is dehumanization despite any *merger* that an author may present. As in Bhabha's conceptualization of mimicry, the Native is never French *and* the Native never appropriates French discourses of power and hegemony (Chapter 4). In short, the Native never writes.

Bestiality, like anthropophagy, is a marker of extreme difference. Sexuality is a central epistemological vector of difference in French discourses that engage in the myth of the Ignoble Savage. European writers often seize upon sexuality as a productive site of distinction, a line of cleavage between an *us* and a *them*, one often expressed in moralizing language. Differences in sexual practices are instrumentalized to buttress categorizations of the Native as animal-like. Elizabeth Povinelli, an anthropologist working on the conflictual relations between Aboriginal Australians and Euro-Australians in the settler-colonial context of modern Australia, offers compelling arguments for how identity and mythic categorizations function in late-liberal capitalism. In Povinelli's theoretical vocabulary concerning 'authentic' Native sexual practices and their reception in Euro-Australian communities, she pinpoints sexuality as a site of moral condemnation

56 *Voltaire, La Condamine, and Buffon*

that overwhelms an otherwise *tolerant* multiculturalism. Briefly providing context is essential for understanding her argument. Povinelli posits that two competing internal forces are present at any given time when those of European origins attempt to comprehend Indigenous alterity: rationality (epistemology) and morality (deontology). Aligning rationality with dominant epistemological evolutions such as the Enlightenment and the Scientific Revolution (and their political and cultural corollaries), the moral functions nevertheless as an overarching, more immediate source of knowledge and decision-making than the rational. In Povinelli's vocabulary, practices considered as morally aberrant are the element that "constitutes the socially and culturally repugnant and the limits of recognition" (*The Cunning of Recognition* 3). Indeed, both anthropophagy and bestiality occupy the liminal, irrational space at the "limits of recognition". However, in the case of Australian Indigenous/Non-Indigenous relations Povinelli emphasizes the preponderance of sexuality as a determining factor in exclusionary moral discourses that reiterate the mythologies of the Ignoble Savage. Moral indignation outweighs attempts at rational tolerance of cultural difference. By defining the Native via examples of bestiality and anthropophagy, Voltaire situates the Amerindian beyond the "limits of recognition". The mythic machine functions as a formalized, coded constructor of *truth* about alterity expressed as a discourse of exclusion, just as Povinelli postulates that "social institutions and relations incite or mitigate against thinking particular modes of otherwise. They influence whether and when critical thought takes place" (*The Cunning of Recognition* 11). The mythic model of the Ignoble Savage typified by representations that focus on extreme behaviors such as anthropophagy and bestiality is an example of when the moral and deontological drowns out the voice of reason, the moment when the mythic is transformed from fantasy and caricature into self-evident, intuitive *truth*. The mythic machine employed by Voltaire undermines the rationality at the heart of the intellectual movement of the *Siècle des Lumières*, undergirding instead the intolerance that Voltaire so loudly decried.

In addition to Povinelli's provoking analyses, my reading of sexuality and hegemonic discourses of normativity has largely been influenced by the work of Scott Lauria Morgensen, whose *queer* critiques of settler-colonialism can be applied to the mythic representational models the French routinely employ in descriptions of the Native. Morgensen's insights into the importance of sexuality and normativity which center on sexuality as defining spaces of European self-definition in contrast to Native practices can deepen understandings of eighteenth-century representations of the Amerindian. In my use of Morgensen, I understand *queer* more broadly than it is typically understood in *queer* criticism: in texts written about the Amerindian in French from the sixteenth century to the present day, differences in sexual practices, which may include what generally is termed *queer* (LBGTQAI, or the term Two-Spirit), but is not limited to those designations. Not only are practices that are traditionally labeled as *queer* instrumentalized in the creation of the myth of the Ignoble Savage, but *any*

Voltaire, La Condamine, and Buffon 57

deviation from French sexual normativity is subject to being *queered* by French authors. Nudity, polygamy, communal bathing, promiscuity, offering wives and daughters as sexual partners to visitors, etc., are *queered* as well as LBGTQAI or Two-Spirit sexualities. It is in this broad sense that I include Morgensen's insight into the centrality of sexual difference in (settler)-colonial ideologies as it manifests in the mythic machine as narrative technology. Morgensen states that:

> colonial heteropatriarchy first redefines embodiment, desire, and kinship to eliminate Native culture, control racialized populations, and secure, in Sherene Razack's term, a "white settler society". (2)

This redefinition of Native sexuality is poignant. This mythic representational model *queers* Indigenous sexual lifeways comprehensively. It is through the generalized *queering* of Native sexuality *and* lifeways that the Civilized-Savage binary crucial for the (self-)definition of the West becomes operational. *Queering* the Native is a condition of possibility for colonial praxis and the mythological discursive structures that bolster it. *Queering* Native sexuality is another narrative technology of "elimination". I use the term "elimination" as employed by Morgensen who coopts his usage from Patrick Wolfe. "Elimination" functions through rhetorical and metaphorical techniques, such as the mythology of the Ignoble Savage, to create an unbridgeable divide between the French and Native, creating a naturalized space within the cultural imaginary for the praxis of colonialism as self-evident, moral *truth*, notwithstanding superficial discursive feigning of tolerance and multiculturalism. Voltaire (and La Condamine's *scientific*) account of Oreillons bestiality is an illustrative example.

The scene that describes Candide's encounter with the Oreillons women is marked with Voltaire's typical dose of satiric humor. The killing of the two primates is portrayed as a heroic act, wherein Candide saves the women from what he perceives as an animal attack. The *queering* of the Native is clear here. While the bestiality of the Oreillons is a sensationalized fiction, it does not function as such for the French readership. The sensationalism associated with La Condamine's report, which is itself buttressed by La Condamine's position as scientist, is a reification of the *fait divers* (random, isolated account) as fact. The humor of the scene dissimulates the (moral/deontological) divide evoked between the French and the Oreillons in the French cultural imaginary. In a word, engaging in sexual acts that are coded as *queer* dehumanizes, situating the Native closer to animality than humanity. Voltaire comically situates saving the women from their animal pursuers opposite his previous *sins* of killing an Inquisitor and a Jesuit as a morally commendable action. Another comedic element of the scene occurs when, after describing them as running naked through the forest while being nipped on the derrière by monkeys, Candide wonders aloud if they might be *femmes de condition* (women of high-standing). This comparison of the Oreillons women to French noblewomen, while intended to

58 *Voltaire, La Condamine, and Buffon*

generate laughter, deepens the furrow between French and Native. While the scene is framed in the comic mode, the representation of Amerindian women engaging in sexual relations with primates is quintessentially dehumanizing, functioning primarily to put into question the status of the Amerindian as human through the technique of *queering*.

Voltaire's version of the Noble Savage myth in the novel *Candide*, the author's reiteration of the myth of Eldorado, situates the *idea* of the Native squarely in the abstract realm of fantasy. A pattern of intertextuality and repetition becomes evident when researching the creation and maintenance of the underlying myths of the Native. Voltaire inscribes *Candide* with a dual framing of the Native. First, the author engages in the mythification of the Oreillons through comic visions of anthropophagy and bestiality, in the register of the Ignoble Savage. Second, Voltaire shifts to the opposite pole of the moral *and* rational spectrum by establishing a correlation between the mythic imaginings of the Amerindian and fabled Eldorado, in the Noble Savage mode. The Eldorado scene exemplifies the mythic nature of the Amerindian in the French cultural imaginary.

Eldorado is an imaginary geography with a long history in representations of the Americas and of Amerindians. In one of the original iterations the myth is linked to the Amerindian body. Alès and Pouyllau explain how the myth takes its roots in:

> the supposed existence of an Indian covered in gold dust, bathing in a lake into which golden objects and gemstones were thrown, it is from this 'Indio dorado' (golden Indian), which henceforth will be known as 'Eldorado', or the 'golden man'. It is from this framework that the 'myth of Eldorado' which acquires a paradigmatic status in the definition of diverse expectations of the conquerors of these unknown lands. (275, my translation)

The fundamental divide between the geographies and the peoples of the Americas and Europe in Voltaire's *Candide* is represented spatially. In the Oreillons scene, the space the Amerindian inhabits is codified as uncivilized. In the Eldorado scene, another spatial break occurs when Candide and Cacambo pass into the city. The ordeal that leads them there, enduring a perilous voyage through rapids and an underground passage, serves as a sign of the mythic geography of the space that the two characters are entering. This is Voltaire's technique for signaling a transition from the known to the unknown, from the imaginary to the mythic (Alès and Pouyllou 281). This moment, when Candide and Cacambo cross over from Oreillons space into Eldorado space, constitutes a shift from the mythologies of the Ignoble to the Noble Savage.

Voltaire's instantiation of the *bon sauvage* is an exercise in philosophical abstraction wherein images are proposed in absolutes that lack any resemblance to the societies of real Amerindian peoples or any other peoples for that matter. The geographic isolation that defines the mythic space of Eldorado and the

Voltaire, La Condamine, and Buffon   59

Eldorado Indians is a problematic aspect of Voltaire's utopic vision that echoes the author's distancing from Amerindian realities. Voltaire's Eldorado is severed from the rest of the Americas, separated from real geographies, indistinguishable from fantasy. Idyllic Eldorado is on the road to Cayenne, a tropical location relatively unknown during the period in which Voltaire writes *Candide*. Voltaire offers a polygenetic-inspired, racially distinctive description of the *indolence* of Amerindians based on the tropical environment in the following passage taken from *Essay on Universal History, the Manners, and Spirit of Nations*:

> In general, America has never been as populous as Europe and Asia, it is covered with immense swamps that make the air unhealthy; the land produces a staggering number of poisons; arrows dipped in the sap of these poisonous plants always cause fatal wounds. Nature made Americans a lot less industrious than men of the Old World. (Chapter 8, my translation)

Voltaire insists on the contamination of American landscapes, in particular tropical ones, such as the region of Cayenne where Eldorado is discovered by Cacambo and Candide. The climate is linked to Native *indolence*. Therefore, when Voltaire describes the wonders of Eldorado, the mythic spaces he invokes are completely incommensurate with the tropical American environment. The connection between the land and its *productions* is broken. Tropical Guyana could not have *produced* Eldorado any more than Amerindian peoples could have, because, according to Voltaire's polygenetic outlook, they are intrinsically linked to the inferior land from which they hail. The protagonist's fears regarding imminent anthropophagy in the area indicate that in the world of *Candide*, the Native is equated with the dangerous poisons that Nature produces. The geography of Eldorado does not belong to the American geography. The unique transition from Oreillons (tropical) space to the land of Eldorado takes the characters on a twenty-four-hour journey on an underground river before they emerge in a space that has little resemblance to the poisonous space they have just left behind.

Through the connection that subsumes the Amerindian within the space that he occupies (Voltaire's polygenism), the idealized *civilization* of the Eldorado myth functions as an exclusionary discourse. Voltaire's vision of the Native indicates that the Amerindian could not have attained to the *enlightened* cultural space of Eldorado. *Candide* demonstrates the endgame of the mythologies that the West constructs around their imaginaries of the Amerindian. The novel distorts Natives via representations based on the two principal mythic lenses of the Ignoble and Noble Savage. Voltaire's mythic discourse of exclusion functions within the narrative technology of the Ignoble Savage *and* the Noble Savage. It is important to understand that the mythic machine dehumanizes even as it idealizes, both polar extremes of the mythologies of the Native distance the Amerindian from the identification that readers of *Candide* associate with their own Frenchness.

60 *Voltaire, La Condamine, and Buffon*

The distinctions between Oreillons space and Eldorado space are evident. The Oreillons inhabit a caricatural wild space, whereas Eldorado constitutes a utopic ideal of civilization. When Candide and his valet enter Eldorado the narrator explains that,

> This place was bounded by a chain of inaccessible mountains. The country appeared cultivated equally for pleasure and to produce the necessaries of life. The useful and agreeable were here equally blended. The roads were covered, or rather adorned, with carriages formed of glittering materials, in which were men and women of a surprising beauty, drawn with great rapidity by red sheep of a very large size; which far surpassed the finest courses of Andalusia, Tetuan, or Mecquinez. (Smollett Chapter 17)

The distancing from Oreillons space could not be more explicit. Whereas in Oreillons space there are no roads, the roads of Eldorado are populated with amazing vehicles with equally beautiful passengers. The physical description of the residents of Eldorado contrasts sharply with the portrait the author offers of the Oreillons, whose name, it should be recalled, is linked to their physical *deformity*. Not only are the Eldorado peoples dissimilar to the Oreillons, the animal life of the region is judged superior to the most prized horse breeds of the Old World. By explicitly comparing the red sheep of Eldorado with well-known and esteemed horse breeds of Spain, Voltaire situates the geographical space and peoples of Eldorado squarely outside the Americas. Cacambo asserts at the beginning of the chapter that they must return to Europe, because American space is *poisonous*. However, after the description of the roads, vehicles, peoples, and sheep just cited, Candide makes an opposite appraisal of Eldorado space, "'Here is a country, however,' said Candide, 'preferable to Westphalia'" (Smollett Chapter 17). These markers of difference between Oreillons space and Eldorado geographies indicate a shift from the mythology of the Ignoble Savage in favor of the Noble Savage framework.

Upon entering the fabled city, the host that Candide and Cacambo meet recounts the genealogy of Eldorado as an isolated element of classical Incan society (106). Connecting Eldorado to the Inca is not random or gratuitous. In Montaigne's essay "On Coaches" it was the Incan roads specifically that astonished. Therefore, Voltaire linking the roadway to this idealized society is a reiteration of an image used by Montaigne nearly two centuries before to construct his own instantiation of the Noble Savage mythology. Voltaire's polygenism also reinforces my reading, because of its stubborn insistence on the unbreakable ontological link between land and people. Consequently, although Voltaire performs a rhetorical oscillation by shifting the mythic significance of the Native in *Candide* from Ignoble to Noble, he does not attribute the wonders of Eldorado ontologically to the Amerindian. It should be noted that Voltaire's myth of Eldorado, while engaging in the myth of the Noble Savage, nevertheless maintains racial hierarchies present in the author's non-fictional pieces, such as the *Essay on Universal History, the Manners, and Spirit of Nations*, which places Europeans at the apex of the human pyramid, while the Native is firmly established as inferior.

In Voltaire's utopic description of Eldorado, there is a departure from the classic motif of the Noble Savage myth that emphasizes the separation between the idealized inhabitants of Eldorado and real Amerindians. Rather than highlight notions of innocence and purity associated with a universalized history, Voltaire performs an entirely distinct mythic transformation. The society of Eldorado represents the enlightened principles espoused by the *philosophe* in the present moment of Enlightenment Europe, and not a supposed golden age of the past. Voltaire's philosophical and literary works are systematically progressive, working to reshape the future. Candide and Cacambo are invited to see the wonders of the city which are described in the following manner:

> they saw public structures that reared their lofty heads to the clouds; the market-places decorated with a thousand columns; fountains of spring water, besides others of rose water, and of liquors drawn from the sugarcane, incessantly flowing in the great squares; which were paved with a kind of precious stones that emitted an odor like that of cloves and cinnamon. Candide asked to see the high court of justice, the parliament; but was answered that they had none in that country, being utter strangers to lawsuits. He then inquired if they had any prisons; they replied none. But what gave him at once the greatest surprise and pleasure was the palace of sciences, where he saw a gallery two thousand feet long, filled with the various apparatus in mathematics and natural philosophy. (Smollett Chapter 18)

Simultaneously representing the rationalist ideal of the Enlightenment (the largest structure in the city is dedicated to the pursuit of scientific research) and the economic interests of Europeans in the wider world (the global capitalist bent of the description), this portrait of Eldorado reveals the shape an eighteenth-century French utopia might take. It is not anodyne that the description is peppered with objects of desire from a colonial perspective. The alcohol is derived from one of the most emblematic crops associated with European expansion into the New World and the slave trade: sugarcane. Taking the metaphor away from the West Indies to the East Indies, the aromas of the public squares are imbued with the exotic spices (cloves and cinnamon) that inspired many voyages of discovery. The capitalistic coincides with the scientific and progressive here in Voltaire's utopic vision of the future as represented by the mythic Eldorado. Lacking the need for legal litigations due to ethic purity, the missing parliament points to traditional articulations of the Noble Savage mythology that describe the Amerindian's innocence as lacking the type of moral corruption that defines Western cultures in the privative mode. However, the forward-looking movement

62   *Voltaire, La Condamine, and Buffon*

that can best be linked to Voltaire's cult of reason as a paragon of the French Enlightenment has to be the edifice dedicated to scientific pursuits, which replaces Versailles with its unique purpose of glorifying and reinforcing the arbitrary power of the Bourbon monarchy.

To Voltaire's mind, this transformative, transcendental tone of Enlightenment thought applies only to the French, not to the Native who is temporally and culturally fixed as a degenerate version of humanity. The extreme, sensationalized representations of Oreillons anthropophagy and bestiality speak to the author's estimation of the position of the Native in the human family. Eldorado is contemporaneous and innovative, an imaginary space infused with the ideologies of the Enlightenment that does not abide the practices described as typical of the Oreillons, and by extension, all Amerindians. Rather than representing the past, Eldorado is a portrait of an ideal future that *Europeans* have yet to realize. It differs considerably from other instantiations of the myth of the Noble Savage which can be identified by their obsession with the purity of origins and the unsullied dream of the past. The fact that Candide and Cacambo do not take away the philosophical and administrative ingenuities of Eldorado but attempt to steal as much gold and precious gemstones as the idiosyncratic red sheep can carry indicates the European's failure to rise to the moral ideals of the mythic city, yet another of Voltaire's winks at the folly of the naïve optimism that the novel reviles. As in the historical examples mentioned in Montaigne's "On Coaches" (the loss of Spanish galleons at sea whose bounteous treasure sinks to the bottom of the Atlantic Ocean rather than fill the coffers of the monarchy), the spoliators do not retain the fortune they extract from Eldorado. They subsequently lose the majority of the booty. Voltaire satirizes greed and avarice by showing the short-sightedness and futility of accumulation in the case of Candide and Cacambo. In addition, he ironizes utopic visions in general, suggesting that Europeans would be incapable of *profiting* from being exposed to *truly* enlightened societies. In the next section, I examine how the mythic frameworks established from the period of first contacts are transferred to discourses that claim a certain *truth* value within the discursive field of science.

3   Buffon and Natural History: The Science of Man and the Systematizing of the Amerindian

The Enlightenment is a formative period wherein the transformation from a broader all-inclusive conceptualization of *sciences* begins to resemble modern notions of the discursive field of science. The *truth* value that will increasingly be attributed to scientific discourse requires examination at this stage, because the vision of the Amerindian espoused by science will have a profound effect on (settler)-colonial praxis. Science continues to exert a heavy influence on the ways in which Indigenous populations are perceived culturally and dealt with by governments and other international organizations today. Examining the scientific reveals that the same mythic paradigms discussed in this volume are constitutive of scientific discourse's representational techniques vis-à-vis the Native. One of the most striking features of the study of the representation of the Amerindian in French diachronically is the virtually unaltered lens through which the French envision the Amerindian over time. While subsequent generations of authors offer new insights in some cases, most works regurgitate old stereotypes without examining their provenance or validity. Different claims and arguments about the Amerindian are put forth in diverse discursive fields; however, the representation of the Native generally vacillates around a core set of preconceptions and judgments (the Noble/Ignoble Savage trope, the nexus between Nature and the Native, primitivism, the Vanishing Indian, Going Native). Paradoxically, the aims and objectives of the individual authors, long considered a determining factor in any objective analysis of the portrayal of cultural Others in literary criticism, appear to matter little in the overall configuration of the Amerindian within this vast corpus. The complexity of the mythic machine as narrative technology fully emerges when the Noble Savage and the Ignoble Savage are recognized as being virtually indistinguishable in their theoretical, analytical, and textual formations. The form of the representation may vary, yet the content remains nearly the same: the original dehumanizing categorizations of the Amerindian are difficult to eradicate epistemologically even when the author's objectives appear to be a positive, relativistic portrayal of the Native (i.e. iterations of the Noble Savage). The mythically dehumanized Amerindian abets dispossession and colonialization, however, the epistemological framework that creates this unique vision of the Native manifests itself most notably in efforts to transform the Amerindian into something which more closely resembles the European model, the *mission civilisatrice*. In the discursive field of science, a major shift that takes place is the expansion of the moral sphere into the biological. In short, the moral judgments made by previous generations of writers become more firmly anchored in the biological being of the Amerindian. This embodiment serves as a bridge whereby the mythic is transferred into a scientific message imbued with *truth*. In Comte de Buffon's *Histoire naturelle*, moral claims are buttressed with a systematic knowledge that seeks to ensconce the European at the apex of what will, a century later, with Darwin, become the evolutionary ladder. Negative depictions of Amerindian societies in the Ignoble Savage mode are coded as natural *and* immoral. These differences become inscribed as *evidence* of European racial superiority in the *Histoire naturelle*. The assertion of an inherent hierarchical paradigm of race in Buffon's *Variétés dans l'espèce humaine* is based on moral and esthetic judgments presented as scientific *truth*. Social scientists take up the same hierarchies, basing their theories on the assumptions introduced by Buffon.

One example that illustrates this phenomenon concerns sexual practices, specifically the practice of offering wives and daughters to visitors as sexual partners. Thevet depicts the practice as pandering by the parents or husband,

64   *Voltaire, La Condamine, and Buffon*

using the term prostitution to denounce the custom from a moralizing standpoint. Buffon takes a similar position in the following passages, but with some significant differences. Although the citations that follow are dealing specifically with Arctic and Subarctic groups, such as the Sami and Inuit, they are applicable in various contexts throughout the Western hemisphere. Therefore, Buffon's commentary on the sexuality of the Other can be equally applied to the Amerindian context:

> Immersed in superstition and idolatry, of a Supreme Being they have no conception; nor is it easy to determine which is most conspicuous, the grossness of their understandings, or the barbarity of their manners, being equally destitute of courage and shame. Boys and girls, mothers and sons, brothers and sisters, bathe together naked, without being in the smallest degree ashamed. When they come out of their baths, which are warm, they immediately go into the rivers. It is the custom among all these people to offer their wives and daughters to strangers, and are much offended if the offer is not accepted. ... As all the different tribes or nations, therefore, resemble each other in form, in shape, in colour, in manners, and even in oddity of customs, they are undoubtedly of the same race of men. The practice of offering their women to strangers, and of being pleased when they are thought worthy of caresses may proceed from a consciousness of their own deformity as well as that of their women. In appearance, the woman, who a stranger has accepted, they afterwards respect for her superior beauty. At any rate it is certain, although remote from each other, and separated by a great sea, the custom is general in all the above countries. (Volume 4, 708–9)

Buffon connects the moral and the biological in ways that defy the reasonableness that allegedly constitutes the ideological foundations of scientific rigor. Sexuality enters the discussion as evidence in support of overarching claims of moral inferiority. Faced with very sexual practices outside their own norms, the Other is banished beyond the "limits of recognition", excluded from humanity based on unassimilable lifeways. Beginning with what Buffon deems an overall lack of decorum (communal bathing and nudity), the discussion quickly shifts to take up the practice of sexual liaisons arising when men offer women to visitors as sexual partners. The author implies the ridiculousness of feeling "honored" by others deigning to engage in sexual relations with one's wife or daughter. The implication is, of course, that this type of sexual morality is so base that is does not even register that when another man has sexual relations with one's wife or daughter one should be offended. Buffon presents this sexual practice as proof of moral and biological failings that serve as markers of distinction between non-Europeans and Europeans, naturalizing European superiority within a racial framework.

Buffon assigns continuity of the practice with all peoples of the North. The sexual practice under discussion occurs among various groups in the Arctic, North America, Central America, and South America. Therefore, the continuity suggested by Buffon in his discussion of the peoples of the North, implies a behavioral, if not biological, unity between those peoples and the Amerindians to the South that share the hemisphere with them. The connection made here between morality and biology is an important feature of Buffon's understanding and textual representations of human racial diversity in the *Histoire naturelle*. The purported immorality of the Amerindian is a necessary feature of Buffon's narrative that serves contrapuntally to the Native's superior physical constitution in comparison with the French. Here, however, Buffon deplores both the biological and the moral. Buffon explains the practice by suggesting that the peoples of the North, recognizing their own physical "deformity", offer women to visitors to which female members of the group are sexually attractive potential mates. Mishuana Goeman's (Seneca) Indigenous feminist critique of construction of gender and racialized mapping is a conceptual framework through which one can re-read Buffon from a Native perspective. Goeman argues that "For Indigenous people travelling through constructed colonial and imperial spaces, the body can be hypervisible as the abnormal body... ...in both physical and mental imaginings" (12). Spatially inflected, Goeman's theory of (re)mapping is a productive tool for reimagining Buffon and natural history's legacy of (mis)representation of the Amerindian Other, in particular Native women and their bodies. Through "narrating geographies that unsettle the heteropatriarchal institutional structures that use race and gender as tools to support settler colonialism", Native writers such as Naomi Fontaine (Innu) challenge the distortion of both Indigenous women's bodies and geographies (26). A discussion of Fontaine's work is central to the final chapter's focus on Indigenous voices and futures. To return to the eighteenth century and natural history's deformations, despite the evident levity intended by the author, Buffon reduces the familial bonds of these peoples to incest, excluding the Native from the moral fold of humanity via an embodiment of the Ignoble Savage within Amerindian women's bodies. The practice of offering wives or daughters to strangers as sexual partners is far more complex and significant than the cursory, dismissive commentary of Buffon would suggest. A common representational tactic is to denounce Native lifeways within the framework of the Ignoble Savage, without exploring the intricacies of practices deemed morally aberrant by European observers. This recalls once again Povinelli's notion of the "limits of recognition". When the moral taboos of Western culture are challenged by a Native behavior (sexuality is a common category, but anthropophagy and human sacrifice are other examples), the Ignoble Savage predominates over the rigorous application of the objective principles underlying scientific empiricism. Albert Hurtado argues that the practice of offering female relatives as sexual partners is not well-understood by Europeans.

Since traders often gave the women and their husbands presents, whites frequently equated the practice of wife lending with prostitution, but the Missouri tribes [Mandan and Hidatsa] and other Plains Indians were involved in

66   *Voltaire, La Condamine, and Buffon*

a far more complicated sexual enterprise than that. For them, the provision of a sexual partner was a matter of hospitality that cemented friendships and trading relationships. Moreover, they believed that coitus transferred power from one man to another, using the woman as a kind of transmission line. The Mandan institutionalized this principle in the buffalo-calling ceremony, a famous rite where old, respected hunters copulated with the wives of younger men who sought to invoke the elder's spiritual aid. These acts also symbolized intercourse with life-giving buffalo, ensured fertility, and drew nigh the bison herds. (Hurtado 60)

The spiritual and cultural aspects of the offering of sexual intercourse with female family members are lost within the mythic machine's narrative technologies, which seek to reduce complexity into simple, binary extremes to categorize and hierarchize human difference. As science becomes more dominant as a discursive field, taking over social territory and capital once within the purview of the theological, the scientist or *savant* gains in prestige in ways that aid and abet the propagation of mythic discourses regarding the Natives of the Americas. While one analyzes Buffon's myopic criticisms of the sexual practices of Amerindians and others, one must also carefully consider the position of Buffon as author or speaker within the French society of the period. With the advent of the sciences as a global system of power and knowledge, the position of authority from which Buffon speaks allows the naturalist to assert the superiority of the European race through the assertion of his own personal superiority vis-à-vis the objects he discusses: the Amerindian. The hierarchy presented by Buffon in this passage, and throughout *Variétes dans l'espèce humaine* and *Histoire naturelle*, situates the European as solely capable of determining physical beauty *and* morality in human societies. Privileging the written concurrently privileges the gaze of the European on the Amerindian Other. It matters little whether a French author ever actually "gazes" upon the object of his text. Having established the superiority of his own judgment (Reason), and by extension that of his fellow Europeans in his quip about ugly Eskimo women, Buffon also discusses the Cartesian dichotomy between the physical (*le corps*) and the spiritual or mental (*l'âme*) as being unequally distributed across racial lines with interesting consequences for the overall image of the Amerindian.

Buffon's articulation of the faculty necessary to embark on a scientific endeavor such as the *Histoire naturelle* is a telling fragment that reveals his philosophy on races and their hierarchical ordering.

Provided by nature with organs, calculated solely for our preservation, we only employ them to receive foreign impressions. Intent on multiplying the functions of our senses, and on enlarging the external bounds of our being, we rarely make use of that internal sense which reduces us to our true dimensions, and abstracts us from every other part of creation. It is, however, by a cultivation of this sense alone that we can form a proper judgment of ourselves. (Volume 4, 571)

What Buffon refers to in this excerpt is that which precisely distinguishes the French from the other races that will be discussed in *Histoire naturelle*. The foundation of the social sciences' claim to truth in the modern world is made here by Buffon in reference to his study of human natural history. The necessary faculty to examine and report upon human racial differences is a double faculty. Primarily, it is derived from the senses and a desire to understand the outside world. This is reason. The second element is what modern scientists would refer to as scientific objectivity. The distancing from oneself and one's physical sensations required to adequately judge humanity is necessary to judge racial difference. From a linguistic standpoint, the repetition of the inclusive 'we' is significant. The author does not claim the capacity for reason and scientific objectivity for himself uniquely, rather he extends it to his readers (the *imagined* French *community*). As we shall see, other races are incapable of this double faculty. Buffon insists on the Amerindian being a part of the human species in certain aspects, while simultaneously excluding the Native from full human status in other key areas. The consecration of the European as model for *full* humanity through writing constitutes a narrative technology. The use of that narrative technology entails a mythologized ideological dehumanization of the Native. That ideology is a key component in the colonial project. Taking its origins in the original myths of the Ignoble and Noble Savage, as well as the Native/ Nature nexus (or Ecological Savage), the scientific *truth* proposed by Buffon in the *Histoire naturelle* is not a novel reality revealed by objective scientific observation, but rather a reiteration and reification of old tropes propagated by the mythic machine, emphasizing radical alterity as the defining feature of the Amerindian. While Buffon's theories take cues from mythic discourses, they also participate in a scientific and philosophic tradition.

Cartesian dualism is an essential aspect of Buffon's (racial) philosophy. The distinctions made between different racial groupes hinge upon each race's profile as it pertains to physical (*le corps*) and spiritual or mental attributes (*l'âme*). Buffon considers the body/spirit dichotomy a crucial first step in understanding the human condition.

The first and most difficult step which leads to the knowledge of ourselves, is a distinct conception of the two substances that constitute our being. To say simply, that the one is unextended, immaterial, and immortal, and that the other is extended, material, and mortal, is only to deny to the one, what we affirm the other possesses. What knowledge is to be acquired from this mode of negation? (Volume 4, 571)

68   *Voltaire, La Condamine, and Buffon*

Buffon establishes hereby the critical importance of the Cartesian framework for any endeavor to comprehend different races. If one revisits the passages above on the sexual practice of offering women to visitors, the physical and the spiritual are key epistemological lenses that allow Buffon to ascribe inferiority. The tone of mockery regarding the *ugliness* and *amorality* of Inuit women is transformed via the recognized and authoritative philosophical theories of René Descartes into an erudite, scientific discourse. From the moralistic judgments originally assigned to the practice in the sixteenth century, the same representation of the Amerindian, buttressed by French philosophical tradition (Cartesianism) and claims of scientific objectivity, reconfigure the mythology of the Ignoble Savage as scientific *truth*. The presence of the moral within the rational discloses its foundational role in empirical scientific objectivity. Not only does Buffon's discourse ally itself with recognized and coded regimes of *truth* in order to lay claim to a certain *truth* value, but the structure and systematization of the domain of natural history itself, and the *Histoire naturelle* as a scientific project and text, support Buffon's efforts to establish his own authorial clout within the field of discourse that is emerging under the name of natural history at this time.

> By virtue of structure, the great proliferation of beings occupying the surface of the globe is able to enter both into the sequence of a descriptive language and into the field of a mathesis that would also be a general science of order. And this constituent relation, complex as it is, is established within the apparent simplicity of a description of the visible. (Sheridan 136)

The 'structure' and 'general science of order' that Foucault points to here are more indicative of the entirety of the animal descriptions of the *Histoire naturelle*, wherein the visible structures of the vast multitude of genera and species are painstakingly articulated, than they are of Buffon's comparisons between human races. It is this 'description of the visible' (the animal) which, in fact, makes natural history's claim to truth because of its 'apparent simplicity'. The contamination of the 'visible' by the moral creates a textual space where it is possible to insert the criticisms that Buffon includes about the non-European as *truth*. In short, without the many tomes of minute description of the anatomy of the various genera of Animalia, Buffon's moralistic and esthetic claims about human racial differences would not convey the same authority or *truth*. Diversity is the special object of natural history, its area of expertise. Therefore, by establishing authority and linking its discourse to a certain regime of *truth* by articulating the 'visible' in the domain of the animal, Buffon can assert his racial descriptions as objective scientific *truth* in the domain of the human. As Foucault states elsewhere, "Natural history is nothing more than the nomination of the visible" (132). However, the 'visible' can make claims to 'apparent simplicity' as its mark of evident *truth*, as it pertains to the description of a leaf or a beaver's tail, but it cannot, of course, hold the same epistemological sway in the relative world

Voltaire, La Condamine, and Buffon 69

of human cultural and ethnic diversity. The key to Buffon's claim to scientific *truth* is the move from the Animal to the Human. Ironically, Buffon does not actually report on what he 'sees' in his descriptions of many of the various animals or human races that he describes in the *Histoire naturelle*. The foundation of natural history's claim to *truth*, that which is 'seen' and subsequently made 'visible' through writing, is absent in Buffon's claims about Inuit women as it is in this excerpt that portrays the Amerindian.

> Besides these savages, who are scattered over the most northern parts of America, we find a more numerous and different race in Canada, and who occupy the vast extent of territory as far as the Assiniboils. These are all tall, robust, and well-made; have black hair and eyes, teeth very white, a tawny complexion, little beard, and hardly a vestige of hair on their bodies; they are hardy, indefatigable travellers, and very nimble runners. They are alike unaffected by excesses of hunger or of eating; they are bold, hardy, grave, and sedate. So strongly, indeed, do they resemble the Oriental Tartars in colour, form, and features, as also in disposition, and manners, that, were they not separated by an immense sea, we should conclude them to have descended from that nation. (Volume 4, 768)

This is Buffon's general description of the Amerindian of North America. His physical descriptions of the strength and overall physical robustness of the Native constitute an important representation of the Amerindian in French letters. An image that first emerged in the travel writing of the sixteenth century (Jean de Léry's writings on the Tupinamba of present-day Brazil is a pertinent example) and will continue to be reiterated by Champlain and the Jesuits in the seventeenth century; the Amerindian as first encountered by the European is typically depicted as healthful and vigorous. Often, comparisons made between the physical attributes of the Native and European describe the Amerindian as healthier than the European. Therefore, couched within the 'apparent simplicity' of Buffon's description, is a history of representation of the Amerindian that remains silent. Not having seen all the different groups of Amerindians he describes, Buffon reappropriates older discourses and images and inserts them into the discursive field of natural history as scientific *truth*. Obfuscating the origin of the information he mines to construct his representations of the Amerindian, Buffon implicitly claims the authority of the eye-witness within a domain that explicitly lauds the 'nomination of the visible' as the ultimate paradigm of *truth* and disciplinary rigor. There is a tension created by the physical description of the Amerindian. How does Buffon hierarchize the Amerindian as inferior in comparison with the European when the Amerindian has a remarkably healthy physical constitution? The answer is in the Cartesian dualism mentioned earlier.

Buffon clarifies his position on body/spirit duality in the *Histoire naturelle* by linking the body with the animal world, thereby relegating it to a lower rung

70   *Voltaire, La Condamine, and Buffon*

of existence. The naturalist insists that reason (*la pensée*) is superior in any comparison between the two fundamental elements of body and spirit (*la pensée* being an Enlightenment-era synonym for Descartes' âme, or soul) (Tome Second, 434). Within Buffon's articulation of the distinction between Man and Animal lies the philosophical groundwork necessary to make the next hierarchical judgment wherein the Amerindian, as well as other ethnic groups, are situated on the table of identities and differences that structures and characterizes the entire discourse of natural history in this period as closer to the Animal than the Human.

> In comparing man with the animal we find in both an organized body, senses, flesh, blood, motion, and a multitude of other resemblances. But these resemblances are all external, and not sufficient to justify a decision, that the human and the animal natures are similar. In order to form a proper judgment of the nature of each we ought to have as distinct a knowledge of the internal qualities of an animal as we have of our own. (Volume 4, 576)

Buffon places the physical part of Man's existence in the domain of the Animal. Natural history's ability to authoritatively pronounce on the distinction between Man and Animal is predicated upon the naturalist's ability to go beyond the 'visible', beyond the exterior, and penetrate the inner workings of that other pole of human existence, the spirit (*l'âme*). The shift that permits Buffon to establish hierarchies and clear-cut distinctions, to classify and catalog human diversity is in the naturalist's unique position as a human being himself. This 'interior' vision is the claim upon which the author's authority is based in relation to his discourse on racial variety in *Variétés dans l'espèce humaine*. However, the interiority necessary to validate the author's representation of human racial categories is only applicable to his own cultural experience as a Frenchman. The special knowledge he claims of his own culture is not applicable universally to other cultures. This is why the structural nature of the discursive field of natural history does not attain the authority to pronounce on other cultures. Buffon attempts to authoritatively judge the Amerindian based upon the exterior view, which he admits is woefully insufficient with regard to understanding the Animal. The claim of authority and *truth* as it pertains to racial hierarchizing and hinges on belonging to the superior "we" mentioned above, i.e. belonging to the European race.

> As all language supposes a chain of thought, it is on that account that brute animals have no speech, for even allowing something in them which resembles our first apprehensions, our most gross and mechanical sensations, they still will be found incapable of forming that association of ideas which can alone produce reflection; and in this consists the essence of thought. To this inability of connecting and separating ideas it is that they are destitute of thought and speech, as also that they neither can invent nor improve any

Voltaire, La Condamine, and Buffon   71

thing. Were they endowed with the power of reflection, even in the most subordinate degree, they would be capable of making some kind of proficiency, and acquire more industry; the modern beaver would build with more art and solidity than the ancient; and the bee would daily be adding new improvements to its cell; for if we suppose this cell as perfect already as it can be, we ascribe to the insect an intelligence superior to our own. (Volume 4, 578)

Buffon's conception of the mark of *true* humanity emerges in this passage. The linguistic reference (a classic determining factor in the Man/Animal debate from ancient times, but also for Descartes) is highly significant. Buffon does not explicitly follow the linguistic argument to its logical ends, yet the conclusions of his position are evident. Privileging language use as evidence of superiority implicitly hierarchizes the written over the oral. If language is superior to no language at all (Man compared to Animal), then a well-developed written language is better than one that is merely spoken (French compared to an Amerindian language). Of course, the linguistically and culturally hermetic space of the text does not allow for any Amerindian rebuttal. Progress is the marker of *true* humanity (read Frenchness or Europeanness). The example chosen by Buffon is architecture. He homes in on two animal structures, the beaver dam and the honeycomb of the honeybee. The Amerindian who is represented as equal or superior physically, but inferior mentally, is metaphorically attached to the animals Buffon cites as examples. Exterior 'visible' objects of culture (architecture) are an obvious proof of superiority in Buffon's science of Man. The comparisons he makes between Man and the animal world are equally relevant in his comparisons between the European and Amerindian. The only space Buffon allows for one to participate fully in what he defines as humanity is a capacity for progress. After all, the bee would only be comparable to the human if it devoted itself daily to trying to improve upon the design of the honeycomb. The implication being, of course, that the Amerindian, along with the beaver and the bee, does not meet the strict requirement of the European definition of progress, with its demand for industry over non-profit based lifeways, the written text over the oral history. According to Buffon's science of Man, the Amerindian is closer to the Animal than the Human. The image of humanity is an evolutionary one that situates the European at the apex of that stadial pyramid. Because the European does not claim to witness progress in Amerindian societies, they are deemed deficient. Moralizing discourse as scientific *truth* within an evolutionary context is especially evident in the citation quoted above concerning the Inuit. Buffon states that the Inuit are "cruder than savage, without courage, self-respect, or modesty: this wretched people only has enough mores to be contemptible" (*Tome troisième*, 375, my translation). The naturalist admits the Inuit into the human family from the Cartesian viewpoint of the physical (*le corps*). However, in the spiritual realm (*l'âme*), the Inuit are animalized and only reluctantly considered as belonging to the species. By refusing to the Inuit the marks of civility,

72 *Voltaire, La Condamine, and Buffon*

Buffon situates them as physically human; morally, they are condemned to the animal. The Inuit merely display the shadow of morality, the unrealized potential for *true* humanity, which only merits the contempt of the *truly* human European writer and readers. To return to Anderson's theories of language and community formation, the author (Buffon) and his linguistically similar readers (the French) are united as a recognizable and *true* human identity via the (re)iteration of the discourse of natural history.

> In general, all of the inhabitants of northern America, including those living in the elevated regions of southern America, such as Mexico, Peru, Chili, etc. were perhaps less active, but equally as hardy as Europeans. (*Supplément Tome quatrième*, 530, my translation)

Buffon's focus on activity is inflected in a specific way. The author signals here, once again the central concept of his racial theory that demarcates the European as the measure of the human species: progress. The Amerindian may be robust, but they are not taking full advantage of their environment, because they do not interact with the environment in the same way as Europeans do. La Condamine's lamentations regarding gold lying about certainly resonate with this strain in Buffon. The natural abundance of Rousseau's state of nature serving as an obstacle to human perfectibility is another echo of this progressive Enlightenment ideal as it compares with Indigenous lifeways in the representations of the Native in the French cultural imaginary. Couched in discursive fields of truth are mythic models of othering that circumscribe how the French apprehend the Amerindian. In addition to his descriptions of the physique of the Native peoples of the Americas in a generalized sense, there is another Amerindian category addressed by Buffon: the peoples of Tierra del Fuego. This group becomes stigmatized as especially animalized in the French cultural imaginary via earlier descriptions of the Patagonians and that mythic inflection is reiterated in Buffon's *Histoire naturelle*. How does Buffon characterize the people of Tierra del Fuego? What role does the mythic mode of the Ignoble Savage play in his scientific discourse about them? In Buffon's *Histoire naturelle* the peoples of Tierra del Fuego serve as an illustration of the worst of humanity in South America. Due to Buffon's adherence to climate theory, the peoples of the far North and the extreme South are the most animalized of all. Therefore, the peoples of the Tierra del Fuego region function as a point of comparison with the Arctic peoples, such as the Inuit. One can see how Buffon's description demonstrates many of the particular characteristics of the naturalist's discursive strategies for situating the Amerindian in a larger French epistemological framework. The contrapuntal comparative imagining of the Native in relation to other ethnicities works to situate the Amerindian in the ordering of knowledge that Foucault claims exemplifies scientific discourses of the classical age.

Voltaire, La Condamine, and Buffon 73

This people appears to be nomadic, because there are abandoned huts that were discovered there before. When the shellfish are depleted in one spot along the coast, they are forced to go set up camp elsewhere. What's more, they have no boats or canoes, or anything of the sort. These are the most miserable and stupidest of all human creatures; and their climate is cold, so much so that two Europeans died there in the middle of summer. (*Supplément Tome quatrième*, 537, my translation)

This quotation marks out the theoretical and *scientific* ground that Buffon wishes to establish as a basis for *truth*. The 'visible'; is highlighted in the naturalist's inferences about the lifeways of the Tierra del Fuegians: nomadism deduced via the visual inventorying of abandoned huts. The visible as site of veridiction is one of the cornerstones of scientific discourse. Through the visual's apparent simplicity, the workings of the hermeneutic and mythic are obfuscated. The gaze the naturalist employs to describe the various features of the animal and plant world is the selfsame objectifying tool that Buffon utilizes in this passage to articulate his judgments about the inhabitants of the southernmost lands of South America. The evidence used by the naturalist is based upon a few abandoned dwellings, coastal shellfish consumption patterns, the absence of certain technologies (namely boats), and the cold weather of the region. The shift to the visual and inferential permits Buffon to claim authority as human, yet he does not maintain the rigorous scientific principles that he sets out for himself to structure and justify the truthfulness of the *Histoire naturelle* as an objective, scientific work. The visual as interpretative is one of the bases upon which scientific discourse presents its findings as self-evident despite their highly hermeneutic nature. Buffon attempts to metonymically situate the descriptions of the Amerindian as scientific *truth* in two ways. First, he claims his authority to speak about other races of the human species because of his inclusive position as human. Bringing the other races close to the European one allows Buffon to feign knowledge of the Other based on knowledge of the Self. Second, the situating of the textual descriptions of the human races in contiguity with observational *truths* about non-human animals and plants asserts another metonymic pressure on the reader to accept Buffon's deductions when the statements that the naturalist makes about the rest of his objects appear self-evidentially factual. The second metonymy reverses the first metonymy. The second metonymy situates the Amerindian closer to the animal than to Buffon and the *truly* human. Europeans' inability to survive the climate even during the summer in the environment inhabited by the Native, underscores the animality of the latter. The Amerindian is physically superior in specific ways (ability to survive in a difficult climatic zone), yet that superiority is systematically dehumanized, deemed an animal quality rather than a human characteristic. Buffon confidently states that the peoples of Tierra del Fuego are surely the stupidest and most miserable of all the

74 *Voltaire, La Condamine, and Buffon*

people on Earth. The evidence for his conclusions appears to be based upon their nomadic lifestyle and their lack of technological progress, a key paradigm for Buffon in determining *true* humanity, through the lens of progress. Additionally, the naturalist infers their cultural value based upon the extremely cold climate. Climate theory is problematized on the following page of the *Histoire naturelle* in an interesting way.

> At any rate, these men of Tierra del Fuego, where one claims that the cold is so great and where they live more miserably than any other place on earth, despite all of that, they haven't lost the dimensions of their bodies: and as they have no neighbors but the Patagonians, which, notwithstanding all the exaggerations, are the tallest of all known men; one must assume, therefore, that the cold of the southern continent has been exaggerated. (*Supplément Tome quatrième*, 538, my translation)

In this citation, Buffon's climate theory is asserted via reference to the Amerindian body in the context of both the inhabitants of the Tierra del Fuego region, and that of another group we have already 'seen': the Patagonian giants. Buffon insists on the humanity of the Amerindians of Tierra del Fuego in a qualified manner. He first refers to them as men despite positioning them closer to the animal realm than the human. Next, he explains the only way in which he considers them to be human: the dimensions of their body. This is, of course, an allusion to another of the great epistemological or theoretical paradigms that inform Buffon's racial philosophy: Cartesian dualism. According to Buffon, the Amerindian of Tierra del Fuego has only the silhouette of humanity. The body (*le corps*) is human-like, retaining the essential dimensions necessary to classify the Amerindian as a member of the human species. However, the spiritual side of the dichotomy (*l'âme*) does not pertain to the Native. Even though Buffon claims an infinite distance between the lowliest example of humanity and the highest example of the animal world, this assertion is not maintained in the *Histoire naturelle*. The most significant aspect of this passage is the reference to the Patagonian giants. Buffon wishes to distinguish himself from the gullible readers who have swallowed wholesale the legend of the gargantuan stature of the Patagonians by qualifying their prodigious height as less than the exaggerations of some authors, while simultaneously asserting that they are the tallest humans on Earth. Buffon's blind adherence to climate theory is evident here. Although he states that the cold is so extreme in Tierra del Fuego that it brought about the demise of two Europeans during the summer months, the existence of the mythologized Patagonian giants means that the climate must not be as cold as other less scrupulous authors have claimed. Buffon attempts to take advantage of opposite poles of the climate theory's principles at the same time, in the same place and climate.

The stunted, culturally degenerate inhabitants of the Tierra del Fuego connote an extreme environment in keeping with the tenets of climate theory. However, the existence of the giant Patagonians throws a wrench in the works of the naturalist's mythic machine. Buffon attempts to explain away the existence of the Patagonians alongside the peoples of Tierra del Fuego by insisting that the climate cannot be as cold as reported. The argument quickly degenerates into an aporic one, because a physically well-developed group (the Patagonians) and an inferior group that is barely hanging on to their human status (the inhabitants of the Tierra del Fuego region) cannot exist in the same geographical region according to the postulates of climate theory. Ironically, the *truth* of Buffon's systematizing epistemological framework for understanding human racial diversity is based upon myth, revealing its *true* nature as imaginary.

Despite Buffon's claims of veridiction and objectivity, the mythic is at the center of French representations of the Amerindian, even within the discipline of science. The mythical apparatus is never completely absent in textual images of the Amerindian. The mythological origins of the representation of the Amerindian are not eradicated by the epistemological movement known as the Enlightenment, with its concurrent rationalism and positivism in one of its proto-scientific descendants: natural history. What one encounters in Buffon's citation above is an attempt at mitigating the mythic component within scientific discourse about the Amerindian, but Buffon's fumbling attempt falls short of demystifying how the French *see* the Native. Buffon's scientific objectivity occurs in a vacuum of textual allusions and culturally biased inferences. If natural history is the "nomination of the visible" as Foucault posits, then the inherent irony of Buffon's racial descriptions about the inhabitants of the Tierra del Fuego region and the legendary Patagonian giants lies in the fact that the naturalist never *saw* either one. The important point to retain here is the way in which mythically inflected and sensationalized representations of the Amerindian play a critical role in the formation of the French cultural imaginary of the Amerindian as a category. The long-established mythic messages about the Native are performing one of the key features of the mythic: *transferability*. From the anecdotal to the philosophic, the mythic machine now lays claim to the scientific. The foundational mythic message, however, changes very little as it passes from the discursive genre of the travel narrative to that of the natural history treatise. The power of the mythic machine is evident here in relation to Buffon's critical understanding of the animal, plant, and human worlds: climate theory. What more poignant example could be found than that of the myth of the Patagonian giants directly influencing Buffon's conclusions about a climatic zone at the southern tip of the South American continent? In addition, the reports of La Condamine about the bestiality of the Oreillons cause a sensational reaction across France and inspires Voltaire to immortalize the mythic report in fiction in his masterpiece *Candide*. Yet, these mythic and sensationalized representations of the Amerindian are formative and enduring in the creation of the French cultural imaginary of the Native. The mythic machine does an extraordinary amount of work maintaining the mythic understanding of the Amerindian Other,

76 *Voltaire, La Condamine, and Buffon*

going so far as to invalidate the very rhetorical principles of scientific discourse, bending the parameters of *truth* to ensure the mythic machine's discursive dominance.

The mélange of the Patagonian giant mythic discourse with that of a scientific discourse that purports to reveal a certain *truth* merely by naming the 'visible' is an example of the significance of narrative in Western knowledge. Science wishes to disassociate its truth claims from the narrative construction of the knowledge it produces, and yet, myth and story are an integral aspect of that construction. Rather than obfuscate a fundamental relationship between knowledge and narrative, Indigenous ways of knowing embrace the connection between knowing and story. Laurelyn Whitt (Mississippi Choctaw) states that,

> Within indigenous knowledge systems, knowledge is typically tied so intimately to experience and imagination as to be inconceivable without them. Stories are acts of the imagination that enable us to enact and reenact experience. One source of their richness as pedagogical vehicles is that they permit us some access to the perspectives of other beings, often those very different from ourselves. We come to know them by relating ourselves to them, by imagining what it is like to be them and to experience the world—including ourselves—through them. (35)

In Whitt's formulation, for Indigenous peoples, knowledge is often tied to personal experience. Writing *Histoire naturelle* is not a personal experience for Buffon in the way that Whitt articulates Native knowledge. Scientific distancing associated with objectification and objectivity is anathema to the personal experience that characterizes Amerindian knowledge. Buffon and the scientific gaze are often at one or more degrees of removal even within the confines of a supposedly empirical project. Buffon does not observe first-hand the peoples that he defines. In many cases, the *Histoire naturelle* resembles more a Renaissance era compendium, an amalgam and re-reading of the written accounts of travelers and experts, rather than the 'nomination of the visible' signaled by Foucault. Buffon's goal of establishing the human, and in particular the European, as the pinnacle of natural history is at odds with the relational bent of Whitt's description of Native ways of learning about the Other, human and non-human. Inclusive rather than exclusionary, Indigenous knowledge systems engage with difference to incorporate other lifeways in an experiential rather than in an observational way. Situating beings within a grander spatializing grid or order of knowledge, which is how Foucault construes science in the classical age, does not consider attempting to comprehend the experiences of the Other and embodying oneself in that experience. Rather, the narrative technology of Buffon's scientific discourse in *Histoire naturelle* seeks to differentiate rather than take the relational as a roadmap, as a best practice for gaining knowledge about the world.

4 Conclusion

In this chapter, the genealogy of the mythic paradigms employed as a lens for understanding the category of Amerindian in the French cultural imaginary has been expanded through investigations into the writings of one of the most influential writers of the eighteenth century. In his renowned novel *Candide*, Voltaire typifies the conflation of the mythic machine. The narrative technologies of the Ignoble and Noble Savage converge through the *queering* of the Native in his descriptions of the Oreillons and the idealizing of New World geographies in the legendary space of Eldorado. In *conversation* with La Condamine, Voltaire's mythic Indian is a fabrication of fiction from *fact*. It is, after all, the novelist's correspondence with the scientist La Condamine that informs Voltaire's bestial portrayal of the Oreillons and their sexuality. In the second section, the *transferability* of mythic discourses across generic lines, from fiction to fact, emerges in an analysis of the proto-scientific writings of the father of natural history, the Comte de Buffon. Continuing the exploration of the mythic machine in the French and Québécois cultural imaginaries, in the next chapter the evolution of the mythic mode into the realms of the Ecological Savage and the Vanishing Indian is elucidated.

Works Cited

Alès, Catherine and Michel Pouyllau. "La Conquête de l'inutile. Les geographies imaginaires de l'Eldorado." *L'Homme.*, vol. 32, no. 122, 1992, pp. 271–308.

Anderson, Benedict. *Imagined Communities: Reflections on the Origin and Spread of Nationalism.* Kindle version. New York: Verso, 2006.

Bhabha, Homi. *The Location of Culture.* Kindle version. New York: Routledge Classics, 2012.

Bourdieu, Pierre. *Langage et pouvoir symbolique.* Paris: Éditions du Seuil, 2001.

Buffon, George-Louis Leclerc de. *Buffon's Natural History: Volume 4.* Frankfurt: Books on Demand, 2020.

———. *Histoire naturelle: Supplément tome quatrième. Gallica.* https://gallica.bnf.fr/ark:/12148/bpt6k10705425.image. Paris: Imprimerie royale, 1777.

———. *Histoire naturelle: Tome troisième. Gallica.* https://gallica.bnf.fr/ark:/12148/bpt6k1067228r.image. Paris: Imprimerie royale, 1749. 27 April 2023.

Coulthard, Glen Sean. *Red Skin, White Masks: Rejecting the Colonial Politics of Recognition.* Kindle edition. Minneapolis: University of Minnesota Press, 2014.

Deloria Jr., Vine. "Ethnoscience and Indian Realities." *Spirit and Reason: The Vine Deloria, Jr., Reader.* Edited by Barbara Deloria, Kristen Foehner, and Sam Scinta. Golden: Fulcrum Publishing, 1999. pp. 63–71.

———. *God Is Red: A Native View of Religion, 30th Anniversary Edition.* Golden: Fulcrum Publishing, 2003.

Douglas, Bronwen. "Climate to Crania: Science and the Racialization of Human Difference." *Foreign Bodies: Oceania and the Science of Race 1750–1940.* Edited by Bronwen Douglas and Chris Ballard. Canberra: ANU Press, 2008. pp. 33–96.

78 *Voltaire, La Condamine, and Buffon*

Duchet, Michèle. *Anthropologie et histoire au siècle des Lumières*. Paris: Albin Michel, 1971.

Goeman, Mishuana. *Mark My Words: Native Women Mapping Our Nations*. Minneapolis: University of Minnesota Press, 2013.

Hugo, Victor. *Œuvres completes*. Kindle version, Arvensa Editions, 2013.

Hurtado, Albert. "When Strangers Met: Sex and Gender on Three Frontiers." *Frontiers: A Journal of Women Studies*, vol. 17, no. 3, 1996. https://www.jstor.org/stable/3346876. 27 April 2023.

La Condamine, Charles-Marie de. *Journal du voyage fait par ordre du roi à l'Équateur*. *Gallica*. https://gallica.bnf.fr/ark:/12148/bpt6k1051290z?rk=42918;4. Paris: Imprimerie royale, 1751. 26 April 2023.

———. *Relation abrégée d'un voyage fait dans l'intérieur de l'Amérique méridionale*. *Gallica*. https://gallica.bnf.fr/ark:/12148/bpt6k1051316r?rk=21459;2. Paris: Pissot: 1745. 26 April 2023.

Lestringant, Frank. *Cannibals: The Discovery and Representation of the Cannibal from Columbus to Jules Verne*. Los Angeles: University of California Press, 1997.

Morgensen, Scott Lauria. *Spaces between Us: Queer Settler Colonialism and Indigenous Decolonization*. Minneapolis: University of Minnesota Press, 2011.

Povinelli, Elizabeth. *The Cunning of Recognition: Indigenous Alterities and the Making of Australian Multiculturalism*. Kindle version. Durham, NC: Duke UP, 2002.

Pratt, Mary Louise. *Imperial Eyes: Travel Writing and Transculturation*. New York: Routledge, 2003.

Sheridan, Alan, translator. *The Order of Things: An Archaeology of the Human Sciences*. By Michel Foucault. Kindle version, Taylor-Francis, 2005.

Smollett, Tobias, translator. *Premium Collection*. By Voltaire, Kindle version, e-artnow, 2016.

Turnovsky, Geoffrey. "The Making of a Name: A Life of Voltaire." *The Cambridge Companion to Voltaire*. Edited by Nicholas Cronk. Cambridge: Cambridge UP, 2009. doi.org/10.1017/CCOL9780521849739. 26 April, 2023.

Voltaire. *Œuvres completes*. Kindle version, Arvensa Editions, 2020.

3 The Vanishing Indian

Manifest and Imperial Destinies

1 Introduction

This chapter focuses on the mythic machine's manifestations in the nineteenth century. Nineteenth-century visions of the Indigenous peoples of the Americas are often articulated via the narrative technology of the Vanishing Indian myth. The original mythic modes of the Noble and Ignoble Savage contain the seeds of the mythic turn to the Vanishing Indian framework. The mythology of the Vanishing Indian portrays the Native as on the verge of extinction. This exclusion of the Amerindian from the future narrative of human history is cited as an ineluctable self-evidence. Through narrations that simultaneously present and *disappear* the Amerindian in a landscape that only admits the Native presence as death, the inherent illogic of the Vanishing Indian mythic machine is revealed as complicit with the colonial project of dispossession and extermination. Having *disappeared* the Amerindian, frontier geographies are opened, allowing for the conquering of the spaces formerly belonging to the Native. The first section of the chapter analyzes the French Western, a derivative form of the more familiar American Western. An influential form that is widely read by the French masses in a rapidly industrializing context, the French Western plays a key role in the *crystallization* of the mythic visions of the Indigenous peoples of the Americas within the French and Québécois cultural imaginaries. While set in the Western hemisphere, the mythic machine's images in the voice of the Vanishing Indian are a tool of self-definition of Frenchness. Nationalist questions of the Self and the Other, as well as colonial and imperial issues are vicariously present in the violent world of the Western. In the final section of the chapter, I return to the *transferability* of the mythic machine's message into disparate discursive regimes, notably scientific discourses. A close reading of the father of sociology, Émile Durkheim's *De la division du travail social* (*The Division of Labor in Society*) reveals the framing of Native sexuality and gender as a pathologized abnormality against which the scientist constructs a normalized and naturalized image of French superiority, supported in his conclusions by the *hard science* of biological racism in the late nineteenth century. Examining Durkheim's utilization of *sexual*

DOI: 10.4324/9781032638751-4

80 *The Vanishing Indian: Manifest and Imperial Destinies*

resemblance through a *queer* Indigenous critical lens, Scott Lauria Morgensen's analysis of the colonial object of berdache anchors my reading of Durkheim's mythically inflected, scientific iteration of the myth of the Vanishing Indian.

2 The French Western

2.1 The Coureur de Bois and Violent Popular Culture

No other figure embodies the connection between the myths of the Vanishing Indian and Going Native more than the coureur de bois. Frontiersman, trapper, Indian fighter, cowboy, etc. are acceptable equivalents for a term that primarily signifies Caucasian participants in the fur trade of New France, but also agriculturally minded *défricheurs*, (land-clearers) who inhabit the mobile edge of colonial settlements. The connotations of the term extend in the French Western to include any person of European descent in frontier geographies, living in proximity and having relations (collaborative and/or conflictual) with Amerindians. The coureur de bois archetype *crystallizes* the myth of the Vanishing Indian into a predominant vision of the Native, reimagining them as a source of self-actualization through spiritual and other adoptions of what are represented, often erroneously, as *authentic* Native lifeways in the mythology of Going Native. This section explores how the coureur de bois is instrumentalized in French Westerns to reiterate the myth of the Vanishing Indian, simultaneously transforming that model into something new: the myth of Going Native. The coureur de bois is a figure that becomes well-known through the Westerns of French authors such as Gustave Aimard, Louis-Henri Boussenard, and, in the Québécois context, Henri-Émile Chevalier. The French Western novel is a derivative form inspired by the American Western, the father of which is James Fenimore Cooper, whose *Leatherstocking Tales* establish many of the conventions that continue to dominate the plotlines and character typologies of the genre to this day. The French Western is not limited to the geographies of what will become the United States, however. For Francophone authors, any frontier space putting Natives and those of European descent in contact constitutes a fertile ground for a Western. For example, while some of Boussenard's tales are situated in the western United States, many of his works take place in French Guyana. His French Guyana carries all the identifiable marks of the Western, pitting the coureur de bois figure against a classic triumvirate of opposing forces: the civilization of which he is a product/outcast, the wild nature of the frontier, and the Native with whom he often maintains an ambiguous relationship. In Aimard's writing, settings include North, Central, and South America. All these localities comprehend the French Western. A transnational viewpoint allows the possibility to engage critically with diverse geographies and milieux, identifying how the mythic machine functions in similar ways in a variety of contexts. The French Western has a greater extension than the American Western which focuses on

The derivative French Western, with its non-American perspective, expands the applicability of the original form while maintaining the genre's core traits. Another way the French Western expands the American genre hinges on Canadian geographies and characters. The coureur de bois is typically of French-Canadian descent. After the Act of Union of 1840 combined Upper and Lower Canada as the unified Province of Canada, French-speaking citizens found themselves submerged in an Anglophone world that increasingly marginalized them. French-Canadian identity becomes a vehicle of critique of Anglo-Saxon notions of global capitalism and race relations. The French-Canadian coureur de bois archetype functions to exculpate French-Canadian presence in contested frontier spaces. Exculpation is a primary aspect of the cultural work the Western novel (and film) performs. The Western naturalizes the presence of settlers on the land through the liminal figure of the coureur de bois or cowboy. In the American Western, these characters are coded as anti-social, producing a counterbalance to the impetus of Manifest Destiny, global capitalism, and settler-colonialism, yet the countercultural actually converges with the colonial project. Indeed, there is synergy between the ideologies of Manifest Destiny, global capitalism, and settler-colonialism. All three are concerned with acquiring new territories for exploitation, exportation, and inhabitation. Land plays a central role in the French Western. Land is paramount in the conflicts in nearly every Western narrative. The frontier is an increasingly smaller space, hemmed in by the Pacific Ocean. In the American context, the frontier is symbolically closed late in the nineteenth century. The massacre of peaceful Sioux at Wounded Knee in 1890 is often cited as the culminating event that completes the Manifest Destiny of the American Republic. Frederick Jackson Turner's frontier thesis, first unveiled as a speech at the World's Fair in Chicago in 1893, is a famous example of the specificity and significance of the frontier vision of geography in American national self-fashioning and mythology. Huhndorf (Yup'ik) pinpoints Turner's frontier thesis as an "elision of… Native history", thereby echoing the logics of manifest manners (Intro). Turner views the frontier as *the* key concept for understanding America, contending that "the existence of an area of free land, its continuous recession, and the advance of American settlement westward, explain American development" (Turner Chapter 1). The frontier is defined by its (re)generative capacity; it is a unique space characterized by "perennial rebirth" (Turner Chapter 1). The categories of Native and settler are critical elements of the articulation of mythic national identities to bring about that "perennial rebirth".

Morgensen, in *Spaces Between Us: Queer Settler Colonialism and Indigenous Decolonization*, tells us that,

> Settler societies engender a normative relationality between the designations "Native" and "settler" that imbues histories of intermingling, interdependence, or the attempted erasure of indigeneity as a marker of national

82 *The Vanishing Indian: Manifest and Imperial Destinies*

difference. The distinction between "Native" and "settler" informs all power in settler societies and their relations with societies worldwide. (1)

For Morgensen, the boundaries erected by dominant discourses simultaneously hone and blur Native and settler categories. The Western focuses on race relations and land tenure, proffering interpretations of those categories in keeping with political movements and their shifting priorities. As such, the Western explicitly addresses itself to the work of (national) identity creation and racialized mythmaking. To return to Andersen's formulation, the Western does the cultural work of creating the parameters of an *imagined community*. "Perennial rebirth" occurs via mythic reiterations of Native and settler. This renaissance does not concern itself with *truth*, but rather adopts an "anarchic approach to meaning" according to Philip Deloria (Standing Rock Sioux), ignoring history and land rights to perpetuate a settler-colonial march westward that does not announce itself as violence but as progress (184). "Perennial rebirth" through the redrawing of distinctions between Native and settler is a symbolic affair that manifests in the discourses of politics, history, religion, (social) science, and literature. The "intermingling, interdependence, or attempted erasure of indigeneity" that Morgensen points to as a primary objective of power-building in settler-colonial societies is a leitmotif of the (French) Western. It is through the figure of the coureur de bois or cowboy that these processes are performed in frontier geographies. The coureur de bois represents the convergence of the three phenomena signaled by Morgensen. Exactly how are these three concepts connected?

Intermingling alludes to proximity and contact. The coureur de bois acting in frontier space with the Native is intermingling. Within frontier economies, the exchange of products and services (such as the Indigenous man or woman who serves as guide to a European [group]) are more than economic exchange. Cultural exchange happens because of economic imperatives associated with global capitalism in frontier geographies. These exchanges are the substance of the Western and the experiences of the coureur de bois. The dual forces of the *francisation* (making French) of the Amerindian and the *indianisation* (making Indian) of the European are present in the historical *and* fictional coureur de bois. With the closing of the frontier in 1890, the "perennial rebirth" that gives the frontier ideology so much potential becomes exclusively symbolic. The French empire in North America ends long before, with the defeat on the Plains of Abraham in 1760 and the Louisiana Purchase. By 1890, the French have long been absent from the settler-colonial frontier, apart from French-Canadian settler-colonialism within Québec itself. Despite the Western's American origins, the French, and other Europeans, continue to (re)produce and consume the frontier. The popularity of the French Western novel is evidence of the extraterritorial, symbolic interest that questions of European and Indigenous identity continue to hold in the Old World long after the independence of the United States and the abandonment of imperial conquest in the Americas.

The Vanishing Indian: Manifest and Imperial Destinies   83

Why does the frontier pique European interest? For Morgensen, the Western novel is not meant to merely entertain. It does the critical cultural work of national identity articulation and exculpation vis-à-vis Native genocide, as well as justification for possession and continued exploitation of stolen land. Its ideology can be applied to non-American geographies, such as empire-building in Asia and Africa. Much has been written about the necessity of replaying frontier dramas to legitimize settler-colonialism in the Americas, but there is a paucity of critical examination of why Europeans who are no longer attached politically/physically to those frontiers continue to be captivated by the genre. Ray Allen Billington points to the influence of James Fenimore Cooper and his *Leatherstocking Tales* as largely responsible for the European obsession with the Western. Speaking about the popularity of the series' first volume, *The Pioneers*, Billington states that,

> All the ingredients of a lusty adventure story were there: the grizzled old trapper Natty Bumppo, chases along forest trails in moccasined feet, wilderness feats of incredible daring, a dainty maiden awaiting rescue from a deadly panther. Natty spoke the untutored vernacular expected of woodsmen, befriended good Indians, was the implacable foe of bad, and was humane to wild animals save when food was necessary. What European with an ounce of adventure in his being could resist? (30)

It is not perhaps happenstance then that at the *Musée du Nouveau Monde* in La Rochelle, France (a critical French Atlantic port for ships traveling to New France and the Americas during the colonial period), French editions of many of James Fenimore Cooper's *Leatherstocking Tales* are prominently displayed (this was the case when I visited in 2010). This emphasis on Cooper and the Western indicates how influential frontier mythology is in the French cultural imaginary. Interestingly, the adventurous aspects of the Western à la Cooper were not seen as fantasy. Billington asserts that,

> Remarkably, Europeans saw Cooper as a realist who accurately portrayed the frontiersmen and Indians- a judgment that would astound modern readers… [The European] audience was eager for reasonably accurate descriptions of the pioneers and the red men, not for the Noble Savages of Rousseau and Chateaubriand. A major market waited works that exploited the towering grandeur of the American forests, the brooding silence of the prairies, the horizonless sweep of the Great Plains; works that pitted leather-clad hunters in spine-tingling battles with painted Indians or savage beasts. Here was a challenge to European novelists, and they met it with such success that Westerns became the standard literary fare of Britishers, Germans, Scandinavians, Frenchmen, Spaniards, even Hungarians and Poles, for a century to come. Carrying realism well beyond Cooper, these authors became the principal image-makers for Europe's literate and semiliterate masses. (31–2)

84   *The Vanishing Indian: Manifest and Imperial Destinies*

Myth confused as reality, fiction swallowed wholesale as fact, is part and parcel of European mythic (mis)understandings of the Amerindian from the fifteenth century until the present day. The *Leatherstocking Tales* open the door to French Western publication in the nineteenth century. Novels appear via regular installments in newspapers to a broad audience, shaping and *crystallizing* the French cultural imaginary of the Native and the Americas. Literature of this ilk becomes readily available to a wider audience through cheaper production techniques. That audience is called to believe in these *realistic* narratives because of a complex historical process of validation that begins with Cooper. Bourdieu's theories on language and symbolic power explain how the Western wields such influence in forging European cultural imaginaries. Bourdieu insists that the power of language does not reside in the linguistic sign itself; the social conditions of enunciation are crucial to apprehend functionalities that language performs. *Literariness* is a subdivision of language that has sparked considerable debate about the specificity of that discourse. The uniqueness of the *literary*, often associated with elite, canonical texts is not the wheelhouse of the French Western. It is a category apart from literariness or *haute culture*. The derivative genre of the French Western is often formulaic, repetitive, poorly constructed, and limited lexically. For these reasons, the academy has largely ignored the French Western as a potential object of inquiry. The rise of literacy and mass media parallels the emergence of popular literatures like the French Western. As mentioned previously, Anderson points to the dual forms of the newspaper and novel as constitutive of the possibility of nationalism in nineteenth-century Europe. The working classes that created the wealth in what is commonly labeled the Industrial Revolution, wealth that was an ineluctable condition of possibility for the emergence of nation states with their naturalizing ideologies of nationalism, mercantilism, imperialism, and racism, are the primary readership of European Westerns. In a different socio-historical context, Bourdieu suggests the attraction that the frontier might represent for workers.

> The morality of might that finds its expression in the cult of violence and quasi-suicidal play (motorcycles, alcohol, or hard drugs) where the relationship with the future is forged for those who have nothing to expect from the future, is, without a doubt, one way to make a virtue out of necessity. ... [the]duty to be tough, for oneself and for others, that leads to the desperate risk-taking behaviors of the aristocracy of the outcast, is a way to take a stand in a world without prospects, dominated by misery and the law of the jungle, discrimination and violence, where morality and emotion do not benefit anyone. (*Langage et pouvoir symbolique* 141, my translation)

Although Bourdieu refers to workers during the *Trente Glorieuses*, his analysis provides some insights into the popularity of the French Western, both in its linguistic similarity to the popular language and its penchant for calling on

The Vanishing Indian: Manifest and Imperial Destinies   85

the reader to identify with heroes and villains that exhibit machismo and the 'cult of violence'. The violence of frontier geographies is a ubiquitous element of the French Western, one mirrored in Bourdieu's account of the French *ban-lieue*, with its toxic masculinity. How does American frontier violence function in French popular culture? What does the frontier signify to the French reader who identifies with the coureur de bois? The (vicarious) violence of the French Western is a key factor in its extreme popularity. For the nineteenth-century French industrial worker, the appeal of the fictional frontier largely resides in its brutality. This violence attracts the interest of working poor during a period of rapid industrialization and mechanization. It may not be violence alone that draws the urban worker in, however. Migration toward urban centers during the second half of the nineteenth and early twentieth centuries is a salient feature of industrialization. Although the environments of the French Western frontier and that of the French countryside are not identical, no doubt the outdoor life of the coureur de bois appealed to rural French sensibilities concerning nature. The French Western glorifies (interracial) violence *and* valorizes lifeways centered on knowledge of and constant interaction with the environment. Both the culture of violence and the natural wonders of the frontier fascinate a readership with reduced mobility, both in the Bourdieusian sense of lack of opportunity for social mobility and advancement, but also in the spatial sense of limited access to natural spaces within the urban centers of the French industrial revolution. Violence and natural grandeur are sublimated in the mythic French Western. The ambiguity of the frontier constitutes a more diverse world, inherently imbued with greater opportunity than the monotonous world of the industrial proletariat.

The construction of American identity has always been linked to interpretations, representations, and mythologies of the Amerindian *and* to European mythologies on Nature and humanity's place in the cosmos vis-à-vis the land *and* other peoples. Richard Slotkin's definition of myth demonstrates how the connection between Europe and the Americas is made in the Western.

> A mythology is a complex of narratives that dramatizes the world vision and historical sense of a people or culture, reducing centuries of experience into a constellation of compelling metaphors. The narrative action of the myth-tale recapitulates that people's experience in their land, rehearses their visions of that experience in its relation to their gods and the cosmos, and reduces both experience and vision to a paradigm. (Regeneration through Violence, 6)

Mythology is a people's perspectival tool and narrative technology for parsing and giving meaning to the world, and in the American case, the land that they inhabit. Although naturalized, these perspectives are arbitrary and culturally determined. European enthrallment with the American frontier and its mythologies, including the Noble, Ignoble, and Ecological Savage modes, the Vanishing Indian and Going Native, is because the whole mythic apparatus is informed by

86   *The Vanishing Indian: Manifest and Imperial Destinies*

the mythic tradition of the Old World, which is then transposed to the New World with many of its fundamental characteristics remaining intact. The transference of older myths into Western hemisphere geographies is a common feature of New World cultural productions. The myths that the New World colonizers create are linked to historically contingent tendencies that developed in the Old World over the *longue durée*, informed by multiple contacts with exotic peoples and ancient mythologies. The chain remains unbroken connecting the myths of the frontier and the Old World. European readers of Westerns recognize the tropes and narrative arcs of the genre. There is little *dépaysement* happening, because the frontier myth is written in a mythic vernacular the reader intuitively understands. In the myths of the Western, influence flows in two directions. The mythmaking apparatus of the American Western is informed (unconsciously) by a shared European cultural inheritance. This transhistorical, transgeographical connection is furthered by the derivation of European versions of the genre that are then (re)mythologized, (re)instrumentalized, and (re)cycled in European discourses, particularly in nationalist rhetoric. There are two points of identification linking the (American) Western to its European audience. One comes from the past, the other is anchored, through political and economic pressures of the present, to a vision of the future. The connection with the past is what I have described as the sharing of a similar mythic vision of the world. The connection with the present and to an idealized, fictive vision of the future is what I have described, with the help of Bourdieu's analysis of popular machismo culture, as the draw of the violence of the frontier to the social class of nineteenth-century European industrial workers. Both temporally determined factors explain the popularity of the myth of the frontier when it is translated into French and transposed to the Old World. How does the Western function in the creation of national identity outside the Americas? There is a direct correlation with the mythologizing of the conquest of the frontier geographies of the American West and the collective consciousness of American identity in the context of American literature. But how does the derivative French Western speak to the reader's understanding of Frenchness? If one thinks envisions the French Western as an adventure in a far-flung locale concerning non-French adversaries, one might be tempted to answer that the French Western can have nothing to do with how a French reader defines Frenchness, but that is not true. The French Western, the mythology of the frontier, and suite of myths about Amerindians engage the reader in specific ways with questions regarding the Self and Frenchness.

2.2   Frontier Nationalist Discourse

Fundamentally, French Westerns connect readers with their Frenchness via the French language. Readers access frontier ideologies through the vehicle of their mother tongue. The translation of the frontier into French imbues the French Western's particular mythologies and intelligibility, legitimacy, and a power of identification. The power of identification is a dual process that begins with the linguistic commonality of the French language. Languages contain registers, purposeful uses or contextualized, situated instantiations of language that all are subsumed in the larger, encompassing category of what is understood by the term *language*. Those registers are determined by many factors, such as varying levels of formality, regional inflection, pronunciation, accent, etc. Examining some basic elements of linguistic register can inform a deeper understanding of the popularity and cultural function of the French Western. The French Western's valorization of violence and its glorification of a specific conception of masculinity *register* with the French working classes in the cultural manner explained above, allowing workers to identify with the hyper-masculinity of the coureur de bois. In addition to this thematic and cultural identification, the French Western's linguistic register engenders reader identification. The French Western is a product intended for the popular class. It is mass produced and mass consumed. Andersen notes that, "the book was the first modern-style mass-produced industrial commodity" (34). The French Western is not a product of elite or even bourgeois cultures. Its prodigious and long-term popularity throughout the nineteenth and twentieth centuries indicates how influential it is in shaping the collective French cultural imaginary of the Amerindian and frontier geographies. Billington concludes that, "Little known to historians of literature, these best-sellers played a larger role than any other writings in shaping the European image of the American frontier" (38). The capacity of the Western to inculcate Europeans with mythic representations of Natives and the Far West cannot be understated. The French Western can garner such cultural power because of the linguistic characteristics that typify the genre. It is characterized both by syntactical and lexical simplicity, common features of popular vernacular and mass culture. In addition to these basic linguistic features, the French Western is predictable and formulaic. Recounting the same plotlines and reintroducing the same characters (with or without changing their names) are two of its most common features.

> For the first time in history a mass audience existed for stories geared to the unsophisticated tastes of the newly educated—stories that were fast-moving, uncluttered by complex plots or characterizations, and packed with the violence and *primitive* emotionalism that appealed to the uncultured. Here was a market for cheap thrillers that no hack writer could resist. (47)

It is precisely for these reasons that the French Western carries linguistic and cultural power, becoming a huge commercial success. The working classes do not read the French Western merely because it has been sufficiently dumbed down, however. The linguistic features allow for the reader's self-identification based on linguistic registers with which the reader is already familiar in their quotidian existence. The French Western is not simply escapism, either, although there is a fair amount of that going on. Permeating the popularity of the French Western, is

88 *The Vanishing Indian: Manifest and Imperial Destinies*

the cultural work that the texts perform vis-à-vis its working-class consumers via the nationalist message that is encoded within the French Western, reaffirming affiliations with Frenchness and the French nation. In addition to the specificity of the nationalist *French* message, there is also an imperial *European* message that blurs the identifications between nation and race, articulating a Eurocentric vision of the world. In the French Western, nationalist and imperialist messages are transposed geographically onto the American frontier and racially onto the Amerindian. Mythologies of the Native are instrumentalized in the articulation of these messages. When examining the European message at the heart of the Western, the insights of Edward Saïd are helpful. Saïd believes that a basic ideological, institutional, and structural element, a building block, of the intellectual project that is *Europe* is the European's belief in their own supremacy.

> the major component in European culture is precisely what made that culture hegemonic both in and outside Europe: the idea of European identity as a superior one in comparison with all the non-European peoples and cultures. (*Orientalism*, 7)

While it is evident that Saïd's work aims to deconstruct that supposition in relation to Europe's accumulated and constructed knowledge of the Orient, the *discovery* of the Americas was equally, if not more influential, in the articulation of European superiority as naturalized fact. If Western culture had long practice in self-defining as superior when looking outward, that experience was intensified after contact is made with the New World. It is not evident that the *discovery* of the Amerindian meant the immediate synchronous *discovery* of a Pan-European identity. As Vanita Seth states,

> Through the works of historians on the idea of Europe, it is possible to recognize in the emergence of a European identity both a historically contingent subject and a highly self-conscious invention. Europe as an identity and a tradition cannot be legitimately defended or appealed to until at least the eighteenth century. …a European consciousness was continually arrested by cultural disparities that rendered the discovery of the new World as a site not for the cultivation of a European identity, but as a battleground for conflicting political claims and religious interpretations. Pre-empting the possible objection that not a secular but a Christian European identity can be appealed to as far back as the Middle Ages… …far from being equal partners, the ambitions of Christendom often undermined the idea of Europe and that the immediate consequence of the decline of Christendom and discovery of the New World heralded not a secular European consciousness but the fragmentation of any monolithic identity. (36)

It is in the crucible of colonial competition that the ideological birth of nationalism should be historically situated. In the New World, competition engenders

The Vanishing Indian: Manifest and Imperial Destinies 89

imperialism as a mode of relation with the Amerindian. The experience of the New World is a formative one in the ideologies of nationalism and imperialism. In the early modern period, following the spread of tales of Spanish treasure in the Americas, that Europe begin to imagine themselves, first as Spanish, English, French, etc. and thereafter as European. Andersen asserts that, "nationalism has to be understood by aligning it, not with self-consciously held political ideologies, but with the large cultural systems that preceded it, out of which—it came into being" (12). It is through the discovery of cultural Others, notably the Amerindian, and colonialism's extractive model of global capitalism that nationalism finds its conditions of possibility. Discovery of the New World is connected to the rise nationalism. Andersen emphasizes the importance of imagination in nationalist ideology, dubbing the nation an *imagined community* bolstered by the cultural products of an incipient mass media network typified by two forms: the novel and the newspaper (25). The French Western is a tool for the proliferation of myths about the Self in nationalistic terms. It is one of the first mass media/cultural products that targets the working classes. Fanon states that, "Colonizer-colonized relationships are mass relationships" (*Les damnés de la terre* 37, my translation). To ripen the conditions of possibility for the imperial ventures of the nineteenth and twentieth centuries and exculpate their immorality in the collective consciousness, a mass media form is needed to articulate racist colonial ideals that harmonize with nationalist interests and ideologies. In this context, the French Western is instrumental in the creation of a national French identity and a European colonial identity. Furthermore, the genre has overtly imperialist themes, which I return to below. French readers' engagement with the geographies, ideologies, and mythologies of the Amerindian in French language reinforces definitions of Frenchness. As Frantz Fanon famously said, "To speak a language is to assume a world, a culture" (*Peau noire, masques blancs* 30, my translation). Through the transposition/translation of the Amerindian in the mythic space of the frontier into the French language, the French Western accesses an apparatus that makes the *imagined community* of the French nation possible. The French reader accedes to the author's "auctoritas" through the linguistic exchange. "Auctoritas" is:

> That legal act consisting of authoritatively affirming a truth that carries the force of law, an act of knowing that, because it is founded, like all symbolic power, on recognition, brings about the very existence it articulates. *Auctoritas*, as Benveniste recalls, is the author's capacity to create. (*Langage et pouvoir symbolique*, 283–4, my translation)

This reference alludes to the power to define the identity of a group, including the way in which an utterance creates a collective identity based on agreed upon mythic representations of the Self/Other dichotomy. Collective assent to the recognizable message of the French Western imbues the genre with a *truth*

90   *The Vanishing Indian: Manifest and Imperial Destinies*

value that is not limited to the fictional world of the novel, but equally inculcates racial ideologies. This is the shadowy power of the mythic machine at work. The mythic mode functions as a narrative technology to create *truths* about the Self and the Other. The self-positionings that derive from the mythological are not constrained to vicarious textual worlds. Indeed, they influence political action in the *real* world. The French Western functions as a *discours performatif,* a performative discourse (*Langage et pouvoir symbolique,* 285).

> Regionalist discourse is a *performative discourse* that seeks to impose the legitimacy of a new definition of where the border lies, to make the *region* known and recognized as it is delineated in opposition to the official defini-tion of the region, wherein the prevailing definition is disregarded and not recognized as such. The act of categorizing, when it succeeds in being rec-ognized or when it is backed by a recognized authority, exerts power in and of itself: 'ethnic' or 'regional' categories, like familial categories, establish a reality via the utilization of the powers of *revelation* and *construction* entailed by the *objectification in the discourse.* (*Langage et pouvoir symbolique* 285, my translation)

The question of territory and identity is central to the discourse of the French Western. After all, the contest of the French Western is primarily concerned with land and who can legitimately inhabit/exploit it, a conflict redramatized between European (descendants) and the Native, reiterating myths about Eu-ropean hypermasculinity and of Amerindian inferiority. The inevitability of European victory reveals the racial component of this overarching structural framework of the Western genre, qualifying it as a narrative technology of the Vanishing Indian myth. Physical superiority linked to hypermasculinity denotes moral superiority in the world of the Western, both are the handmaidens of geno-cide. This vision of morality vis-à-vis the Native reinforces an inherent mes-sage of European moral superiority coded as masculine that becomes intimately linked in the Western reader's mind to the very violence (military *and* moral) that makes that victory possible. One cannot deny the influence of the French Western in the imagination of the French culture; the genre's most famous au-thors were some of the most popular cultural producers of their time. The his-tory of extra-territorial conflict, competitive colonialism, imperialism, and the evolution of the ideological certainty of European superiority are coterminous. It is only through geographical displacement and direct physical contact with the non-European Other that the European comes to believe in his intrinsic su-periority. The ideological history of racism dictates that Europe's subsequent discoveries of the Other accumulate knowledge about the world outside to build a clearer image of the world within, the Self. The Crusades, the Conquest of the Americas, and the African Slave Trade are stages of *crystallization* of the ideol-ogy of European superiority from postulate to established (scientific) *truth*. The

The Vanishing Indian: Manifest and Imperial Destinies   91

French Western plays an important cultural role in that process. The Western's repetition of mythologies of the Amerindian (Noble/Ignoble Savage, the Ecological Savage, the Vanishing Indian, and Going Native) is an accumulative, performative process that institutes and institutionalizes a racial hierarchy that situates the European at the apex. In short, the repetition of the conquest of the Native reiterates and buttresses assumptions about European superiority. In addition, the ritualized performance of European victory and Amerindian defeat, coupled with appropriation of Native lands, entails an exculpation and valorization of imperial conquest. After the Reconquista, the specter of Europe as possible victim of colonization is exorcised, in part through the ritualized performance of European victory, not only in imperial conquests of the, but for the masses in the pages of the French Western. When Albert Memmi says that, "The mythic portrait of the colonized will include, therefore, an incredible laziness, that of the colonizer, the virtuous taste of action" (99, my translation), he refers to the mythic portrayals not only of France's specific colonial victims in the Maghreb, but also to a characterization that the French public has long accepted within the cadre of the inculcation of the French Western's portrayal of the Native/European relation and racial hierarchies. The submissiveness of the lazy (a trait often attributed to the Native in the French Western) connotes the stain of imperial defeat. The racial marking of the non-European as indolent is a common feature of all colonial/imperial discourses. This leitmotiv peppers representations of the Amerindian from Columbus' first letter back to Ferdinand and Isabella to the present day. But, as Memmi pertinently asked, "can you accuse an entire people of being lazy?" (100, my translation). Memmi's germane question deconstructs the preconceived notions that inform the West's claim to racial superiority by revealing the stereotype as myth. Myth is the pith of the French Western; it is composed of little else. This overgeneralization is what Memmi calls the "the mark of the plural".

> The colonized is never characterized in a differentiating way; he is only fit to be drowned in collective anonymity[... ...]. He is hardly still a human being, tending to quickly be considered an object. At the far end of the spectrum, the greatest desire of the colonizer, the colonized should no longer exist except to fulfill the colonizer's needs, which is to say, he is transformed into a pure colonized thing. (104–5, my translation)

The repeated performance of the domination, subjugation, and/or massacre of the Amerindian in the French Western is correlate to the imperial outlook that Memmi astutely records in the twilight of the French Empire's grip on Northern Africa. The vision of the world that emerges in the French Western promotes, naturalizes, and normalizes imperial attitudes toward non-Europeans globally.

Gerald Vizenor articulates what he terms survivance against physical *and* metaphorical violence. Survivance is in many ways a negation of negation,

92   *The Vanishing Indian: Manifest and Imperial Destinies*

a refusal to accept the very denial of existence that Memmi posits. Vizenor contends that, "Survivance, then, is the action, condition, quality, and sentiments of the verb *survive*, to remain alive or in existence, to outlive, persevere with a suffix of *survivancy*" (*Survivance: Narratives of Native Presence*, Chapter 1). Just as genocide, dispossession, displacement, and internment on reservations occurs in the historical past and present in the Americas, metaphorical correlates are propagated as part of an overarching European ideology of imperialism and conquest in the various derivatives of the American Western throughout Europe and its colonies. Karl Kroeber, speaking about Gerald Vizenor's understanding of the category *Indian*, explains that, "He insists that there are now no real indians. Indians are counterfeit people, simulations created by whites to complete intellectually the genocidal terrorism they have practiced so enthusiastically since 1492" (*Survivance: Narratives of Native Presence*, Chapter 2). The (French) Western is instrumental in the objectification at the heart of the inauthenticity that Vizenor targets, the intellectual completion of the genocidal terrorism in the real world. The Western does the cultural work of that *intellectual* completion of what *Indian* signifies for Americans and French alike. Indian signifies victim. Indian is marred and defined by what Vizenor calls "tragic victimry". John Gamber describes the mythologies of the Euro-Western as, "the limiting and hegemonic portrayals of tragic victimry and static manners foisted upon Native peoples" (*Survivance: Narratives of Native Presence*, Chapter 12). Vizenor refers to them as, "the simulations of absence and cultural dominance" (*Native Liberty: Natural Reason and Cultural Survivance*, Introduction). What is taken from the Native in the Western? Both Memmi and Vizenor call it by the same name: liberty (Memmi 104, Vizenor, *Native Liberty: Natural Reason and Cultural Survivance*, Chapter 2).

The French Western is part of a larger cultural shift. Imperialist ideologies become a mainstay in French culture. The phenomenon is labeled by many historians as *colonial culture*. Colonial culture in France is characterized by a variety of forms.

> Multiple cultural markers helped form and shape colonial culture: travel literature and adventure novels (with the press reporting the feats of explorers and the discovery of the world), critical institutions (such as the first colonial associations), geographical societies, and commerce-related organizations with new ambitions and aspirations, alongside the dramatic rise in research and interest on the Other and the Elsewhere (such as in colonial ethnography and physical anthropology). Together, these elements formed a complete discourse animated by social practices, which, popular throughout the nineteenth century and well into the first half of the twentieth century, serve to reveal the conditions of the cultural possibility of imperial expansion. (Blanchard et al. 3)

The Vanishing Indian: Manifest and Imperial Destinies 93

Colonial culture infiltrates the French cultural imaginary through the multitudinous vectors of literature, art, science, public education, mass media, public spectacles (such as the Universal Expositions, ethnographic exhibitions, and "human zoos"), etc. This encourages colonial attitudes based on hierarchized, racialized discourses of French superiority, non-European inferiority, and the responsibility of the French to complete what came to be known as the *mission civilisatrice*, the civilizing mission (Blanchard et al. 5). The French Western plays a similar role, in concert with other discourses that are more narrowly concerned with the specific geographies of the emerging French Empire. The conquest of the Amerindian Other in the French Western is an ersatz for French imperial ventures in various geographies. The French Western's ascendant popularity throughout the period of French imperial expansion is directly related to the genre's central role within the larger cultural shift of the birth and invigoration of *colonial culture*. Mass cultural products like the French Western expand *colonial culture* beyond an infinitesimal portion of French society (statesmen, industrialists) to the masses, *crystallizing* Frenchness as part of what came to be known as *la plus grande France* (France *and* its colonies). The French Western novel is critical for the expansion of colonial culture, "the technical means for 'representing' the kind of imagined community that is the nation" (Andersen 25). A positive feedback loop exists between the articulation of colonial culture and nationalist discourses. The reinforcement of the definition of the Other is concomitant with the definition of the Same. Pratt tells us that,

> While the imperial metropolis tends to understand itself as determining the periphery (in the emanating glow of the civilizing mission or the cash flow of development, for example), it habitually blinds itself to the ways in which the periphery determines the metropolis- beginning, perhaps, with the latter's obsessive need to present and re-present its peripheries and its others continually to itself. Travel writing, among other institutions, is heavily organized in the service of that imperative. So, one might add, is much of European literary history. (6)

The French Western participates in "determining the [French] metropolis" in much the same way that travel literature and other cultural forms participate in the elaboration of French *colonial culture*. For Pratt, the definition of the Other and the Self are inextricable processes that are central to culture. The connection between French imperialism and the French Western's American geographies and Amerindian antagonists is not as surprising as one might believe when one considers that the hero of nearly every French Western novel is ethnically marked as French or a French-Canadian *coureur de bois* (Billington 32). The hero's Frenchness is expressed as superiority in comparison, not only with the Amerindian, but crucially with the American (or other groups of European

94 *The Vanishing Indian: Manifest and Imperial Destinies*

descent), as well as Asians and Africans who feature more rarely but are not entirely absent from the genre. A pertinent example of can be found in the work of Louis Boussenard, a prolific author of French Westerns. In a rare exception to the rule of always casting a compatriot as the protagonist, in *Chasseurs canadiens* (Canadian Hunters) (1886), Boussenard casts an Englishman as the leading character. However, this choice is utilized to critique the British. Adopting a similar premise as that employed in *Around the World in 80 Days* by Jules Verne, Boussenard begins with a wager about whether the Bighorn Sheep is technically a sheep or a goat. This scientific question sends the Englishman Sir Georges Leslie to the Rocky Mountains to photograph specimens of the animal and quickly return. The text is peppered with criticisms of the Englishman, who is little more than a collection of stereotypes that reinforce French views of the English as stuffy and avaricious. The wager that begins the novel, echoing the bet that sets Phileas Fogg off, reflects the concerns of European imperialism. The wager engages with key aspects of imperial power. Knowledge of the non-human is an integral feature of imperialism. Alfred Crosby draws a connection between Europeans' tendency to introduce their own suite of plants and animals into newly conquered lands and their ability to learn about and adapt native flora and fauna to their own ends. The history of early test sites for the European imperialist project, such as Madeira (where Columbus once owned a residence), demonstrate the importance of wildlife in exploration. Taking advantage of the local fauna, such as the native pigeon, which was "so unused to humans they could be caught by hand", the Portuguese quickly overexploit the local environment by not only eating nearly all the available wildlife, but also by destroying the forests that once covered the island (Crosby 76). Introducing rabbits, thought to be a foolproof source of protein the colonists further decimate local plant and animal populations, the whole representing a general pattern that European imperialists are doomed to repeat in many colonial contexts (Crosby 71–103). Throughout the history of European imperialism, knowledge of wildlife is linked to the killing of the very animals one wishes to know. Killing is inseparable from knowing. This maxim holds true for the human species. The Guanches, the original inhabitants of the Canary Islands (another early test site for European imperialism), are an example of the lethality of contact. Taking advantage of the disunited nature of Guanche groups on the seven islands, Europeans rapidly exterminate the Native populations (Crosby 87). The encounter of Europe with the exterior world is a bloody affair. When Boussenard utilizes the Linnaean distinction of sheep versus goat to poke fun at English punctiliousness, he does not question the morality of killing. After all, the French-Canadian *coureur de bois* who acts as guide to the Englishman has a similarly violent relationship with the animal world, that of the hunter. The difference between the calculating precision of the Englishman and the heroics of the *terre à terre* French-Canadian huntsman is a nationalist one. Violence is integral to knowledge acquisition. In *Chasseurs canadiens*,

The Vanishing Indian: Manifest and Imperial Destinies   95

animal violence and human violence are parallel, both encompassed by the gaze of an English colonial. Not only does the Englishman seek to win his bet against his other compatriots by discovering the *scientific truth* about the Big Horn, but Sir Georges' curiosity extends to the anthropological. This is most striking in a gruesome scene wherein he attempts to record the murder and cannibalistic consumption of a Native man by other Amerindians. In the preceding chapter, Boussenard lays the groundwork for the scene in an earlier chapter by announcing the Englishman's wish to be an eye-witness to cannibalism. A Native group called the Blood People are attracted by a discarded trout that Leslie has thrown into the river. They retrieve the carcass and devour it raw. Both scavengers and consumers of raw meat, the Blood People are represented as animalistic in the Ignoble Savage mode. The supposedly bloodthirsty tribe is not a source of fear but are met with enthusiasm fueled by the Englishman's acquisitive violent curiosity. After the Blood People dance and sing for the Englishman, he immediately records what he sees. The observational obsession of the Englishman is evident throughout; he sketches new phenomena even employing recent inventions: the camera and the phonograph (Boussenard, *Chasseurs canadiens* 42–3). Capturing the visual and acoustic is the Englishman's goal in the staged cannibalism scene. Inspired by the presence of the Blood Men, the Brit's attention is drawn to an Amerindian porter who happens to be nearby when the idea occurs to Leslie that if he does not *happen upon* a scene of cannibalism, he might be able to *make one happen* by bringing his ingenuity and wealth to bear. With a cynicism that Boussenard attributes to all Anglo-Saxons, Leslie asks an American member of the expedition if he likes money and the immediate answer is yes. The Englishman offers ten pounds sterling to wound the Amerindian porter sufficiently to ensure that he cannot escape. Leslie's intention is to incite the Blood People's renowned hunger for human flesh by offering them an easy victim. The American shoots the Native porter in the leg. The Amerindian porters on the expedition are provided gratis by the British government. Leslie remarks that they are less interesting than beasts of burden such as the mule, because they are free, revealing the Brit's racist attitudes (Boussenard, *Chasseurs canadiens* 32–3). The Blood People and the heartless, avaricious Englishman are defined in relation to the superhuman French adventurer or the *coureur de bois*. The Western requires the connivance of the reader in the definitions of the Other *and* the Self to do the cultural work of imposing its mythic nationalist message. The coded linguistic system of the Western is both descriptive and prescriptive. It calls on the reader to recognize and accede to the definitions that it assigns to all groups. The French reader reading the French Western, following the adventures of the French hero with whom he *identifies*, is implicitly interpellated to consider all Others inferior to the Self. *Identification* with the superiority of the French and *rejection* of the non-French Other are the prescriptive nationalist messages of the French Western that contribute to the greater shift of *colonial culture*.

96 *The Vanishing Indian: Manifest and Imperial Destinies*

2.3 The Mythology of the Vanishing Indian

In the Western, the Noble Savage is the Amerindian who helps to further advance the frontier objectives of the European, often entailing the betrayal of their own culture. The advancement of the frontier is coupled semiotically with the mythology of the Vanishing Indian. In the spatio-anthropological geographies of the Western frontier, the Noble Savage and Ignoble Savage alike coalesce through violent resistance, collaboration, and/or desperate resignation into the figure of the Vanishing Indian on the frontier which is always also *vanishing*. The myth of the Vanishing Indian is a paradoxical harbinger of the end of the mythic frontier itself. The *closing* of the frontier does not spell the end of the mythologies that it engenders. Rather, these myths continue to evolve, their semiotics grafted onto other contexts. The Western with its mythologies of the Vanishing Indian and frontier is a remarkably versatile and flexible coded linguistic system capable of adapting to a variety of socio-cultural situations. In the human geography of the Western, the Native is ambiguous. The Native is always Noble *and* Ignoble, romanticized and savage, and therefore non-Human; the Amerindian is defined by this instability built by the mythic machine, the objectifying of the Native as narrative technology in the Western suggesting the dispossession and genocide of the Amerindian. Literary annihilation, to return to Vizenor's terminology, abets settler-colonialism via the narrative technology of the Vanishing Indian. Next, I will examine the myths of the Vanishing Indian and the Nexus of Native and Nature in the works of Gabriel Ferry, Gustave Aimard, and Henri-Émile Chevalier.

Eugène Louis Gabriel Ferry de Bellemare (1809–1852), better known by his *nom de plume*, Gabriel Ferry, is perhaps the first French author to publish a French Western. It can be difficult, however, to determine the authorship of some of the texts published under the pseudonym Gabriel Ferry, because of the unusual situation of the publication of several of his works. After the author's death in a fire aboard the British steam liner *L'Amazone* in 1852, some of Gabriel Ferry *père*'s works continue to appear, whereas other novels leave the presses under the same name, while they are actually the work of the author's son, Gabriel de Bellemare, Gabriel Ferry *fils*. I will treat *Les aventures d'un Français au pays des Caciques* (The Adventures of a Frenchman in Cacique Country) (1881) as the work of Gabriel Ferry *père*, although there is no definitive answer regarding its authorship. Throughout the novel, the author refers to travels through Mexico long before the moment of diegesis, which I believe supports my attribution of the text to Gabriel Ferry *père* rather than to his son. If determining the authorship of certain publications proves difficult, what is certain is that texts appearing under the name Gabriel Ferry enjoy enormous success during the second half of the nineteenth century in France. Many of the author's novels are reprinted several times. *Le coureur des bois* (1853) has nine editions printed alone. The popularity of Gabriel Ferry other authors of the French Western reinforces how critical a role they have in shaping the French

The Vanishing Indian: Manifest and Imperial Destinies   97

cultural imaginary of the Amerindian. The representations of the Native that one encounters in this corpus circumscribe how the French understand the category of Native. Despite the title, the Amerindian is missing from the text. The *pays des Caciques* is conspicuous for the absence of Natives in the novel. The text is a nineteenth-century reboot of the *roman picaresque* set in post-revolutionary Mexico. The comic action of the text takes place in a New World geography which is nearly devoid of the Native. When Ferry does mention Amerindians of Mexico, the descriptions he offers are terse and deprecatory, in the Ignoble Savage mode. The author references Natives dressed in rags, recounts a priest of Spanish descent grabbing an Amerindian by the hair to ask him for directions, describes the tyranny of Amerindian village leaders vis-à-vis the Native population, mocks examples of Indigenous religious syncretism, situates Amerindian culture temporally in the European Middle Ages, and portrays the Natives as gullible, naïve children (76, 87, 89–91, 96–7). This panoply of narrative conventions and mythic clichés constitutes an exhaustive list of the representations of the Amerindian in the novel (284 pages), a novel which nevertheless claims to take place in the *pays des Caciques*. A critical question that *Les aventures d'un Français dans le pays des Caciques* inspires: what is the significance of the absence of the Amerindian in the *pays des Caciques*? The absence of the Amerindian is redolent of the myth of the Vanishing Indian. The irony of the novel's title doubles as an assertion of the superiority of those of Spanish descent in Mexico. Ferry portrays the Mexico of circa the 1840s, a country having already successfully completed its own *mission civilisatrice*. Ferry ellipses the presence of the Amerindian and obfuscates the complex ethnicities at play in a nation with a large population with Amerindian ancestors. The mestizo and creole population make up the majority of the Mexican population. However, Ferry reiterates the illusion that the only identities that exist in Mexico are those of the colonizers and the colonized, the Spanish and the Amerindian. This narrative technology is reductive and recreates a neatly compartmentalized binary, which lends itself easily to French (European) ideologies of race. José Armando Prats identifies who Westerns depict the Native through *imminent presence* and *virtual absence* in the landscape (24). Prats refers to the space that the Amerindian occupies in the American Western movie as the *vanishing point* (123, 140–1). While his analysis treats the cinematographic Western as its object of inquiry, its application is equally appropriate in the case of the French Western, as integral to what I have been referring to as the Vanishing Indian myth; it is *the* defining, teleological representative figure of the French Western. While the myth of the Noble Savage continues to be an operative narrative technology, regularly employed to represent the Native, the Vanishing Indian myth takes over as the dominant representational paradigm wherein the Amerindian ironically exists textually as a non-entity, present only in absentia, while he becomes the unique subject of a paradoxical guilt-laden collective nostalgia. The *disappearance* of the Native defines the myth of the Vanishing Indian and opens up a narrative space that

98   *The Vanishing Indian: Manifest and Imperial Destinies*

can then be filled by the French subject/narrator/reader. This phenomenon is perhaps no more evidently exemplified than in *Les aventures d'un Français dans le pays des Caciques* by Gabriel Ferry. The myth of the Vanishing Indian becomes the central metaphor of the frontier, precisely at the moment when the Native and the frontier *disappear*. The domination of Nature and the extinction of the Native are at the heart of the French Western, enmeshed and conflated with extractive violence. The Vanishing Indian myth evolves in conjunction with techniques of representing Nature and civilization. I begin with this strange example of a book about Natives that does not really contain many Amerindian characters to emphasize how the *disappearance* of the Amerindian is central to the mythic illogic of the French Western.

One of the most influential and prolific writers, author of several novels and novellas, who pens a large part of the corpus of nineteenth-century French Westerns, is Gustave Aimard, né Olivier Gloux (1818–1883). At times writing alone, but also collaborating with Jules Berlioz D'Auriac (1820–1913), Aimard writes several novels per year during the apogee of his career, publishing more than fifty novels in his lifetime. Aimard spends considerable time abroad, gaining first-hand experience with Native lifeways. He often refers to his personal travels in his novels, adding a veneer of *truth* to his fictions. It is not only experience with the lands and peoples of the Americas that inspires the author, however. The popular literature he discovers serves as a direct model for his writing. Some of Auriac and Aimard's works are actually known plagiarisms of relatively unknown American Westerns. This does not negatively affect their popularity or sales.

As I stated above, the prevailing myth that informs the French Western is the Vanishing Indian. The *disappearance* of the Native from the land is the teleological impetus of the genre, its inherent illogic. The myth of the Vanishing Indian is often articulated in parallel with the myth of the nexus of Native and Nature (or the Ecological Savage). This mythic framework echoes the seemingly positive inflection of the Noble Savage mythology by situating the Amerindian in an idealized harmonious symbiotic relationship with the non-human environment. Gustave Aimard's first French Western, *Les trappeurs de l'Arkansas* (The Trappers of the Arkansas) (1858) is illustrative of the French Western's vision of the mythic nexus of Native and Nature. In the incipit Aimard expounds on the meaning of contact and conquest in South America.

> The traveler disembarking for the first time in South America experiences a feeling of undefinable sadness, despite himself. Given that the history of the New World is nothing other than a regrettable martyrology, in which fanaticism and avarice walk continually side by side. The search for gold was at the origin of the discovery of the New World; once the gold was found, America was nothing more to its conquerors than a waystation where these greedy adventurers came, a dagger in one hand and a crucifix in the other, to reap

The Vanishing Indian: Manifest and Imperial Destinies 99

an ample harvest of that ardently coveted metal, after which they returned to the fatherland to show off their riches and bring about new emigrations with their unbridled displays of luxury. (Aimard, *Les trappeurs de l'Arkansas* 3, my translation)

The haunting melancholy that afflicts the European who arrives in the Americas is the nostalgia and guilt-laden sting of the Vanishing Indian myth. Nostalgia and guilt are central elements of the Vanishing Indian's narrative technology. The history of the New World is described in this passage as nothing more than a martyrology. Aimard perfunctorily condemns the violence inherent in colonialization, while all the manifestations of its avarice and excesses are duly cataloged. However, Aimard's text belies this apparent stance. The novel focuses almost exclusively on the agency of Europeans. The actions of European subjects constitute the major plotlines while the many Native dead of the martyrology are generally silent/silenced in the work. What Aimard offers the reader is the opposite of a martyrology of the Amerindian peoples. He writes about the Americas to portray the triumph of progress and Western civilization. The *disappearing* of the Native is a necessary prefatory condition to create the space for the European to demonstrate their *superiority*. This passage serves as a framing for the French reader's understanding of American geographies and the novel that follows. The geographies of the Americas are presented as devoid of Amerindians. The martyrology is a germane metaphor for the Vanishing Indian myth because it accurately encapsulates the functioning of the narrative technology itself. Signaling the death of countless Amerindians, the martyrology alludes vaguely to the destruction of entire cultures in a single word, a synecdoche of genocide. In Aimard's *Les trappeurs de l'Arkansas* (and the French Western in general), the written history of the Native consists in chronicling their extinction, which is actually a heroic tale recounting the victory of settler-colonialism and capitalism. At the close of the passage, the author articulates one of the most critical aspects of the Vanishing Indian myth, namely its teleological nature. Aimard anchors his novel in a vision of the Native as already extinct. This performative framing informs the French cultural imaginary that the Amerindian is inferior, dehistoricized, and *disappeared*. This might seem paradoxical for a text full of Amerindian characters, however, this is one of the overarching ironies of the French Western, where the Native is characterized by their *imminent presence* and *virtual absence*. They only exist at what Prats has called the *vanishing point*. The Amerindian must *disappear* to open up the land. This is doubly paradoxical because the land, i.e. Nature is mythically represented as being in symbiotic relation with the Native.

Nature seems to have showered its gifts in heaping handfuls in this country. The climate is pleasant, temperate, salutary; gold, silver, the most fertile land, the most delicious fruits, medicinal herbs are abundant there, the

100 *The Vanishing Indian: Manifest and Imperial Destinies*

most effective salves are found there, the most useful insects for dying, the rarest marble, the most precious gems, game and fish of all sorts. But in the vast solitudes of the Gila River and the Sierra Madre independent Indians, Comanches, Pawnees, Pimas, Opatas, and Apaches, have declared a terrible war on the white race. In the Indians' unrelenting and incessant wanderings, they make the whites pay dearly for all the riches that their forefathers robbed from the Natives and that they repeatedly lay claim to still. (*Les trappeurs de l'Arkansas* 6, my translation)

The double image of Arcadian Nature and recalcitrant Natives is at the heart of the French Western's mythic geographies. Despite the ideological and discursive pretense of the *mission civilisatrice* to assimilate and incorporate the Amerindian, the Vanishing Indian myth insists upon the (violent) *disappearance* of the Native. The *disappearance* of the French Western novel refers to the biological elimination of the Native through both symbolic and physical violence, what Vizenor calls *literary annihilation*. If one reads this passage in conjunction with the first Aimard passage that I discussed above (this excerpt appears shortly after the earlier passage), one recognizes that the Comanche, the Pawnee, the Pima, the Opata, and the Apache are foreordained to be fresh entries in the *martyrology*. These citations appear at the beginning of Aimard's first French Western as framing devices that shape the reader's (mis)understanding of the Amerindian and American geographies. According to the inherent illogic of the myth of the Vanishing Indian, the conflict between Native and European is presented as belonging to history, to the past. There is no possibility of the reversal of its ineluctable, unilateral movement. The Amerindian's role in this narrative technology is to *disappear*. This role is *crystallized* by the mythic structures of the French Western. The circumscription of the Amerindian in the French cultural imaginary in the French Western relegates the Amerindian to a closed space, without a past and without the possibility of a viable future. The Vanishing Indian myth performs the *disappearance* of the Amerindian by presenting the Native as extinct or nearing extinction, culturally *and* biologically. Bhabha argues that hegemonic discourses temporalize the Other in specific ways.

Hegemony requires iteration and alterity to be effective, to be productive of politicized populations: the (non-homogeneous) symbolic-social bloc needs to represent itself in a solidary collective will—a modern image of the future—if those populations are to produce a progressive government. (43)

According to Bhabha, cultural blocs need to build a "solidary collective will" through discursive techniques employed to create a commonly accepted "modern image of the future". In the history of the mythological representation of the Amerindian in French letters, the collective French cultural imaginary identifies the Amerindian as incapable of producing a "modern image of the future".

The Vanishing Indian: Manifest and Imperial Destinies   101

One of the most prevalent narrative technologies of the French Western is the utilization of a specific lexicon of conventional images and metaphors in order to indicate an "authentic" Amerindian in these fictional, mythologized representative modes. The use of this lexicon points to the established existence of a coded French cultural imaginary of the Amerindian. The accumulative practices of representation of the Amerindian during the preceding centuries in create a set of tropes that are then employed by authors in the formulaic Western. These "manifest manners", to use Vizenor's terminology, emerge from a long tradition of representation of the Amerindian that becomes *crystallized* into a vocabulary with its own semiological purchase within the French cultural imaginary, its own ability to be immediately recognized and (mis)understood as *truth*. This *crystallization* is inherent in systemic adherence to the stereotyped caricatures that make the French Western possible. The use of the mythic lexicon of the Native is a narrative technology that functions as a condition of possibility of the evolution of the Noble Savage myth into the preponderant image of the Amerindian in the nineteenth century: the myth of the Vanishing Indian. As Vizenor reminds us, these are merely simulations or 'indians'. For example, let us examine the corpus of Henri-Émile Chevalier (1828–1879). Chevalier is significant because of his association with Québec and early French-Canadian literature. Despite his French nationality, Chevalier can be considered an early Québécois novelist. The author spends nearly ten years in the former French colony, before finishing out his days in France. Chevalier writes two cycles of novels that focus on Amerindians. Most of them are centered on specific groups, such as *Les Pieds noirs* (1861), *La Huronne: scènes de la vie canadienne* (1861), *La Tête plate* (1862), *Les Nez percés* (1862), *Les Derniers Iroquois* (1863), and *Poignet d'acier: ou les Chippiouais* (1863). Chevalier's work is significant, because it is an early example of Québécois literary representations of the Native. Chevalier helps shape the French and Québécois cultural imaginaries of the Amerindian. However, if one reads Chevalier's novels supposedly based on distinct tribes, one recognizes that there is little or no difference between the Iroquois, the Huron, the Blackfoot, the Flathead, or the Chippewa. Chevalier includes a few well-placed stereotypes to create a veneer of verisimilitude. Nineteenth-century Amerindian characters of the Western are formulated within an intertextual tradition of representation that rests on the perpetuation of myth. The representation of the Amerindian in Chevalier's texts speaks more to the cultural expectations of the reader than to Native lifeways or identities. This long representational tradition vis-à-vis the Native is an all-encompassing system, both esthetic *and* epistemological, that circumscribes the possibilities of what an Amerindian can be in any given discourse. Speaking to the collective and persistent nature of myth, Roland Barthes explains that, "When myth touches the whole of society, if one wishes to liberate the myth, it is the entire society that has to distance itself from it" (231, my translation). Barthes points to an important aspect of the mythic machine's hold on the French cultural imaginary: it is not easy to free oneself of mythic *knowledge*

102 *The Vanishing Indian: Manifest and Imperial Destinies*

that one unconsciously accepts as *truth*. Academics deconstructing myths does not go far enough to eradicate dangerous mythic messages. It will take the whole of the collective to address and reject the myth to be liberated from the insidious hold of these flawed fantasies. The dual nature of this tradition, it being both in the realms of literature, art, and science, as well as epistemology and cultural imaginings, is precisely what constitutes the representation of the Amerindian in French as myth. Myth explores the unknown artistically in an attempt to understand, in an attempt to provide guidelines or explanations for reducing the irreducible and unknowable to the known and comprehensible. Myth is strategically at play in the literary representations of the Amerindian from the early period of first contacts until the present day as a narrative technology which seeks to hierarchize the peoples of the world, positioning the French (European) at the pinnacle of the pyramid and the Amerindian at the nadir. The power of myth to invoke belief, to create a codified cultural imaginary that nonetheless makes certain claims to *truth*, is remarkable. The only discourse which can be associated with a "modern image of the future" is that of the subject writer, decidedly not that of the object, the Amerindian Other. The inherent illogic of the French Western is one of conflict; however, the outcome is never in doubt. The reader always already knows who will win in the end. The mythic machine creates knowledge of the unknown and disseminates that knowledge as *truth* for the benefit of the linguistic community in general, the *imagined community* as an echo of the French and Québécois cultural imaginaries of the Amerindian. The writer of the French Western presents himself as having access to specialized knowledge of the Amerindian and the Americas. In the case of two of the most popular writers in the genre, Aimard and Chevalier, their textual descriptions are validated as *authentic* by their personal travel experiences in the Americas. In this travel-inflected claim to special knowledge about American geographies and peoples, the author implicitly aligns themself with the protagonist of European descent, the White Hero. The White Hero is, of course, the protagonist that accomplishes the goals of Western civilization on the frontier. It matters little whether the White Hero is amical or inimical toward the Amerindian characters that support or resist them, the representation of various Amerindians, individually and collectively, depends largely on their stance vis-à-vis the European's goals of expropriation and conquest, both types of White Hero inevitably serve the progress and colonization. According to Prats, not only is specialized knowledge of the Amerindian a key feature of the White Hero, but a certain ability to assimilate the Amerindian in their very essence, to appropriate their identity as Amerindian is often associated with the White Hero. In portraying the White Hero, writers of the Western usually imbue the archetype with *authentic* Amerindian qualities. The intimate familiarity that the White Hero has with the Amerindian, whether the relationship is one of friendship or conflict, does not greatly alter the prevailing metaphorical link between the White Hero and the Native, allowing them to conquer the Amerindian, through good will *or* warfare

The Vanishing Indian: Manifest and Imperial Destinies   103

(Prats 174–5). One of the stereotypes of the Native that make up part of the lexicon of clichés in the French Western novelist's repertoire is his capacity to pass undetected by the untrained, unobservant eyes and ears of those of European descent. It is common to include a description of European adventurers on the frontier being wholly surprised by the sudden appearance of an Amerindian or even several Natives, appearing seemingly out of nowhere, catching the European off guard and unawares. Therefore, when Aimard begins his novel *Le grand chef des Aucas* (The Great Chief of the Aucas) (1889) with a description of his White Hero by evoking this trope, it functions within the context of the French Western as an authenticating technique.

> Without the lightest sound making me suspect his unexpected arrival, four steps in front of my face, a man was looking at me, leaning on his rifle. ... ... The man reminded me of that race of hardy adventurers that travel across America in all directions. A primordial race, hungry for air, space, liberty, hostile to our notions of civilization. And because of that very thing, they are destined to fatally disappear before the immigration of the laborious races, whose powerful tools of conquest are steam and the application of mechanical inventions of all kinds. (6–7)

Using the lexical item of the undetectable Native as an authenticating image of the White Hero, Aimard goes on to situate the European, specifically the character Valentin who is identified as a *coureur de bois* who has intimate knowledge of American geographies gained through twenty years of experience living among Indigenous peoples. The *disappearance* of the Native before the advancing European frontier's immigrant masses is echoed here in the teleology of the *coureur de bois*' inevitable obsolescence. The White Hero is likened to the Amerindian precisely because of his knowledge of him. The adoption of Native lifeways, even in part, condemns the *coureur de bois* to be *disappeared* in parallel with the Native. An integral aspect of the mythology of the Vanishing Indian is its correlative mythology of the Vanishing White Hero. The ability to adopt another group's lifeways is only possible for the European, however. It is the cultural inheritance of the White Hero alone, never the Amerindian, to arrive at the mastery of the Other through knowledge of him (Prats 200–2). One function of the mythic machine in the French Western is its denunciation of one of the most prized ideological tenets of the *mission civilisatrice*: assimilation of the Amerindian. The incommensurability of the Vanishing Indian myth's teleology with any attempt at Native assimilation exemplifies the ways how the French Western is complicit with the ideologies of conquest. The structure of the French Western is narrowly teleological. The end point envisioned by the genre is the extinction, or *disappearance*, of the Amerindian as a distinct cultural and/ or biological group. All Amerindians, Noble and Ignoble Savages alike, resisters and collaborators, are condemned to be represented within the circumscribed

104 *The Vanishing Indian: Manifest and Imperial Destinies*

representational limitations of the myth of the Vanishing Indian as part of the inherent illogic of the mythic machine.

In the mode of the Vanishing Indian, the "insensitivity" of the Native is another prevailing stereotype throughout the history of the representation of the Amerindian. Native insensitivity can be placed in one of two general categories, physical or emotional. Out of the long list of hackneyed images of the Amerindian, the double valence of the cliché of Native insensitivity permits us to demonstrate the paradoxical nature of the stereotype. The dual nature of the insensitivity trope is recognizable from the early period of first contacts. Physical insensitivity can be described in certain contexts as a positive trait, whereas emotional insensitivity is nearly universally negative. The ability to withstand great physical exertion and pain, or extreme weather conditions has long been a standard figure French authors employ to describe the Amerindian. Chevalier, describing a half-Native character, tells us, "He was small, stocky, with a robust frame, hard and flexible like steel, and of a constitution that feared neither the pangs of hunger nor the burning of thirst, neither the bite of boreal cold, nor the heat of the tropical sun" (*La Tête-Plate* 3, my translation). The superhuman is evident in the geographical designations of the northern forest and the (sub)equatorial tropics. This double geography is not a *real* space likely to be inhabited by the same person. They would not occupy the North and the tropics simultaneously; however, they presumably could withstand either, given their remarkable physical insensitivity. In Aimard's *Le Grand Chef des Aucas*, the author makes a similar generalization, "Physical fatigue didn't seem to have a hold on the iron-like constitution of the Indian" (309, my translation). In the context of ritualized torture, insensitivity in the face of physical pain is portrayed as one of the most important indicators of masculine honor in Native societies. Refusing to cry out or react while undergoing torture is reiterated many times over the course of the history of the representation of the Amerindian. The opening scene of *La Tête-Plate* (The Flathead) (1862) by Henri-Émile Chevalier is a perfect example of the figure.

> "The Chinooks are little women. They don't know how to beat their enemies any more than they know how to torture them. I've killed two times four of their warriors."
>
> "That's a lie, Serpent-Tail", replied one of the chiefs, hitting the prisoner with his tomahawk.
>
> A stream of blood squirted from the wound on his face. Without uttering a complaint, he continued:
>
> "Yes, in my cabin, hang the scalps of two times four of those that the Chinooks call their braves that died crying like timid fawns."
>
> Another blow of the tomahawk hit him in the chest. His muscles quivered, his teeth gnashed and sweat beaded up on his forehead, but the pain didn't cause him to cry out one single time; he didn't convulse at all.

> "The Chinooks, he went on stoically, have arms as weak as their minds. It's hare's blood that runs in their veins. How could they defeat valiant Clallomes, when they can't even knock a Clallome down when he is tied up? I snatched your wife, Eye-of-the-Wolverine, and she served as my slave."
>
> Following these words, the Indian he had been talking to jumped up in rage. Pulling a long knife from its sheath, he rushed toward the prisoner to stab him with it. One of his companions stopped him.
>
> "No, don't kill him yet", he said, "we will show him how the Chinooks treat owls of his kind". (3, my translation)

The Chinook have taken a prisoner, Queue-de-Serpent, or Serpent-Tail. The text begins in a context of ritualized torture. The novel's incipit enters this space *in media res* with the prisoner, following traditional protocol, insulting his torturers hoping to procure a quick death, a coup-de-grâce brought on by prodding the torturers to rage. When the tomahawk blows come, the physical insensitivity of Serpent-Tail appears incredible. Within the insults and provocations that Serpent-Tail hurls are other elements that speak to the inhumanity of the Amerindian: murder (the many scalps the prisoner has taken) and sexual depravity (the sexual enslavement of another's wife). Moreover, the entire scene signals the inhumanity of the Amerindian in the Ignoble Savage mode. I am referring, of course, to the torture itself. This example from Chevalier underlines the negative aspects of the physical insensitivity trope. The convergence of this figure with the repetition of *crystallized* images of violence, sexual license, and torture present the Amerindian as non-human, via the narrative technology of the myth of Ignoble Savage. The French reader cannot identify with Serpent-Tail *or* his torturers. The Native necessarily inhabits a space devoid of culture and humanity (physically, emotionally, and psychologically). This scene is one of framing; it informs and delimits the reader's possible (mis)understandings of the Amerindian. Throughout the remainder of the text, and in other French Westerns, the Amerindian is circumscribed by the insensitivity trope, denied *true* humanity. When Aimard or Chevalier employ the insensitivity cliché to describe the Amerindian it is a signifier of everything Amerindian in the French and Québécois cultural imaginaries. The mere mention of insensitivity evokes a semiological system with its own hegemonic ideologies, hierarchizing the insensitivity of the Native as inferior to the sensitivity of the European. European weakness trumps Native stamina and endurance through the power of myth, according to the inherent illogic of the mythic machine. This is how the narrative technology of myth functions. The physical superiority of the Amerindian (the European is usually depicted as relatively incapable of withstanding the same pain, work, or weather) is subverted. The physical insensitivity trope animalizes the Amerindian in the Ignoble Savage mode. The positive turns negative within the representational vision of the Native repeated in the French Western. The effectiveness of the mythic machine lies in the capacity of every portrayal (positively

106 *The Vanishing Indian: Manifest and Imperial Destinies*

or negatively inflected) to echo the logic and ideologies of French superiority vis-à-vis the Amerindian.

Emotional insensitivity is the opposite side of the insensitivity stereotype. Insensitivity to situations that require an emotional reaction in the tragic mode of European drama is tantamount to savagery of the Ignoble variety. A typical iteration of the trope is the figure of an Amerindian (usually male) that does not pay sufficient heed to the bonds of family, committing acts of violence against his progenitors, partner, or progeny. The central position of sexuality in the heart of the family entails a normative rejection of non-family affirming practices by Natives. For example, in *La Tête-Plate* by Henri-Émile Chevalier, the author engages in the ethnographic mode, framing Amerindian culture for his French(-Canadian) readers with an anecdotal tale about a Chinook chief named Casanov that murders his wife after the death of the couple's son (15–6). Similarly, in *Le Grand Chef des Aucas*, Aimard creates a scene characterized by Native emotional insensitivity. The chief Antinahuel, in a fit of anger, forgets the sacred bonds of family, and violently murders his own mother by dragging her behind his stallion (Aimard 145–6). Later in the narrative, Aimard presents the moral standard espoused by the Araucanians, "Araucanians have a profound affection for their family. The thought of leaving their relative or friends behind, exposed to the ravages of war, sunk them into the depths of despair" (*Le Grand Chef des Aucas* 392, my translation). While Antinahuel's violent act constitutes an aberration according to the cultural norms of the Araucanians, the function of the emotional insensitivity trope is to mark the category Amerindian as inhuman and inferior. Despite the existence of examples of moral, courageous, even heroic Araucanians in the novel, the emotional insensitivity of Antinahuel stains the Araucanian as a people, and the Amerindian as a category in the ideology of the mythic apparatus. Native emotional insensitivity situates the Amerindian in a non-human space, outside of culture. Like the Noble and Ignoble Savage myths, the myth of the Vanishing Indian replaces difference with one teleological conclusion about the past, present, and future of the original inhabitants of the Americas: *disappearance*. It matters little whether certain groups attempt to assimilate to European lifeways or resist militarily, the Vanishing Indian myth insists on the essential vulnerability of all Amerindians. Every Native is condemned according to the ideology of the Vanishing Indian and its martyrology. Within the inherent illogic of the French Western, progress is the conqueror of the Amerindian, not the settler-colonial descendants of Europeans. Thereby, European violence against Amerindians is justified and morally displaced as an ineluctable, temporal continuance, rather than a disruptive, methodical genocide. After all, how can one blame the European harbingers of progress for paving the way? Situating progress (and not the actual individuals who commit acts of violence against Natives) as the impetus behind the advancing frontier, the physical manifestation of Manifest Destiny, condemns the Amerindian for their incapacity to create a "modern image of the future", which necessarily reiterates

The Vanishing Indian: Manifest and Imperial Destinies   107

the ideologies of extraction and exploitation connoted by progress itself. Native lifeways are often directly antithetical to such a vision of Nature and humanity's place in it. The Vanishing Indian myth is the necessary opposite number of the myth of progress. Both neglect the reality of culture and identity in favor of mythic messages that blur moral definitions in relation to physical and cultural acts of genocidal violence. The *absence* of the Native can have dramatic consequences for the definition of the modern European subject, however, particularly in the nascent discourses of the social sciences. In the next section, I examine the role of Amerindian difference, namely sexuality, in the articulation of modern sociology in the text *De la division du travail social* by Émile Durkheim.

3   Émile Durkheim: Sexual Resemblance and the Foundations of Modern Social Science

Émile Durkheim is considered by many as the father of modern sociology. Within his voluminous corpus, the monograph *De la division du travail social* (1893) occupies a seminal position regarding the formulation of the author's sociological thought. It is in this text, for example, where the author introduces the concept of the *"fait social"*, or social fact, which he posits as the most basic object of sociological inquiry. With the unique importance of *De la division du travail social* in the development of Durkheim's thinking individually and in the history of the establishment of the discipline of sociology, more generally, this text as an illustrative example of the vision of modern (French) social sciences' vision of the Native. This monograph is indicative of the mythically informed preconceptions that participated in the formation of the author's *scientific* understanding of the Amerindian. In this section, I focus uniquely on how Durkheim employs his *knowledge* of the Indigenous peoples of the Americas to speak about European modernity as hierarchically superior to the *primitive* Native. Durkheim's articulation of what he calls the *problème* that he is addressing in *De la division du travail social* is heavily dependent upon presenting Amerindian sexuality and gender roles in specific ways. The author instrumentalizes sexualized iterations of the mythologies of the Ignoble Savage to posit the Native as *retrograde*. This narrative technology allows Durkheim to then position the European as the scion of modernity. Employing naturalized European sexual normativity as a benchmark of civilization, Durkheim constructs his argument around the *aberrance* of Native lifeways. I begin by demonstrating how the division of social labor defines civilization according to Durkheim. Next, I show how the author establishes a connection between the organic or the biological, embodying the object of the social fact. This sets up the rhetorical space which subsequently allows Durkheim to reference Native bodies and sexualities as evidence of *primitiveness* in comparison to modern French anatomies. After explaining how the biological is linked to the theoretical in Durkheim's argument, I identify how the author makes connections between physical modernity and moral

108 *The Vanishing Indian: Manifest and Imperial Destinies*

superiority, relegating the Amerindian to an inferior status, both ontologically (biologically) and morally. My analysis reveals how the father of sociology dehumanizes and detemporalizes the Native as a basis for the creation of a foundational discourse of the social sciences, a discourse which purports to produce objective *scientific truth.*

One of the fundamental assumptions of Durkheim's sociological thought is the hierarchy of modern and *primitive.* The modern is unquestionably superior to the *primitive* to his thinking. As a starting point for much of the nineteenth century's *scientific* inquiry into Indigenous peoples worldwide, this Western arrogance is virtually uncontested. The following citation succinctly expresses many of the connotations of the epistemological choice of valorizing the modern and deprecating the *primitive.*

> We need have no further illusions about the tendencies of modern industry; it advances steadily towards powerful machines, towards great concentrations of forces and capital, and consequently to the extreme division of labor. ... [Economists] see in it the supreme law of human societies and the condition of their progress. (Simpson 56)

Eurocentric visions of Western modernity are characterized as an idealized image of progress here. Durkheim does complicate that position by remarking that suicide and crime rates are more prevalent in *civilized* societies, yet he does believe that the concept of division is crucial to society, linking that to a higher morality than that which might otherwise be attainable in non-divided societies. While Durkheim attempts to maintain an objective distance from the idealization of progress and division throughout the text, he nonetheless concludes that the division of labor and societal progress are illustrative of biological and moral *truth.* As I referenced in the first chapter as part of my discussion of myth, Wole Soyinka pinpoints the centrality of compartmentalization in the West as it pertains to mythic discourses that nevertheless make claims of *truth:*

> [It] is a recognisable Western cast of mind, a compartmentalising habit of thought which periodically selects aspects of human emotion, phenomenal observations, metaphysical intuitions and even scientific deductions and turns them into separatist myths (or 'truths) sustained by a proliferating superstructure of presentation idioms, analogies and analytical modes. (37)

Soyinka rightly argues that the act of division, in a variety of contexts is a defining trait of Western culture. I reintroduce Soyinka's insight here, because the division of labor and the compartmentalizing penchant of the Western mind are synergistic. They reinforce one another with increased cooperative energy as modernity *progresses.* After all, any way of thinking is bound to have direct effects on a people's way of living. Soyinka's use of the term "technology" is

The Vanishing Indian: Manifest and Imperial Destinies 109

significant because compartmentalized epistemologies, understood by Soyinka as "technology", are reflected in the industrial technologies of labor that Durkheim props up as markers of civility. Division, or as Soyinka calls it, "compartmentalization", becomes an overarching site of veridiction in *De la division du travail social*. The analogy performs facile *transferability* when Durkheim switches codes, leaving behind labor to talk about the biological, specifically the bodies of the Native and the French.

Having offered division in labor as the precondition of and evidence for progress, in the next step in Durkheim's argument the author associates the law of division to the body and the individual, stating that, "[the] law of the division of labor applies to organisms as to societies" (Simpson 57). The *truth* of Durkheim's analysis, while highly speculative and conjectural, is transferred from one domain, the very specific discussion of European economics in modern industrial societies, to the domain of universal human biology. The biological and cultural are teleologically determined by the sociologist's insight and framing of the function of human societies. This is a crucial connection that the author makes in order to later make observations and draw conclusions based on the *truth* of Indigenous bodies as proof of the existence of the "social fact", which is the very basis of the disciplinary methodology of sociology as posited by Durkheim in this seminal work in the field. It is critical to deconstruct the articulation of Durkheim's argument, in order to expose the mythic origins of the *scientific truth* it naturalizes. Durkheim elaborates on and seeks to concretize the *transferability* of his insights into the French social realm from what he sees as a universal *truth* of biology.

> It is no longer considered only a social institution that has its source in the intelligence and will of men, but is a phenomenon of general biology whose conditions must be sought in the essential properties of organized matter. The division of labor in society appears to be no more than a particular form of this general process; and societies, in conforming to that law, seem to be yielding to a movement that was born before them, and that similarly governs the entire world. (Simpson 57)

Durkheim naturalizes the ideal of progress and the division of labor as a biological phenomenon. Taking a particular economic mode which is historically specific to modern industrial developments in the West as his starting point, the author extrapolates this mode as *the* defining essence of biological life in general. Thereby, Durkheim situates progress, as he understands it economically (capitalism's extractive model), as an evolutionary *truth*. This is a particularly illustrative example of the narrative technology of naturalizing one's viewpoint through mythic rhetoric. Having proven the validity of progress as universally beneficial and biologically imperative, Durkheim goes on to instrumentalize the Native as counterpoint, as an example of peoples who have not accepted the

110 *The Vanishing Indian: Manifest and Imperial Destinies*

course of Nature as he envisions it. In this way, the Amerindian is categorized as *retrograde*. This vision of the inevitability of division and its biological origins *naturalizes* not only economic and legal aspects of *civilized* societies, but also assumes a specific sexual normativity, namely Western sexual expectations and morality.

The next rhetorical move Durkheim makes is to *transfer* the biological and economic *truth* that he has discovered to the moral question.

> [Is] the division of labor, at the same time that it is a law of nature, also a moral rule of conduct; and, if it has this latter character, why and in what degree? (Simpson 58)

Durkheim goes on to answer yes to this question. Having established the biological *truth* of division, Durkheim's argument makes a jump that cannot easily be justified or explained using the rigorous methodology of the *scientific*, despite the author's assurances to the contrary and his explanation of the "social fact". Not only is division a primordial biological reality, but it also represents a universal moral imperative. Therefore, when Durkheim subsequently employs myths of the Ignoble Savage by citing *retrograde* Native sexual practices, the Amerindian is presented as resistant to progress both biologically *and* morally. Earlier in this study, I referenced two concepts that it might be useful to recall at this point of my analysis of Durkheim. Bruyneel describes "colonial time" as a Western epistemology of the Native that presents the European as "advancing" and the Amerindian as "static" (2). Durkheim's argument is informed by this way of thinking. In addition to Bruyneel's theory, I have also cited Bhabha and the necessity for hegemonic powers to create a "modern image of the future" for themselves, while simultaneously denying such futurities to the colonized (Chapter 4). In making the Native doubly *retrograde*, belonging to "colonial time", without a "modern image of the future", Durkheim's representational models participate in the overarching mythic paradigm of the period: the myth of the Vanishing Indian, excluding the Native from the future. Classifying the Amerindian as *retrograde* within a discourse of *scientific truth*, Durkheim demonstrates the *transferability* of the myth of the Vanishing Indian. From the French Western's depiction of the Native at the *vanishing point* to the foundational myths of sociology in Durkheim's *De la division du travail social*, the Vanishing Indian myth is characteristic of the collective French vision of the Amerindian of the period.

The *disappearing* of the Native within Durkheim's text passes through the author's articulation of modernity and primitiveness as a question of morality. The author sees progress, which comes about through the division, as the moral impetus of history and evolution, stating that, "Briefly, in one of its aspects, the categorical imperative of the moral conscience is assuming the following form: *Make yourself usefully fulfill a determinate function*" (Simpson 59, emphasis in original). This is the moral imperative that Durkheim's work locates as the teleological end or function of division. Either perform an economic function, as determined by the profit-driven requirements of the system, or fall into obsolescence, *disappearance*, and social death. In short, if you are not contributing, you are irrelevant, nonexistent. As such, although he has not introduced the Native explicitly into his analysis, Durkheim positions the Native *a priori* as *retrograde*, biologically and morally incapable of complying with the prescribed social order. It must be admitted, however, that Durkheim does not offer up progress as *the* biological, moral, and economic imperative of human existence without careful consideration of possible detractions. He does make brief mention of the possibility that modern industrial society might not be an indisputable model for healthy living. Durkheim cites Lémontey, a political thinker during the period of the French Revolution, who, like Rousseau before him, compares modern, civilized life and that of the Amerindian, and decides in favor of the latter's existence (Simpson 59). Durkheim also points to suicide as a predominantly Western phenomenon as a possible critique of progress and the division of labor, later penning the monograph *Le suicide* (1897) which painstakingly researches the phenomenon in French society. However, in the final analysis, Durkheim's argument in *De la division du travail social* supports the modern industrial societal model as the epitome of the multifaceted *truth* of progress with the division of labor in society as the arbiter of *truth* on every plane of existence.

In a close reading of the articulation of his arguments, Durkheim's logic becomes apparent. By carefully examining the steps the author takes to reach his conclusions, one can expose the mythic nature of his discourse and its resonance with the evolution of the mythic machine that we have been tracing in this volume.

Our work, then, will be divided into three principal parts:

To determine the function of the division of labor, that is to say, what social need it satisfies.

To determine, then, the causes and conditions on which it is dependent.

Finally, as it would not have been the object of such grave accusations if it had not really deviated fairly often from the normal condition, we shall try to classify the principal abnormal forms it presents, so that they will not be confused with the others. (Simpson 60)

In this passage, Durkheim lays out the structure of his argument and his methodological presumptions are evident. In the third element of his exposition, he signals how the abnormal will help to better understand the normal. Using nosology as an analogy, the author presents that which is abnormal, the *retrograde* Amerindian, as pathological vis-à-vis the healthful, progressive "functioning" of the French. By taking up the abnormal or pathological as his object, Durkheim asserts an ontological difference. Within this ontological, or biological

112 *The Vanishing Indian: Manifest and Imperial Destinies*

difference, abnormality is associated with immorality. This continues and builds upon Durkheim's metaphorical focus on the biological and the individual body. By insisting that the reader accept the connection between the physical body and civilizational progress as it becomes manifest through the division of labor in society, the author lays down the groundwork for the rest of his argument, in which he instrumentalizes descriptions of Native sexuality as abnormality and immorality, in order to *crystallize* the ontological and moral superiority of the European. Morality is of key concern in *De la division du travail social*, (the root 'moral' appears 424 times in the text) because Durkheim recognizes the tension between modern industrial economic progress and moral decadence (as evidenced by his scholarly interest in suicide as a negative consequence of progress). After claiming that industry and art are both questionable as to their logical and historical association with good moral standing, science is posited as the standard bearer, or source of morality, for the social order that is the object of Durkheim's investigation.

> Of all the elements of civilization, science is the only one which, under certain conditions, presents a moral character. That is, societies are tending more and more to look upon it as a duty for the individual to develop his intelligence by learning the scientific truths which have been established. (Simpson 64)

The development of intelligence is, perhaps unsurprisingly, located squarely and uniquely in the domain of science and *scientific truth*. The passage clearly illustrates the universalizing and totalizing claims of Durkheim's discourse. Presenting science as the flagbearer of modern morality is problematic when one considers the mythic origins of the discourse's specific brand of *truth*. In contrast, Indigenous ways of knowing have often been relegated to the irrelevant or demonic. Laurelyn Whitt (Mississippi Choctaw) explains,

> Oppressive relations of power have shaped the histories of diverse knowledge systems and continue to inflect the present in ways that obscure or override their diversity. The existence and value of indigenous knowledge systems have, for example, been systematically denied. In the origin stories of the dominant culture, indigenous peoples have superstitions, myths, or belief systems based on ignorance. They do not have knowledge systems. (31)

Native knowledge is not considered a viable form of knowledge because it does not accept many of the tenets at the heart of empirical science's relation to the world. Rather than objectifying through physical and analytical "division", Indigenous peoples often see the environment, for example, as "alive, spiritually replete" (Whitt 29). On the same theme, Vine Deloria Jr. (Standing Rock Sioux) signals the need to "radically transform scientific knowledge". The path forward for science must "demonstrate how everything is connected to everything else"

(Spirit and Reason 39). For Deloria Jr., the neutrality of the world as posited by science is nonsensical, contending that, "a sense of purpose must become part of the knowledge that science confronts and understands. The present posture of most Western scientists is to deny any sense of purpose and direction to the world around us, believing that to do so would be to introduce mysticism and superstition" *(Spirit and Reason 39)*. Echoing the exclusionary discourse of science mentioned by Whitt, Deloria Jr. laments the arrogance of science's perfunctory dismissal of Indigenous knowledge. In her critique, which focuses on biocolonialism, Whitt points to the lack of diversity in ways of knowing within the strictures of the elaboration of Western science. This lack of diversity is a result of the symbolic violence of the myth of the Vanishing Indian within the social sciences' (self-)positioning vis-à-vis the non-European object. In much the same way that the Native is *disappeared* in the French Western, Indigenous culture and knowledge *disappears* in the "oppressive relations" instigated between Western and Indigenous knowledges. Therefore, it is critical to reexamine the naturalizing and totalizing discourses of hegemonic knowledge structures such as science. As I mentioned previously, science abets the colonial project of extermination.

To return to Durkheim's exposition, I have been following the train of Durkheim's thought regarding progress and its purported attachments to human biology and morality. Thus far, he does not directly allude to the Amerindian; however, it is necessary to clearly understand the context into which the representation of the Amerindian is inserted in Durkheim's overall articulation of one of the foundational texts of sociology. I will now analyze the direct references to the Amerindian in the opening sections of the text, where Durkheim proposes the "social fact" as the base unit of knowledge, not only in sociology, but, as the quote above shows, in all human intelligence generally. It is around sexuality and gender roles that the representation of the Native specifically intervenes in Durkheim's analysis.

[One] may conjecture that the same homogeneity was found at the beginning of human evolution, and see in the female form the aboriginal image of what was the one and only type from which the masculine variety slowly detached itself. Travelers report, moreover, that in certain tribes of South America, man and woman, in structure and general appearance, present a similarity which is far greater than is seen elsewhere. Finally, Dr. Lebon has been able to establish directly and with mathematical precision this original resemblance of the two sexes in regard to the preeminent organ of physical and psychic life, the brain. By comparing a large number of crania chosen from different races and different societies, he has come to the following conclusion: "The volume of the crania of man and woman, even when we compare subjects of equal age, of equal height and equal weight, show considerable differences in favor of the man, and this inequality grows proportionally with civilization,

114   *The Vanishing Indian: Manifest and Imperial Destinies*

so that from the point of view of the mass of the brain, and correspondingly of intelligence, woman tends more and more to be differentiated from the male sex. The difference which exists, for example, between the average cranium of Parisian men of the present day and that of Parisian women is almost double that observed between male and female of ancient Egypt". (Simpson 69)

After having discussed whether resemblance causes humans to come together, or whether the attraction of opposites is the maxim that most correctly describes the origin of human society, Durkheim shows how resemblance is coded as *primitive* and division leads to sexual differences. Gender differentiation is closely linked in the argument to progress and its moral and biological universal imperatives. Durkheim cites *hard science*, namely cranial measurements, to situate Indigenous peoples of South America in a temporality that is equated with that of Ancient Egypt. By positing an ontological relationship between Ancient Egypt and contemporary Amerindians, Durkheim engages in the tradition of situating the Native temporally in the past, within the inherent illogic of the Vanishing Indian myth. As evidence of the *scientific truth* of the ontological superiority of the French, Durkheim reiterates one of the most characteristic metaphors of the mythic paradigm of the Vanishing Indian. The site where Durkheim locates this mythic ontological difference is significant. It is sexuality that defines that difference, biologically and morally. After all, the lack of a modern, European division of labor is the cause of the extraordinary *resemblance* between Amerindian men and women of South America, according to Durkheim and his *scientific* sources. The pinpointing of Native sexual resemblance as a site of ontological difference is echoed in discourses of anthropology and settler sexual normativities in the twentieth century. Morgensen localizes *berdache* as an important element in the *queering* of the Native. Berdache, which Morgensen labels a "colonial object", highlighting the constructed nature of the concept, is typically an androgynous male Amerindian. Morgensen explains how *berdache* functions in settler-colonial discourses.

It [*berdache*] cohered an object of knowledge that described a gender-transitive and homosexual subject, defined by male embodiment, who received social recognition in Native American societies. Over time, the object projected a uniformity of sex, gender, sexuality, and indigeneity that let it represent principles of human nature and culture. Disagreement over its definition regularly called its qualities into question, but that very deliberation promulgated *berdache* as a key object of colonial desire for Indigenous and sexual truth. (55)

While Durkheim does not directly reference berdache as a specially revered Native identity, the author's articulation of Native sexuality utilizes the same narrative technologies as the more modern discourses targeted by Morgensen's

The Vanishing Indian: Manifest and Imperial Destinies   115

analysis. In particular, the "uniformity of sex, gender, sexuality, and indigeneity" that the construction of berdache allows Westerners to claim, is precisely the way in which Durkheim employs Native sexualities to "represent principles of human nature and culture". Not only does the father of sociology locate ontological difference in what he interprets as androgyny, but he utilizes that distinction as a founding site of *scientific truth*, namely European superiority over Amerindians. In comparison to the Ancient Egyptian and contemporary, androgynous Amerindian, it is the "big-brained" Parisian man and the "tiny-brained" Parisian woman that serve as the model for the division of sexual labor, progressive modernity, and civilization as Durkheim understands it.

> [The division of labor] combines both the productive power and the ability of the workman, it is the necessary condition of development in societies, both intellectual and material development. It is the source of civilization. Besides, since we quite facilely assign an absolute value to civilization, we do not bethink ourselves to seek any other function for the division of labor. (Simpson 63)

The division of labor, based on Durkheim's interpretation of modern and *primitive* gender roles, is presented as a profit-enhancing, intellect-building wellspring of civilization. Thereby, the propagation and maintenance of the modern industrial economic system is revealed as the sole function of the division of labor. The superior male and inferior female that results from such a system manifests itself in many ways within the author's argument. Durkheim's analysis has direct consequences politically, not only biologically for women, in particular. In addition to his citing of the small brains of contemporaneous French women, Durkheim signals female political agency as *retrograde*, going against the principles of progressive division.

> There is even now a very great number of savage people where the woman mingles in political life. That has been observed especially in the Indian tribes of America, such as the Iroquois, the Natchez; in Hawaii she participates in myriad ways in the men's lives, as she does in New Zealand and in Samoa. (Simpson 69)

In this excerpt, Durkheim lists various Amerindian groups in addition to Pacific Islander groups. Native female agency, what Durkheim describes as their "participation in the life of men", is positioned as a behavioral correlate of the extraordinary "sexual resemblance" of Amerindian societies. As such, it is morally condemned because of the inseparability of the biological and moral in Durkheim's thought. The political agency of Native women is categorized as *retrograde* in Durkheim's *scientific* analysis. Presented as evidence of European superiority, the relatively smaller brain sizes of French women are the marker

116 *The Vanishing Indian: Manifest and Imperial Destinies*

of civilized progress, whereas the sexual and biological androgyny, embodied by the political agency and "participation in the life of men" of Native women is stained with the primitiveness of the Ignoble Savage. Durkheim goes on to equate the concept of "sexual resemblance" with a weakening of familial bonds. As mentioned in the previous chapter in my discussion of the representation of the Native in French *scientific* texts of the eighteenth century, family is often denied to the Native, this lack being cited as a sign of inhumanity. Durkheim's *De la division du travail social* participates in that tradition.

> Thus, among the same peoples, marriage is in a completely rudimentary state. It is quite probable, if not absolutely demonstrated, that there was an epoch in the history of family when there was no such thing as marriage. Sexual relations were entered into and broken at will without any juridical obligations linking the union. (Simpson 70)

As in other examples, such as early written accounts by Europeans which state that Amerindian peoples do not respect familial bonds, claiming that Natives practice anthropophagy on family members, Durkheim presents contemporaneous Amerindians as lacking the very basis of society: family. The irony of this argumentation as part of a justification for the advantages of the civilized division of labor, which itself can be cited as weakening and destroying the bonds that hold family units and communities together through hyper-individualism and atomization is staggering. Nonetheless, what Durkheim characterizes as irresponsible Native "promiscuity" and "retrograde" sexuality becomes *the* site of the ontological difference between the normalized, naturalized French and the *queered* Amerindian. Through a discourse of *truth*, based on Durkheim's speculations and quotations of cranial measurements, or *hard science*, Native practices are *queered* and *disappeared* by employing the narrative technologies of a representational mode that engages with the history of the myths of the Ignoble Savage and the Vanishing Indian in the mythic machine. As La Condamine and Buffon in the eighteenth century, Durkheim focalizes on Native sexuality as a marker of difference. As Morgensen argues, sexuality is a determining factor in the epistemological understanding of the alterity of the Amerindian, as well as a tool of European (settler) self-definition (2).

In this section I have shown how Émile Durkheim instrumentalizes the mythologies of the Ignoble Savage and the Vanishing Indian in the articulation of his primary argument in one of the foundational texts of sociology, *De la division du travail social*. Through a close reading and analysis of the early sections of the work, I have demonstrated how the author conflates progress biologically and morally in order to argue for the superiority of European bodies and minds in contradistinction to Native bodies and minds. Framing the foundations of sociology by *queering* Native sexualities and gender roles through a turn to *hard science*, Durkheim makes *truth* claims about Amerindian

The Vanishing Indian: Manifest and Imperial Destinies 117

peoples that naturalize the purported superiority of the West. Having been systematically eradicated via the mythic machine's Vanishing Indian, the Native as simulacrum returns to the fore in the following chapter as the objectified, mythologized catalyst of European subjects' phantasmagoric voyage in twentieth- and twenty-first-century iterations of the mythology of Going Native in both French and Québécois literatures.

Works Cited

Aimard, Gustave. *Le grand chef des Aucas*. *Gallica*. https://gallica.bnf.fr/ark:/12148/bpt6k56602921?rk=42918;4. Paris: F. Roy, 1889. 27 April 2023.

———. *Les trappeurs de l'Arkansas*. *Gallica*. https://gallica.bnf.fr/ark:/12148/bpt6k445691g.r=gustave%20aimard%20les%20trappeurs%20d%27arkansas?rk=21459;2. Paris: Amyot, 1858. 27 April 2023.

Anderson, Benedict. *Imagined Communities: Reflections on the Origin and Spread of Nationalism*. Kindle version, Verso, 2006.

Bhabha, Homi. *The Location of Culture*. Kindle version. New York: Routledge Classics, 2012.

Billington, Ray Allen. *Land of Savagery, Land of Promise: The European Image of the American Frontier in the Nineteenth Century*. New York: W.W. Norton & Company, 1981.

Blanchard, Pascal, Sandrine Lemaire, Nicolas Bancel, and Dominic Thomas. "Introduction". *Colonial Culture in France Since the Revolution*. Translated by Alexis Pernsteiner. Edited by Pascal Blanchard, Sandrine Lemaire, Nicolas Bancel, and Dominic Thomas. Bloomington: Indiana UP, 2013.

Bourdieu, Pierre. *Langage et pouvoir symbolique*. Paris: Éditions du Seuil, 2001.

Boussenard, Louis. *Aventures d'un gamin de Paris au pays des bisons*. *Gallica*. https://gallica.bnf.fr/ark:/12148/bpt6k1116809/f1.item.r=boussenard%20aventures%20d'un%20gamin%20de%20Paris%20au%20pays%20des%20bisons. Paris: Colin, 1892. 29 April 2023.

———. *Chasseurs canadiens*. *Gallica*. https://gallica.bnf.fr/ark:/12148/bpt6k944831s/f1.item.texteImage. Paris: Librairie Marpon et Flammarion, 1886. 29 April 2023.

Bruyneel, Kevin. *The Third Space of Sovereignty: The Postcolonial Politics of U.S. – Indigenous Relations*. Minneapolis: University of Minnesota Press, 2007.

Chevalier, Henri-Émile. *La Tête-Plate*. *Gallica*. https://gallica.bnf.fr/ark:/12148/bpt6k5832216x.r=henri-%C3%A9mile%20chevalier%20la%20t%C3%AAte-plate?rk=21459;2. Paris: Librairie Poulet-Malassis, 1862. 27 April 2023.

Crosby, Alfred. *Ecological Imperialism: The Biological Expansion of Europe, 900–1900*. New York: Cambridge UP, 1991.

Deloria, Philip J. *Playing Indian*. New Haven, CT: Yale UP, 1998.

Deloria Jr., Vine. *Spirit and Reason: The Vine Deloria, Jr., Reader*. Edited by Barbara Deloria, Kristen Foehner, and Sam Scinta. Golden: Fulcrum Publishing, 1999.

Fanon, Frantz. *Les damnés de la terre*. Paris: Éditions La Découverte, 1985.

———. *Peau noire masques blancs*. Paris: Éditions du Seuil, 1952.

Ferry, Gabriel. *Le coureur de bois, ou Les chercheurs d'or*. *Gallica*. https://gallica.bnf.fr/ark:/12148/bpt6k30402523.r=gabriel%20ferry%20le%20coureur%20de%20bois?rk=21459;2. Paris: Librairie Hachette et Cie, 1881. 27 April 2023.

118   *The Vanishing Indian: Manifest and Imperial Destinies*

———. *Les aventures d'un Français au pays des Caciques. Gallica.* https://gallica.bnf.fr/ark:/12148/bpt6k96419s?rk=21459;2#. Paris, Maurice Dreyfous, 1881. 27 April 2023.

Gamber, John. "Tactical Mobility as Survivance". *Survivance: Narratives of Native Presence.* Kindle version. Lincoln: University of Nebraska Press, 2008.

Huhndorf, Shari M. *Going Native: Indians in the American Cultural Imagination.* Kindle version. Ithaca, NY: Cornell University Press, 2015.

Kroeber, Karl. "Why it's a Good Thing Gerald Vizenor is not an Indian". *Survivance: Narratives of Native Presence.* Edited by Gerald Vizenor. Kindle version. Lincoln: University of Nebraska Press, 2008.

Memmi, Albert. *Portrait du colonisé/Portrait du colonisateur.* Paris: Éditions Gallimard, 1985.

Morgensen, Scott Lauria. *Spaces between Us: Queer Settler Colonialism and Indigenous Decolonization.* Minneapolis: University of Minnesota Press, 2011.

Prats, Armando José. *Invisible Natives: Myth and Identity in the American Western.* Ithaca, NY: Cornell UP, 2002.

Pratt, Mary Louise. *Imperial Eyes: Travel Writing and Transculturation.* New York: Routledge, 2003.

Saïd, Edward. *Orientalism.* New York: Vintage, 1994.

Seth, Vanita. *Europe's Indians: Producing Racial Difference, 1500–1900.* Durham, NC: Duke UP, 2010.

Simpson, George, translator. *The Division of Labor in Society.* By Émile Durkheim. Kindle version, Digireads.com Publishing, 2019.

Slotkin, Richard. *Regeneration through Violence: The Mythology f the American Frontier, 1600–1860.* Norman: University of Oklahoma Press, 1973.

Turner, Frederick Jackson. *The Frontier in American History.* Kindle Version, Henry Holt and Company, 2011.

Vizenor, Gerald. "Aesthetics of Survivance: Literary Theory and Practice." *Survivance: Narratives of Native Presence.* Edited by Gerald Vizenor. Kindle version. Lincoln: University of Nebraska Press, 2008.

———. *Manifest Manners: Narratives on Postindian Survivance.* Lincoln: University of Nebraska Press, 1999.

———. *Native Liberty: Natural Reason and Cultural Survivance.* Kindle version. Lincoln: University of Nebraska Press, 2009.

Whitt, Laurelyn. *Science, Colonialism, and Indigenous Peoples: The Cultural Politics of Law and Knowledge.* Cambridge: Cambridge UP, 2009.

4 Going Native
The Myth of Being Indian

1 Introduction

This chapter focuses on the narrative technologies of the mythic machine's Going Native mode, which situates the Amerindian as a site of veridiction. Potentially opening the door for self-actualization of collective redemption, Going Native mythologies engage with, perpetuate, and extend the mythic genealogy investigated in previous chapters. Going Native is an appropriative, neocolonial mythic discourse that makes claims of universal *truth* and the transcendence of Western epistemologies, yet mythic (mis)understandings remain central to the confirmation of racial hierarchies that marginalize Indigenous peoples. I begin with a discussion of the mythic (re)writing of two earlier works that represent Amerindian: *Vendredi, ou les limbes du Pacifique*, winner of the Grand Prix du Roman of the Académie Française in 1967, by Michel Tournier and *Rouge Brésil* by Jean-Christophe Rufin. Tournier's novel is a rewrite of the Daniel Defoe classic *Robinson Crusoe*. Rufin's Prix Goncourt winner for 2001 takes a second look at the French Admiral Villegagnon's failed colonial venture in the sixteenth century in Tupinamba territory in what becomes the Rio de Janeiro region of modern-day Brazil, the same voyage that brought André Thevet to the New World. Next, I shift focus to examine Québécois Francophone representations of the Amerindian, beginning with a chronicle of the (mis)representation of the Native over time. By including French-Canadian authors' visions of the Native, I widen the scope of my research to encompass a more proximate geographical context that offers a unique opportunity to comparatively analyze French and Québécois mythologizing of the Native. In addition to reworking or resisting classic images, Québécois authors Robert Lalonde and Jacques Poulin's novels disseminate mythic iterations of the Going Native myth centered on Amerindian sexuality. Through the insights of berdache as theorized by Morgensen deeper understanding of the connections between political discourses and Going Native narratives is revealed. In both *Le dernier été des Indiens* (1982) by Lalonde and Poulin's *Volkswagen Blues* (1984), mythologized Native sexualities transform the Amerindian into agents of change for French-Canadian protagonists. Coopting

DOI: 10.4324/9781032638751-5

120   *Going Native: The Myth of Being Indian*

Native *non-normative* sexualities, these authors locate *truths* in mythically distorted images of the Amerindian. In the following section, coincidentally, it is the same Amerindian group, the Tupinamba, that figures largely in Rufin's *Rouge Brésil* that is now the ethnographic object of Claude Lévi-Strauss' *Tristes Tropiques* (1955). Deconstructing the mythic intertextuality of Lévi-Strauss' "specialized knowledge" about the Native, alongside the anarchist anthropology the famed anthropologist's students, Pierre Clastres, I demonstrate how social *scientific* discourses are constructed based on epistemological displacement and the inherent illogic of mythic distortion of the Amerindian in the French cultural imaginary.

2   Going Native in Mythic Rewriting: *Vendredi, ou les limbes du Pacifique* by Michel Tournier and *Rouge Brésil* by Jean-Christophe Rufin

As we have seen throughout our foray into the evolution of the narrative technologies of the French and Québécois cultural imaginaries, myths of the Native are often rewritings; at times little more than repetitions of earlier representations. Michel Tournier's novel, *Vendredi, ou les limbes du Pacifique* is a rewriting of one of the most fundamental texts in the Western canon, *Robinson Crusoe* (1719) by Daniel Defoe. Defoe's classic maintains considerable cultural purchase in Anglophone society today, with several literary and cinematic reboots appearing regularly. *Robinson Crusoe* has not only influenced the English-speaking world, however. The novel is well received throughout Europe, including France. *Robinson Crusoe* has shown itself to be one of the most imitated plotlines in literature, television, and cinema, leading to the coining of the term *robinsonnade* to describe any similar storyline in French. The mythic story of Crusoe also informs the French cultural imaginary concerning the peoples and geographies of the Americas. It is perhaps hardly surprising, then, that the highly awarded author Tournier chooses to reimagine the tale in his novel *Vendredi*. The title of the novel and its inversion of the roles of the protagonist and Friday, an Araucananian of both Amerindian and African descent is revealing. Switching the focus of the title away from the English protagonist toward the Indigenous man Friday signals a clear theoretical (re)positioning Tournier's rethinking of Defoe's work. In the original, the main character is defined by his struggle to maintain his integrity against Nature *and* against Friday's corrupting influence. Crusoe survives years of exile only to emerge virtually unchanged by the ordeal. Defoe's Crusoe remains intact psychologically and culturally, an Englishman from the first to the last page. This is the most significance difference between Defoe's and Tournier's versions. Tournier foregrounds transformation and transcendence in *Vendredi*, insisting upon Crusoe's complete reinvention of his identity. Tournier's Crusoe is changed by the dual influences of Nature and Native, by his struggle and communion with the island of Speranza and the observational

Going Native: The Myth of Being Indian   121

philosophy that develops from his interaction with Friday. Tournier's title, therefore, refers to Friday, not Crusoe. The implication, attested in the plot, is that Friday's *primitive* vision of the world is the more viable philosophy. Tournier presents Friday's *naïveté* remedy to the corruption of Crusoe's Judeo-Christian, Freudian cultural heritage, portrayed as a hindrance rather than an aid to Enlightenment or personal fulfillment. Crusoe's actualization, his Going Native, exemplified by his final decision to remain on the island rather than return to civilization, as he does in Defoe's version, is Friday's doing. However, a closer reading reveals two factors that belie Crusoe's supposed conversion. First, the transformation of Crusoe from Englishman to Native begins long before Friday's. Despite his manic efforts to control the microcosm of Speranza through rules, measurement, ritual, and intensive agricultural exploitation (an evident ersatz for colonialism and its economies of extraction), Crusoe's attitudes toward nature evolve prior to Friday's appearance.

> In fact, the observation of the Charter and the Penal Code, the draining penalties he forced himself to suffer through, respecting a strict schedule that left him no time to rest, the ceremonial aspect of all the important acts of his life, the whole corset of conventions and dictates that he imposed upon himself so that he wouldn't stumble, didn't keep him from dreading the untamed, wild presence of the nature of the tropics, and, within himself, solitude's work of eroding away his civilized soul. (82, my translation)

It is the environment that first begins to transform Crusoe via the narrative technology of the mythic machine. The myth posits that contact with the Native leads to transcendence. The *primitive* heals the (soul) wounds of the *modern*. Yet, there is nearly always an environmental corollary to the mythology Going Native. The European protagonist's metamorphosis is double; it is only through a transformative relation with Nature *and* Native that the realization of the narrative arc of Going Native is completed. The relationship that Crusoe cultivates with the island of Speranza, at once mother (Crusoe descends into the depths of a cave in an obvious metaphor for a Freudian return to the womb) and lover (Crusoe engages in sexual intercourse with various natural elements, including a mossy patch at the interstice of two branches and a sandy knoll, which leads to the emergence of a new plant species). The dual catalyst of Crusoe's Going Native is a familial connection with Nature and a pupillary one with the Amerindian. Crusoe's relationship with Friday, before the latter accidentally sets off an explosion that destroys the elaborate English colonial edifice instituted by his *master*, is characterized by domination and violence. Always secondary, Friday is a subaltern, a failed attempt at assimilation, and a direct threat to the order so dear to Crusoe. The typical structure of the mythic mode of Going Native would entail Friday facilitating the transformation of the Englishman into a version of the Noble Savage. That is confuted not only by the European/Native relationship

122 *Going Native: The Myth of Being Indian*

as colonizer/colonized, but remains equally problematic after the dramatic explosion that ends Crusoe's efforts at controlling the island *and* Friday. In this second, ostensibly more egalitarian, stage of the Crusoe/Friday relationship, Tournier essentially presents scenes centered on Friday's interaction with Nature. Friday's interactions with an ibex anchor this plotline, purportedly illustrating Indigenous ways of interacting with the non-human. The reader only has access to Crusoe's observations and explanations in the form of entries in his *Log-Book*, however. The inner workings of Friday's mind are opaque. Friday fashions a musical instrument and a kite from the cadaver of Andoar, a male ibex killed by Friday in a playing out of *primitive* masculinity vis-à-vis Nature, are two symbols of the *aerial*. In *Vendredi*, the *aerial* symbolizes Crusoe's Going Native transformation. Equally, the instrument and kite are evidence of Friday's epistemological difference vis-à-vis Crusoe and his capitalist heritage. The effort spent producing these objects is anathema to capitalist ideals of efficiency and productivity. Furthermore, Friday's transformation of the remains of Andoar are meant to be indicative of an Indigenous worldview regarding the natural environment. Crusoe draws these conclusions based on observations of Friday's behavior and, *according to his own epistemological categorizations and imperatives*, claims to have undergone a profound transformation; he has now successfully Gone Native after recognizing the error of European lifeways. Irony is a central element in all of Tournier's fiction. The author mocks Crusoe's *intelligence* and arrogance. In the end, it is Friday who escapes the island. Friday is captivated by the modern world via his experiences with the crew of the *Whitebird*, the ship that finally arrives at Speranza, that he chooses to join the Western world. The irony resides in the effect of Crusoe's influence on the Native. When the explosion destroys the veneer of civilization, it is the consequence of two converging elements of the dysfunctional relationship between Crusoe and Friday. The dual elements of the colonial project that conspire to bring Crusoe's exploitative system down are regulation and imitation. First, Crusoe's hoarding of tobacco requires a rule that Friday not smoke, leading to Friday smoking clandestinely. Seeking a hidden place, Friday enters the grotto where stores of gunpowder are housed. In smoking, Friday imitates Crusoe. In the logic of the *mission civilisatrice*, this impetus to imitate the *superior* European's behavior is an ambiguous aspect of contact. The ironic result of Crusoe's colonial efforts is not Friday's adoption of Christianity and capitalism, rather he picks up the bad habit of smoking which leads to the destruction of the entire edifice of Crusoe's careful microcosmic reconstruction of Western culture. The second factor that undermines Crusoe's supposed transcendence from civilized to *primitive* is the ending of the novel which leaves Crusoe with a young boy from the *Whitebird*, the ship that finally arrives to *save* him. The *Whitebird* takes Friday aboard and leaves a cabin boy who is grateful to escape the captain's violence. On the surface, it may appear that Crusoe's satisfaction at the end of the text is based upon not being alone. However, the dénouement equally raises doubts as to Crusoe's

Going Native: The Myth of Being Indian 123

Going Native arc. The discovery of the Estonian cabin boy's presence is a repetition or (re)writing of the introduction of Friday into Crusoe's insular world. Rather than being met with fear, Crusoe aims his rifle at Friday upon first seeing him, intending to kill him, but missing and killing one of Friday's pursuers instead, the young cabin boy, an ersatz protégé or son, the long-awaited progeny of Crusoe's fecundation of the island, is met with joy as the fulfillment of Crusoe's destiny. The boy is rechristened *Jeudi* (Thursday) in the novel's final sentence, "From now on, Robinson told him, your name will be Thursday. It's the day of Jupiter, the god of the Sky" (Tournier 254, my translation). The reference to the sky alludes to Crusoe's transformation, his Going Native mythology is inscribed as an awakening to *aerial* realities that his former self was incapable of realizing, lost in a telluric world of excessive order and exploitation. The protagonist moves through three phases of development, from the telluric, to the vegetative, finally reaching Enlightenment in the *aerial*, which is symbolized by the kite and instrument that Friday fabricates from the ibex's skull. The ibex is significant because upon first arriving on the island, Crusoe encounters a similar animal, killing in blind rage, symbolizing the brutality of the European vis-à-vis Nature. The irony in the final scene pertains to the symbol of Crusoe's complete transformation from civilized to savage, the sky god Jupiter's affiliation with the name *Jeudi* is proof that Crusoe has not, in fact, been able to successfully slough off his cultural heritage. Crusoe's elation at discovering Thursday's presence emanates from a fresh opportunity to inculcate (i.e. to control, to colonize) represented by the young boy. Thursday is a new subaltern for Crusoe to dominate. The first action taken by Crusoe when Friday arrives is to give him a name. Naming is tantamount to possession. Naming is a claiming of control or objectifying the object named. There is, of course, a fraught history in the Americas of European naming and fallacious claims of possession. While Thursday's escape from the ship frees Crusoe from living out his remaining years in solitude, it also provides him with an opportunity to pass on the knowledge that he has gained from Nature and Native. The paternalistic aspects of Crusoe's relationship with Thursday are not essentially different from the parameters of the relationship with Friday and are redolent of the inherent illogic of the Going Native mythic paradigm. While ostensibly transformative, the narrative technology actually reinforces the European colonial worldview. Huhndorf (Yup'ik) contends that the "primary cultural work [of the Going Native myth] in fact is the regeneration of racial whiteness and European-American society" (Introduction). Rather than present an *authentic* Amerindian as model for self-actualization, the narrative technology of Going Native is complicit with colonialism and the exclusion of the Native. Does Tournier's (re)writing of Defoe's masterpiece dramatically alter the relationship between the European and the Amerindian (or Eastern European)? The answer, of course, is no. The text is not about *Vendredi* as Tournier's title might suggest. This Going Native is illusory. Crusoe requires the presence of the Other, but not to learn from them. The need the Other satisfies is

124   *Going Native: The Myth of Being Indian*

appropriative. Crusoe appropriates Nature and Native to make certain claims about his identity, however, these claims have no real connection to Nature or Native. Going Native in Tournier's *Vendredi* and in Rufin's *Rouge Brésil* occurs within a closed hermeneutic system of Western epistemologies. Rather than representing liberation from Western cultural heritage, Crusoe's Going Native reiterates classic myths of the Amerindian, the Noble Savage and the nexus of Nature and Native. Crusoe attempts to become what the French cultural imaginary has taught him an Amerindian is: a Noble Savage. The irony at the end of Tournier's text, the naming of his new colonized object, Thursday, points toward a continuation of the economic, philosophical traditions of Crusoe's heritage rather than any new or hybrid identity. Crusoe builds a false *aerial* philosophy based on mythic (mis)understandings of the Amerindian Other. The crucial element of Crusoe's Going Native experience is missing from the pages of Tournier's text. The edifice of Crusoe's transcendence is built on an observational rationalism that does not grant Friday subject status. Rather, it circumscribes Friday as object. Crusoe's (symbolic) *possession* of the (mythology of the) Amerindian is total. Tournier, writing during the emergence of the deconstructionist project of postmodern literature and the popularization of New Age spiritualties based on *knowledge* of Indigeneity, clearly sees the binary systems behind Western conceptions of identity and culture. He holds them up as a mirror, to mock and ridicule without taking the next step beyond that binary worldview. Tournier is content to expose the mechanism without proposing blueprints for a new (mythic) understanding. *Vendredi, ou les limbes du Pacifique* is a product of its time. Published in 1967, the novel reflects the deconstructionist turn, but not the more creative, iconoclastic bent of later postmodernist literary works. Tournier's project dissects *and* employs the mythologies that have been the focus of this volume over preceding centuries.

Having lost the Native as articulated in the Noble Savage within the mythology of the Vanishing Indian, one turns to the past, to a time before the mythologized Indian vanished, or was *disappeared*. Ironically, now that the West has annihilated the last trace of the Amerindian, the teleological terminus of the Vanishing Indian myth, the only response is to become Native oneself. The Going Native myth is a return to the Noble Savage myth after passing through the *disappearance* of the Native. All the mythologies in this study are in genealogical *and* synchronic relation. The Vanishing Indian and Going Native mythologies develop from the Noble/Ignoble Savage and the nexus of Native and Nature. Additionally, many elements of that mythic genealogy continue to have purchase in French and Québécois representations of the Amerindian. The once Noble Savage is reduced to nostalgic symbol via *disappearing* through the narrative technologies of the Vanishing Indian. Henceforth, the Noble Savage can only be played by the European. In (symbolically) destroying the Native (Vizenor's) "literary annihilation", myth revives them in the Westerner whose *knowledge* of the Amerindian (actually knowledge of the mythic system of representation of the Amerindian) allows them to metaphorically return to Rousseau's state of nature and to become Native. Having created (the myth of) the Amerindian (the Noble/Ignoble Savage, the Nature and Native nexus, the Vanishing Indian) in the French and Québécois cultural imaginaries, that fabrication is now appropriated by the colonizer. Rufin's *Rouge Brésil* reflects the appropriative narrative technologies of the mythic machine's representation of the Amerindian.

Rouge Brésil, the winner of the 2001 Prix-Goncourt is another example of (re) writing an earlier representation of the Amerindian, an expedition led by the French Admiral Villegagnon to Brazil in the 1550s. Rufin's plot centers on the myth of Going Native. For Tournier and Rufin, the Amerindian represents a privileged site of identity (re)formation. The protagonist of *Rouge Brésil* is the young Frenchwoman Colombe, a feminized version of the patronym of Christopher Columbus, *Colomb* in French. This (re)writing of Columbus' name is an example of the long tradition of reimagining the history of the contact between Europeans and Amerindians in a more positive way, a literary obscuration of historical genocide. Montaigne engages in the practice in "Des coches". Rousseau's play, *La découverte du nouveau monde*, is based upon this revisionist tradition. Rufin interpellates a tradition does not adhere to historical or cultural realities, employing instead the narrative technologies of the mythic machine to construct an alternate history. In Rufin's *Rouge Brésil* and Tournier's *Vendredi*, gender roles and sexuality are central to the author's exploration of Western identity. The young woman Colombe experiences a sexual transformation catalyzed by her contact with the Tupinamba, a sexually inflected instantiation of the Going Native myth. Before contact with Natives, Colombe dresses as a boy to join Villegagnon's expedition and accompany who she believes is her brother Just to the New World. Presenting the French as repressive, the Native Tupinamba represents a healthier environment wherein Colombe can explore sexuality. Part of Colombe's sexual Going Native is nudity. Her nudity reveals her gender to the French prior to her forced repatriation into the colonial space of the French-controlled island off the coast. Rufin introduces feminist and ecocritical critiques into the sixteenth century. However anachronistic, Rufin's text balances the demands of the genre of the historical novel and the modern criticisms he highlights well. Both issues are exclusively linked to French perspectives that take no account of Tupinamba worldviews. Rufin appropriates elements of the historical accounts of André Thevet, Jean De Léry, and Admiral Villegagnon to structure an essentially twenty-first-century French discussion about women's rights and the climate crisis. Nudity, a salacious aspect of early travel accounts of encounters with Amerindians, plays a privileged role in Colombe's Going Native. Not only does Colombe's nudity constitute an assumption of gender as woman, it also conveys a certain power in the world of Rufin's novel. While Colombe's nudity empowers, Amerindian nudity signifies neither power nor liberation. Rather, Native nudity is associated with sexual exploitation by members of Villegagnon's party and by Colombe's mentor in the process of Going Native,

126 *Going Native: The Myth of Being Indian*

a Frenchman named Pay-Lo. Pay-Lo has several Amerindian lovers with whom he sires numerous progeny. Pay-Lo's sexual promiscuity is presented as typical of Tupinamba practices. Gender roles, sexuality, and the myth of Going Native are knotted in *Rouge Brésil*. Both Pay-Lo and Colombe adopt gender roles in keeping with Tupinamba praxis. However, their adoption of aspects of Native sexuality presents a contradiction. Pay-Lo's sexual liaisons with many Amerindian women can readily be construed as exploitative, directly opposing the modern French, feminist critique present elsewhere in the novel. Rufin's insertion of anachronistic elements of modern social critique creates tension that underpins the Going Native plotline. Confusion derives from the ambiguity associated with Colombe's Going Native experience. By contrast, in *Vendredi*, Crusoe's transformation is a consequence of contact with the Nature *and* the Amerindian Friday. Tournier's Going Native myth emphasizes the influence of the Native, *not* Nature in the transformative process, locating catalytic power with the Native. Contact with the Native leads the European to Enlightenment and self-actualization through Going Native. Concerning this mythic itinerary, Rufin's text is more ambiguous regarding the source of transformative power. In *Rouge Brésil*, the author presents a triumvirate of influences that operate as on Colombe: Pay-Lo (the Frenchman who has completed his own journey of Going Native allowing him to act as guide), Native Tupinamba women, and Nature. All three elements assist in Colombe's transcendence. Although all three are present, Rufin privileges Pay-Lo's role in Colombe's spiritual journey. Like in *Vendredi*, Rufin's Amerindian characters are conglomerations of stereotypical details taken from the *crystallized* lexicon of mythic representations of the Native. They are not attributed the complexity of the European characters. Huhndorf (Yup'ik) explains that the European protagonist of the Going Native journey is the "center of consciousness" of the narrative, whereas the Amerindian is "more or less incidental to the story" (Intro). This is true in *Rouge Brésil*, where the Going Native myth is effectuated via contact with a Frenchman, rather than a *true* Amerindian character. As in Tournier's *Vendredi, ou les limbes du Pacifique*, Rufin's title references both Native and Nature, *Rouge Brésil*. Both texts suggest a perspectival shift away from European paradigms, yet both direct the reader's attention to primarily Western concerns, relegating the Native to an "incidental" role, temporally linked to "colonial time": "static" and incapable of transformation (Bruyneel 2). Going Native is a unilateral and univocal mythology. Going Native is unilateral because it is unidirectional. Only the European can Go Native through specialized *knowledge* of Native cultures. It matters little whether that knowledge is accurate or mythic. Little is mentioned regarding Tupinamba or Araucanian existence in either novel. French categories and philosophical imperatives are the focus. Indigenous characters are necessary, yet secondary elements. However, it is Pay-Lo who takes center stage in Colombe's (meta) physical transformation. Rufin's version of Going Native is unique in comparison with the Tournier's which represents the classic narrative technology.

The microcosmic solitude of Speranza facilitates a reductive vision of contact and reciprocal influence in identity (re)formation. In *Rouge Brésil*, the action takes place among numerous peoples with different affiliations and roles. This creates ambiguity because the reader cannot pinpoint the exact source of transformation. Rufin provides a key: Pay-Lo. In a further complication of the feminist critique, the elderly Frenchman mentors the young Frenchwoman, providing her with the special *knowledge* needed to fulfill her Going Native experience. Colombe's guru in Going Native is a Frenchman. There is little evidence that might indicate that author Rufin intends his articulation of this mentor-mentee relationship in identity metamorphosis to be read as irony; however, the reader must ask how *authentic* Colombe's Going Native can be when she is converted by an elderly Frenchman and not by Amerindians. My claim is not that Rufin does not present Native women and Nature as aspects of Colombe's conversion experience. They are present and do participate; however, they play a "more or less incidental" role. The guide in the transformation is Pay-Lo. Perhaps unsurprisingly, given the mythic simulation of the "indian", to use Vizenor's term signaling mythological invention, that the European with *knowledge* of the Amerindian constitutes the perfect mentor in the Going Native process. The proof that Rufin's European characters act as guides, helping other Europeans in their Going Native, is evident in the novel's dénouement. When Just is reunited with the transformed, *Native* Colombe, another transformation occurs. The faux-incestuous love story plays out via yet another mythic Going Native miracle. Just, who undergoes inculcation at the hands of Villegagnon himself as the admiral's chosen protégé, pliable and subservient to the Admiral's extractive, colonial mentality, rapidly switches sides upon seeing the new, nude, liberated, and *Native* Colombe. The culmination of the mawkish love story is Just's own Going Native. Like Colombe, it is not knowledge of Native lifeways that activates Just's about-face and the abandon of his Western colonial heritage; it is the assistance of a more experienced European that effectuates the necessary transmogrification. Just's mentor is Colombe, not Amerindians. The irony is lost within the romantic plotline and Rufin's preference for a happy ending without too many complications, yet there have been few moments in the long history of the representation of the Amerindian in French literature that have provided a clearer glimpse of the mechanics of the narrative technology of the mythic machine's mythic misrepresentation of the Native. Close examination of the mythic representations of the Amerindian reveals that French authors' metaphorical constructions of the Native are little more than two-dimensional, unilateral and univocal conversations with/about French cultural paradigms. In addition to providing pertinent examples of the structuration of the Going Native myth, the latest evolution, or (re)writing, of the Noble and Ignoble Savage and Vanishing Indian myths to be analyzed, *Rouge Brésil* and *Vendredi, ou les limbes du Pacifique* offer another look at a theme that has been an integral element of textual representations of the Amerindian since the period of first contacts: the nexus of

128 *Going Native: The Myth of Being Indian*

Native and Nature in the French cultural imaginary. Associated with the myth of the Noble Savage, the nexus of Nature and Native is a crucial mythic mode that participates in the genealogy that we have traced from the period of early contacts.

3 The Nexus of Nature and Native in Mythologies of Going Native

A significant element of Tournier's critique via the *wisdom* of the Native is how the author depicts European and Amerindian praxis vis-à-vis Nature. As in Rufin's Going Native, Tournier's articulation of the mythic nexus of Native and Nature reveals the narrative technologies of the mythic machine. It is not exposure to Native lifeways, to a novel practice in the environment that inspires Crusoe's transformation. It is the voyage within the Freudian *womb* of the island that allows the European protagonist to discover the *truth* hidden in the *primitive* depths of his own identity, crucially not via *knowledge* of the Amerindian. Tournier presents Crusoe and Friday as opposed in their approaches to the environment, notably non-human animals. The most evident example of an ecocritique in Tournier's text is centered on the ibex. The author uses characters' interactions with the animal to contrast European and Native. When the protagonist comes to his senses following the shipwreck and begins to explore the island, a vague shape comes into focus. It is an ibex buck, though Crusoe is not able to *recognize* it.

> Little by little the object in the green half-light transformed into a kind of wild goat, with long hair. Head high, ears thrust forward, it watched him approach, standing rigid, in stony stillness. From the big statue of fur blocking the path, burst forth a snicker like a ventriloquist's laugh. His fear compounding with his extreme exhaustion, Robinson was seized by a sudden rage. He lifted his cudgel and brought it down between the animal's horns with all his might. There was a dull cracking sound, the beast fell to its knees, then tipped over onto its side. It was the first living thing that Robinson had encountered on the island. He had killed it. (17, my translation)

This passage defines Western attitudes vis-à-vis Nature equating the non-human animal with the mythologized Amerindian, referring to the ibex as savage, wild, and hirsute. Both descriptions reach far back into conceptions of the Ignoble Savage as the European Wildman (Dickason, *Myth of the Savage*, 70–80). Subsequent developments support a reading of the wild ibex as metaphor for the Native. The ibex is depicted as prideful and confident. He holds his head high and even dares to laugh. This is too much for the Englishman to bear. Overcome by a nameless rage, Crusoe cracks the ibex's skull. Tournier points out Crusoe's myopic *savagery*, importantly not the non-human animal nor the Amerindian.

Going Native: The Myth of Being Indian 129

The ibex represents Nature and Native. Indeed, Crusoe attempts to kill Friday when he first sees him. Another significant element: Crusoe's inaction regarding the animal's dead body. A difference between European and Native attitudes toward the environment is linked to the use of resources. For Crusoe, killing the non-human animal and leaving its corpse to rot is normative behavior. Tournier implicitly critiques Western ecological praxis here, signaling disrespect of the non-human animal. An historical case that exemplifies this Western/Native difference is the bison. Great Plains Natives are known for their use of every part of the buffalo to fulfill a variety of material needs, wasting nothing. The opposed image of the European's wanton cruelty and squandering: the European shooting into the herd from the window of a train car, paying someone to fetch the skins, and leaving the rest to rot. Euro-Americans equated the decimation of the buffalo with the extermination of the Amerindian. Tournier introduces Crusoe's violently wasteful relationship with Nature to posit Friday's ecological practices as counterpoint. Let us examine how Amerindian ecological practice is represented in the mythic modes of the nexus of Nature and the Native and Going Native. First, the anonymity of ibex in the Crusoe scene is absent; Friday names the ibex Andoar. This detail is not insignificant, given the importance of naming. I mentioned above that Crusoe's act of naming the island, Friday, and Thursday is an appropriative gesture. Between Friday and the ibex, it is one of mutual recognition, seeing the human in the non-human. Friday's naming is antithetical to Crusoe's naming. In *Vendredi*, naming serves as a model for how the characters envision the human and non-human. Second, there is inherent respect in Friday's relation with Andoar. Tournier inscribes this respect between Friday and non-human animals earlier in the text, explaining how Tenn (the only other survivor of the shipwreck, a dog) behaves differently toward Friday than toward Crusoe. In another scene, Friday nurses the runt of a brood of vultures, much to Crusoe's dismay. Indeed, vultures are marginal beings in the Englishman's. Crusoe leaves the ibex corpse lying on the ground. In contrast, Friday transforms Andoar's body into something new, something of spiritual, not economic value. Tournier presents the Native as creating meaning *with* non-human animals, not extracting value *from* them. Friday consecrates Andoar's bodily remains by creating a kite from his dried skin and a musical instrument from his skull. Rather than focusing on *material* needs (as with the bison example, Friday's transformation of Andoar's body speaks to *culture*. Tournier takes a stereotype, the use of every available resource, and reemploys it to insist on the Native possessing *true* culture. According to the Crusoe's Western rationale both objects are useless. However, both are critical in Crusoe's Going Native experience. They symbolize the final stage of Crusoe's metamorphosis: the *aerial* stage. Commencing in the *telluric*, passing through the *vegetative*, and culminating in the *aerial*, Crusoe's self-actualization can only be completed with Friday's mentorship and the lessons learned from the transformation of the ibex remains are a turning point in the mythology of Going Native in the novel. Crusoe switch into Native in the

130   *Going Native: The Myth of Being Indian*

Noble Savage mode is illusory. Crusoe names the young Estonian boy Thursday, reflecting an attempt to *return to nature*. Thursday coming before Friday, represents an impossible reversal in the temporal order reflective of Crusoe's desire to become Amerindian-like. *Primitive* being the antidote to *modern*, this temporal reversal is part of the inherent illogic of the mythic machine. While Tournier presents Friday as having a healthier understanding of humanity's position in the non-human environment, he provides no insight into Friday's inner thoughts, relegating Friday to a secondary status, "more or less incidental to the story" (Huhndorf, Introduction). Instead of identifying with Friday as the "center of consciousness", the reader is left with Crusoe's New Age philosophical (mis) understandings. Appropriating actions and objects that he does not understand such as the kite and the musical instrument, Crusoe incorporates them into his own redemptive journey from *modern* to *primitive*, European to Native, thereby completing the mythic narrative arc. However, the Englishman's new philosophy does not take Friday's worldview into account. This practice echoes the same extractive ideology behind Crusoe's behavior vis-à-vis the natural world, in keeping with what Vizenor has termed "manifest manners". George B. Handley urges caution and critical awareness when examining Western discourses that aim to *return to nature* via contact with the *primitive*, identifying a link between modern environmental discourses that idealize Indigenous peoples and the mythology of the Noble Savage.

> The privileging of animism and the essentializing of the native or black subject can lead to a categorical dismissal of the diasporic subject and of hybridity, and the valorization of wilderness can lead to an unfruitful dismissal of history, technology, and culture. (Handley, "The Postcolonial Ecology of the New World Baroque", *Postcolonial Ecologies: Literatures of the Environment*, Chapter 5)

Handley rightly recognizes the univocal and unilateral nature of Western discourses of Indigenous ecology, calling this narrative technology a "categorical dismissal of the diasporic subject", a description that certainly fits the Amerindian-African Friday. Friday's trajectory remains unclear, illustrating the erasure of his subjectivity, but also an "unfruitful dismissal of history, technology, and culture". By silencing Friday's subjectivity and history in favor of Crusoe's Western mythology of Going Native, the Amerindian is ironically present only as the reflection of Crusoe's own attitudes and concerns, not as subject or agent, but as object. Such ahistorical framings of Native ecology have become commonplace in modern environmentalist discourses. As such, "viewing American Indians as keepers of the land is finally simply an escape mechanism, something that does not in itself bring about any actual behavioral change toward the environment" (Schweninger, *Listening to the Land: Native American Literary Responses to the Landscape*, Introduction). While Tournier's focus may be to

Going Native: The Myth of Being Indian 131

debunk mythologies by ironizing Western binary logics, the mythologies of the nexus of Nature and Native are part of the mythic apparatus, shaping the French and Québécois cultural imaginaries. A more appropriate perspective on Friday's actions after having killed Andoar, a view that takes into account Native ecologies and lifeways, would focus on the concept of reciprocity. George Tinker asserts that, "Violence cannot be perpetrated, a life taken, in a Native American society, without some spiritual act of reciprocation" (qtd. in Schweninger, *Listening to the Land: Native American Literary Responses to the Landscape*, Chapter 3). However, Tournier's description of Friday's spiritual actions only reiterates the Crusoe's perceptions within the myth of Going Native. The mythic machine functions via amalgamation. The equation of Native and Nature is an ingredient in the Going Native narrative. Native lifeways, ecology and spirituality are absent except for in their narrow applicability to Crusoe and his imperatives as articulated according to the inherent illogic of Going Native. Huhndorf (Yup'ik) surmises that Going Native, "support[s] European-American hegemony. While those who go native frequently claim benevolence toward Native peoples, they reaffirm white dominance by making some (usually distorted) vision of Native life subservient to the needs of the colonizing culture" (Introduction). In *Vendredi*, the mythology of the nexus of Nature and Native is the "distorted vision of Native life" that Crusoe appropriates in order to realize his self-actualization. As Philip Deloria (Standing Rock Sioux) explains, "Indians represented spiritual experience beyond representation. Ironically, books... proved the standard means of gaining access to that experience" (168). Echoing Huhndorf, Deloria pinpoints the problematic structure of the mythic machine's Going Native as a secondary source built on a mythologized simulation of the "indian" that grants, in its book form, access to specialized *knowledge* about the Native. In the end, the only *knowledge* transmitted is a mirroring of Western ideologies and (mis) understandings of the Amerindian Other. Tournier enjoys deconstructing preconceived ideas and challenging binaries. Tournier's texts are fraught with irony that forces the reader to question received ideas about the Other and the Self. However, Tournier does not transcend the act of deconstruction. He does not present a viable third option, in a dialectic movement that goes beyond the deconstructed binaries at the core of his work. An Indigenous critique of Crusoe's extractive ideologies can be found in the Anishnaabe's legendary monster, the Windigo, an appropriate lens for understanding Western economies and attitudes toward Nature and Native. Robin Wall Kimmerer (Potawatomi) evokes the Windigo as an interpretive model for better comprehending the differing praxis of Indigenous and European peoples vis-à-vis the environment.

The market system artificially creates scarcity by blocking the flow between the source and the consumer. Grain may rot in the warehouse while hungry people starve because they cannot pay for it. The result is famine for some and diseases of excess for others. The very earth that sustains us is being

132 *Going Native: The Myth of Being Indian*

destroyed to fuel injustice. An economy that grants personhood to corpora-
tions but denies it to the more-than-human-beings:: this is a Windigo economy. (376)

In Kimmerer's analysis, the extractive logic of Crusoe's nascent global capitalism and the current climate crisis can be seen more clearly through the Windigo's
madness and insatiable hunger, metaphors for the avarice of Western economics.
For Kimmerer, the answer is cultivating gratitude which "plants the seed for
abundance" (376). The third viable option missing from Tournier's Going Native mythology's deconstructive take on the binaries of European ideologies is
based on reciprocity in Kimmerer's analysis.

Each of us comes from people who were once indigenous. We can reclaim
our membership in the cultures of gratitude that formed our old relationships
with the living earth. Gratitude is a powerful antidote to Windigo psychosis.
A deep awareness of the gifts of the earth and of each other is medicine. It
celebrates cultures of regenerative reciprocity, where wealth is understood
to be having enough to share and riches are counted in mutually beneficial
relationships. (376)

The false remedy of the mythic machine's narrative of Going Native, the imaginary movement from *modern* to *primitive* is countered in Kimmerer's philosophy by the "powerful antidote" of gratitude. Indigenous cultures emphasize a
direct knowledge of the non-human world, one that cannot be obtained through
fanciful voyages of self-discovery in a mythic mode of (mis)representation and
(mis)understanding of the Other. Gratitude is not available in books, but through
experience. Kimmerer posits a "regenerative reciprocity" as a more equitable
way to interface with Nature as "people who were once indigenous" ourselves.
Recommending an experiential mending of broken ties and rekindling "our old
relationships with the living earth", Kimmerer's is constructed on solid ground,
rather than on the shifting sands of European mythologies.

4   Representations of Nature and Native Sexuality in *Rouge Brésil*

In contrast to *Vendredi*, *Rouge Brésil* criticizes Western environmental destruction by attacking Western attitudes, directly citing extractive practices linked
to the bourgeoning global capitalism of the sixteenth century. *Rouge Brésil*
"rais[es] the question of nature in colonial context" (Racevskis 78). If Tournier's ecological critique aims more broadly, Rufin has a narrower target. *Rouge
Brésil* addresses local problems associated with trade of brazilwood deforesta-
tion, and the ecological limitations of the island ecosystem where Villegagnon
elects to situate his camp. The island of Speranza, represents Edenic abundance.

Going Native: The Myth of Being Indian   133

The small island of the *France antarctique* colonial venture is evocative of consequences of excessive extraction. Villegagnon chooses an island without a reliable potable water supply or any appreciable means of subsistence. Echoing the inherent illogic of the Ignoble Savage myth, Villegagnon's decision comes from fear of the Natives on the mainland. One of the many ironies in *Rouge Brésil* centers on violence and danger. Villegagnon bases several decisions on anxiety about the Ignoble Savage's brutality, yet Rufin emphasizes the destructiveness of *French* practices vis-à-vis Nature and Native. The author's critical stance goes beyond the environmental to ridicule the entire Western superiority complex. Mocking the French, *Rouge Brésil* succeeds as a rewriting of De Léry's *Histoire d'un voyage faict en la terre du Brésil* (1578) because Rufin's text reiterates, in a more modern timbre, one that takes into account issues of environmentalism and feminism, the acerbic wit of the original. However, the author's primary focus is the European, again the "center of consciousness" with the Amerindian as "more of less incidental to the story" (Huhndorf, Introduction). The existence of real Natives is secondary and only transmitted through the mythic mode in a form that can be *recognized* in the French cultural imaginary. For Rufin, the critique of the environmental crimes of the French colony is offset against the *simplicity* of the Tupinamba, in the Noble Savage mode. Nude Tupinamba women and cannibalism are mentioned and condemned, yet little is learned of Tupinamba lifeways. As in *Vendredi*, ecological Going Native narratives fail to account for Amerindian histories and subjectivities. Presenting the Native as spiritually ecological without engaging with Amerindian practices performs a double "dismissal" of Indigenous culture (Handley, "The Postcolonial Ecology of the New World Baroque", *Postcolonial Ecologies: Literatures of the Environment*, Chapter 5). This "dismissal" is evident in *Rouge Brésil*, where rather than realizing an ecological transformation through contact with the mythology of the nexus of Nature and Native, Colombe is guided by the European Pay-Lo on her journey of self-actualization, a process that is always concerned first and foremost with the human Self rather than the non-human environment. Colombe's transcendence demonstrates that ecological Going Native should be interpreted as European myth rather than Native reality when Native lifeways are silently "dismissed". What does it mean to position the Native as symbolic spokespeople for safeguarding Nature? Reminiscent of the Noble Savage, the mythology of the nexus of Nature and Native is a slippery epithet with many consequences. Shepard Krech III pinpoints the advent of the nexus of Nature and Native, what he calls the Ecological Indian, in the 1960s and early 1970s. Krech seeks to revise Western understandings of the Ecological Savage.

> [Its] relationship to native cultures and behavior is deeply problematic. The Noble Indian/Ecological Indian distorts culture. It masks cultural diversity. It occludes its actual connection to the behavior it purports to explain. Moreover, because it has entered the realm of common sense and as received

134 *Going Native: The Myth of Being Indian*

wisdom is perceived as a fundamental truth, it serves to deflect any desire to fathom or confront the evidence for relationships between Indians and the environment. (27)

In Krech's analysis, "common sense" and "received wisdom" signal what I refer to as cultural imaginary. The mythology of the Ecological Savage is transformed from narrative technology into a "fundamental truth" about the Native, preventing deeper understanding of Amerindian ecological practices. In *The Ecological Indian*, Krech demonstrates how Amerindian peoples *did* historically alter their environments. Krech's motivation is to show that through environmental destruction, the Native does attain culture as understood from a Western perspective. While Krech opposes the "dismissal of history, technology, and culture" that Handley laments in reductive discourses of *primitive* ecological symbiosis, he overshoots his attempts to valorize Native cultures by insisting on their environmental destructiveness. One of the essential characteristics of myth is how it precludes reciprocal understanding. Mythic exclude the Native from the category of *human*. In the nexus of Nature and Native, might there be a space wherein Amerindian ecologies might be understood neither as minimal nor as destructive? Deterministic binaries of the mythology of the nexus of Nature and Native or *culture* definitions that rely on environmental damage do not accurately represent Native views of Nature. Environmental harm should not be a criterion for designation as fully human. Native peoples interact with the environment in a variety of ways, that diversity must be examined and considered if understanding of Amerindian cultures is to be anchored in reality, not distorted by the mythic machine.

As in the Noble Savage myth, (a)temporality is crucial to the nexus of Nature and Native. Idealizing Natives as ecologically exceptional prevents them from participating in life as subject. The mythic Ecological Savage is relegated to "colonial time", a "static" temporality that does not allow for advances to be made concerning the climate crisis (Bruyneel 2, Schweninger, Introduction). While I do not contend that non-Indigenous cannot learn about more balanced ecological practice from Amerindians, the mythologizing and authenticating of the Ecological Savage is appropriative and reductive. The myth of the Ecological Savage, a twentieth-century manifestation of the nexus of Nature and Native, proposes problematic temporalizations of Natives, disallowing them a "modern image of the future" by presenting them as rural, agrarian, or hunter/gatherer when large percentages of Amerindians inhabit urban areas. The Ecological Savage is complicit with settler-colonial ideologies of the *inferiority* of the Amerindian with echoes of *terra nullius*, closer to Nature often signifying outside culture. Ecocritical analyses should maintain a healthy critical wariness of facile conclusions about Indigenous peoples. A fine balance must be reached between valorizing environmental practices that uphold values of reciprocity and gratitude vis-à-vis the "more-than-human" world and repeating hackneyed mythic representations

Going Native: The Myth of Being Indian   135

of Amerindians as Ecological Savages. Solutions for the environmental crisis will necessarily come from many traditions. Proposed answers that come from Indigenous peoples must be considered without ceding to the mythologizing of a "return to nature", related to myth of Going Native. Having discussed Nature and Native in *Rouge Brésil*, another feature must be examined: sexuality.

Native sexuality has been instrumentalized as a marker of essentialist difference in since first contacts. Difference based on sexuality is also a key component of the mythology of Going Native in *Rouge Brésil*. While Native sexualities often fall in the Ignoble Savage category, it is appropriated by Rufin as a path to self-actualization. Native sexualities or French simulations of Native sexualities are critical to European's Going Native experience. Sexuality and sexual normativity inform Rufin's text in many ways. Colombe's androgyny can be interpreted through what Morgensen calls "the colonial object berdache" (55). Morgensen views settler-colonialism as a critical site of anthropological inquiry into the formation of non-Native *queer* identity, primarily in the late twentieth century. "Settler colonialism is naturalized whenever conquest or displacement of Native peoples is ignored or appears necessary or complete, and whenever subjects are defined by settler desires to possess Native land, history, or culture" (16). It is precisely in association with the desire to "possess Native culture" that French (and Québécois) iterations of the myth of Going Native reiterate settler-colonial ideologies. Sexuality is a privileged site of essentialist difference that is constructed in discourses by engaging the "colonial object berdache" (Morgensen 55). Berdache is an anthropological conceptualization for theoretically understanding Native sexuality. It is instrumentalized to generalize about Native sexuality and its (im)morality according to Western (mis)understandings of Amerindian peoples. As a theoretical object, it attempts to generalize Native roles wherein sexually ambiguous, transgender, and/or homosexual individuals (typically male) are granted special, often revered, status in Indigenous cultures.

> While appearing to describe Native Americans, berdache presented a primordial mirror to the civilizational modernity of colonial and settler subjects. It cohered an object of knowledge that described a gender-transitive and homosexual subject, defined by male embodiment, who received social recognition in Native American societies. Over time, the object projected a uniformity of sex, gender, sexuality, and indigeneity that let it represent principles of human nature and culture. Disagreement over its definition regularly called its qualities into question, but that very deliberation promulgated berdache as a key object of colonial desire for Indigenous and sexual truth. (55)

Morgensen pinpoints the function of berdache as a tool for European self-definition. Propping up berdache as the moral opposite of European sexual normatives allows the European to define themselves ontologically in contradistinction to Amerindian peoples. Berdache not only *queers* those Natives who are

136 *Going Native: The Myth of Being Indian*

trans-genitive or homosexual, but *queers* all non-normative Indigenous sexual practices, such as nudity or offering women to visitors as sexual partners. One of Morgensen's most important insights is his understanding of the conflation of berdache with sexual uniformity or androgyny. While initially employed to construct difference, subsequently berdache is coopted to connect *modern* non-Native homosexuality to *primitive* Native sexuality, constituting a sexual iteration of the Going Native myth. Through both *queered* Native nudity and androgyny, Colombe, having completed the process of Going Native, can be interpreted as an instantiation of the colonial object berdache. The young female protagonist must dress as a boy to gain admittance on Villegagnon's ship. Cross-dressing is not directly related to any announced transgender identification by that character. Rather, crossdressing is presented as repressive. Colombe's unveiling of her femininity is portrayed as a liberating act, a coming out. Colombe's "coming out" as heterosexual female, symbolized as sexual freedom and *truth* by her Native nudity, can be interpreted as *queering* crossdressing. Cisgender normativity is reinforced within Rufin's plot. However, Rufin is making a feminist critique rather than attempting to naturalize cisgender. It is Colombe's right to assume her heterosexual female identity that Rufin wishes to assert. How does Colombe realize or perform her sexuality, her gendered *truth*? It is through the mythology of Going Native that she "comes out" of the prison of her Western heritage. Nudity, in contradistinction to repressive, patriarchal, and colonial crossdressing, is the key to Colombe's philosophical and sexual transformation. Nudity has a long history in the representation of the Amerindian, often being cited as a marker of essentialist difference in the Ignoble Savage mode. Rufin's representation of Amerindian nudity is a departure from the negatively inflected coding of that tradition. Native nudity the key to sexual *truth* in *Rouge Brésil*. The author replaces the negative image of the nude Ignoble Savage for the redemptive model of the nude Noble Savage, which serves as catalyst for the myth of Going Native.

> [She] was especially happy to have dropped the mask and doubly affirmed her freedom: by unveiling her true identity and by showing that, being a woman, she didn't need to be locked into any of those other prisons, of modesty, false prudishness, and frilly dresses. In that moment, running through the bouquets of euphorbia and frangipani, her body hardened and stroked by ritual paint, young and taut like the swollen leaves of the rubber tree, she felt like she was at the crossroads of all the strength and softness, of hardness and tenderness. No place on earth, no other time could have given her this freedom, this power. As the pale blue of the water of the bay became visible above the trees, she felt her soul take on the same pastel tint without casting a shadow on her happiness. (Rufin 379, my translation)

Colombe's process of Going Native is related specifically to Native sexuality through nudity. Native nudity is a catalyst for self-actualization. Rather than

Going Native: The Myth of Being Indian 137

being labeled uniquely feminine, Colombe exhibits androgynous characteristics. This is hinted at in the designation of her body as "hardened". Racevskis contends that Colombe inhabits a liminal space as to her performance of gender roles, calling her a "purposefully androgynous character" (76). In conjunction with crossdressing, Colombe's performance of male coded behaviors is significant. Colombe, having successfully Gone Native, represents how the French cultural imaginary views the Native through the mythic lens. Her character is a positively inflected (i.e. Noble Savage) manifestation of the tradition of mythic representations of the Native. As a nude female hunter, Colombe is a *modern* Western articulation of the androgyny associated with the "colonial object of berdache", and more generally of its *queered* correlate Native nudity, which functions as a critical element of the mythology of Going Native in *Rouge Brésil*. Berdache is a useful critical tool in analyses of mythologies of Going Native, because it further elucidates ways in which textual representations of the Amerindian are appropriative despite seemingly valorizing Native practices. Through berdache as an integral element of sexually inflected stories of Going Native, as in *Rouge Brésil*, the original myth of the Noble Savage is reinforced and reiterated in a new form, one which utilizes new narrative technologies. The colonial and colonizing constructions of berdache and Going Native do not transcend earlier mythic paradigms; they only provide a new variation of the same simulations of the "indian". After approximately four and a half centuries (the time separating the writing of De Léry's *récit de voyage* and Rufin's novel), mythic paradigms remain largely unchanged. Myth continues to be the lens through which the French envision the Amerindian. Whether narratives of Going Native are articulated via visions of Nature as informed by the myth of the Ecological Savage or non-normative sexualities that are positively inflected through the colonial object berdache, foundational myths from the earliest periods of contact continue to circumscribe French (mis)understandings of the Amerindian. In the next section, I shift focus away from France, turning my attention to the literature of Québec and an examination of how French-Canadian authors engage with the representational tradition of myth.

5   The Mythic Indian in the Québécois Cultural Imaginary

Throughout this study, I have predominantly examined texts written by French authors. While many of these writers have important ties to Québec, notably Samuel de Champlain and Henri-Émile Chevalier, all the authors in the corpus are commonly categorized as French. In this section, I explore the literary tradition of Québec and its contribution to the evolution of Francophone mythologies of the Native, or as they are known in Canada: First Nations. The literature of Québec is linguistically and culturally linked to the French literary tradition. Reaching maturity during the twentieth century, it is often considered a distinct *national* literature by Quebeckers and critics alike. In the domain of

138 *Going Native: The Myth of Being Indian*

French Studies in the North American academy, Québécois literature often finds itself situated under the umbrella of Francophone (World) Studies. By analyzing the literary representation of the Amerindian in the context of French-speaking Québec, I widen the scope of this study to include not only a *Francophone* voice, but one which has a much closer proximity to Natives. This section aims to situate Francophone Québécois literature's mythic (mis)representations of the Native both historically and transnationally. Before directly analyzing texts that portray the Amerindian, it is worthwhile to sketch a history of the representation of the Amerindian in the literature of *la Belle Province*. What follows does not purport to be a comprehensive survey of what would be a corpus much too large to address in the context of this volume. Rather, this concise chronicle of the Native in French-Canadian literature highlights some major texts. The third chapter focused on the mythic machine's narrative technology of the Vanishing Indian, demonstrating the influence of that lens as an interpretive model for apprehending the category of the Amerindian in the nineteenth century. The poem with which I commence this history of the Native in Québécois literature employs the same mythic lens.

François-Xavier Garneau is born in the city of Québec in 1809 into a well-established family whose presence in French-Canada dates to the seventeenth century. A self-taught intellectual who cut his literary teeth reading the works of Milton, Shakespeare, Montesquieu, and Voltaire, Garneau is most renowned as the father of Québécois history (Roy 165–6). Garneau wrote a seminal work on Canadian history, the first of its kind, emphasizing a French-Canadian perspective. It would become the definitive history for French-Canadians for decades to come and is still read nearly two hundred years later. Garneau's poem "Le dernier Huron" published in 1840 is inspired by a painting from one of Canada's most important portraitist and painters of religious themes of the nineteenth century, Antoine Plamondon (1804–1895). Plamondon's *Le dernier Huron* (The Last Huron) (1838) is a "symbolically charged image of a human being in communion with nature" (National Gallery of Canada). The mythic modes of the Vanishing Indian and the Ecological Savage are clearly present. The poem is compelling for many reasons. First, it becomes a sensation at the time, likely causing Plamondon's eponymous painting to gain levels of celebrity it might not have otherwise enjoyed. The popularity of the poem is evidence of its influence upon the *crystallization* of the Amerindian in the Québécois cultural imaginary. Second, the poem engages with prevailing mythic paradigms regarding the Native, including the Vanishing Indian. Indeed, the title frames the piece in the mythic mode of *disappearing* the Amerindian and the Vanishing Indian mythology is echoed throughout. In the initial stanza, Garneau laments the "extermination" of New France's staunchest Amerindian allies of the seventeenth century, abandoned to their fate of near total destruction at the hands of the Iroquois (Haudenosaunee).

Going Native: The Myth of Being Indian   139

TRIOMPHE, destinée! Enfin, ton heure arrive.	TRIUMPH, destiny! At last, your time has come.
O peuple, tu ne seras plus.	O people, you shall be no more.
Il n'errera bientôt de toi sur cette rive	The only part of you that will soon wander this riverbank
Que des mânes inconnus.	Shall be the unknown spirits of the dead.
En vain le soir, du haut de la montagne,	At night, in vain, from the mountain top,
J'appelle un nom: tout est silencieux.	I call out a name: all is silent.
O guerriers, levez-vous; couvrez cette campagne,	O warriors, rise up; cover this countryside,
Ombres de mes aïeux!	Shadows of my ancestors! (Allpoetry, my translation).

There are several elements that are redolent of the mythic mode of the Vanishing Indian, notably the ineluctability of the extinction of the Huron. The "unknown spirits of the dead" recall the martyrology of the French Western, a contemporaneous cultural production. In addition to the *disappearing* of the Native, "Le dernier Huron" engages in the Noble Savage mythology that is often concurrent with the guilt of the Vanishing Indian leitmotiv.

Libres comme l'oiseau qui planait sur leurs têtes,	As free as the bird that flew over their heads,
Jamais rien n'arrêtait leurs pas.	Nothing ever stalled their march.
Leurs jours étaient remplis et de joie et de fêtes,	Their days were full of joy and celebrations,
De chasses et de combats.	Of hunts and battles.
Et dédaignant des entraves factices,	And scorning false fetters,
Suivant leur gré leurs demeures changeaient;	Following their will, their abodes changed,
Ils trouvaient en tous lieux des ombrages propices,	Everywhere they went they found propitious shade,
Des ruisseaux qui coulaient.	And flowing streams. (Allpoetry, my translation).

140   *Going Native: The Myth of Being Indian*

In this stanza, the idealization of the innocence of the Noble Savage mythology is present. Associated with birds and a life of continual happiness, the "Noble" origins of the Noble Savage myth are reiterated. Hunting and waging war, the purview of the nobility in the Old World, is grafted onto the Amerindian. Characterized by freedom, the Native inspires jealousy because of the Amerindian's ability to slough off "false fetters", a reference to a modernity maligned throughout the poem. The poet even praises nomadic lifeways, a step rarely taken by European authors, even those who employ the Noble Savage. The bucolic description of the landscape here is in marked contrast with a landscape described in the second half of the seventh stanza.

Plus de forêts, plus d'ombres solitaires;	No more forests, no more solitary shadows;
Le sol est nu, les airs sont sans oiseaux;	The ground is bare, no birds are in the sky;
Au lieu de fiers guerriers, des tribus mercenaires	In the place of proud warriors, mercenary tribes
Habitent les coteaux.	Inhabit the hillsides. (Allpoetry, my translation)

In this passage, the landscape is a hellscape that the author equates, not with the Native, but with the rise of industrialism in the Saint Lawrence River valley. This period is characterized by an ever-growing encroachment of economies of extraction into the heretofore primarily agrarian society of Québec. "Le dernier Huron" dramatizes social crises of mid-nineteenth-century Québec *and* laments the demise of the Huron. The piece's focus on contemporary Québécois dilemmas belies a facile interpretation that would situate the Amerindian as the "center of consciousness". The poem is an iteration of the Going Native myth. In the first stanza, the author refers to the ghostly remnants of the Huron lamented throughout the stanza as Garneau's own "ancestors". In the final verse of stanza eleven Garneau calls the "extinct" Huron "relatives and friends" (Allpoetry, my translation). In the following stanza, the author proclaims that, "I am the only one who remains to transmit their memory to the people of our time" (Allpoetry, my translation). The elaboration of the Vanishing Indian and Going Native myths is often concomitant. The (symbolic) violence of the *disappearing* of the Amerindian can be linked to replacement, wherein the non-Native writer *speaks for* the Native group. The narrative technology of Going Native obfuscates the complicity between Going Native's supposed valorization of "Indigeneity" and symbolic extermination in the mode of the Vanishing Indian. Although the following comments are made in reference to the American context, Philip Deloria's (Standing Rock Sioux) insights are valuable for reading Garneau.

Going Native: The Myth of Being Indian 141

> The dispossessing of Indians exists in tension with being aboriginally true. The embracing of Indians exists in equal tension with the freedom to become new. And the terms are interchangeable. (191)

In this significant early text in the history of the representation of the Native in Québécois literature, the author coopts Native identity to lay claim to an aboriginal belonging to the land, thereby seeking to pass as "aboriginally true". The poem speaks in the tragic mode regarding the "extinction" of the Huron *and* the erosion of traditional French-Canadian lifeways. In the final stanza, Garneau prophesizes the renaissance of the Native, laying waste to the "pompous cities" of modernity (Allpoetry, my translation). The author asks, "Who knows? Maybe then the Indians and their forests will be reborn on these banks" (Allpoetry, my translation). Returning to an anti-modern golden age is not so much about the return of the Huron, victims of symbolic *disappearance* via the Vanishing Indian myth, but the "freedom to become new" that Deloria pinpoints as a necessary ingredient in taking on the identity of the Amerindian Other. This poem celebrating rural values is the harbinger of one of the most significant movements in the history of Québécois literature: the *roman du terroir*. The most famous example of that genre is undoubtedly *Maria Chapdelaine* (1913) by Louis Hémon, the next text I will discuss in this chronicle of the mythic literary representations of the Amerindian in Francophone Canada.

Although the author Louis Hémon is a Breton and not a French-Canadian by birth, the novel *Maria Chapdelaine* is a quintessential text of the Québécois canon. Portraying the French-Canadian equivalent of a pioneer tale, the perennial *défricheur*, or land-clearer, Samuel Chapdelaine is the novel's patriarch. Samuel continually moves further from "civilization". The text is situated on the frontier, a liminal space that juxtaposes Nature and Culture. Three suitors of the young eponymous heroine serve as archetypes of different life paths. The three characters are emblematic of the past, present, and future at the beginning of the twentieth century. Lorenzo Surprenant, an émigré living near Boston, represents modernity and a radically different lifestyle from the agricultural work that the novel praises as the heart of the Québécois national character. The surname Surprenant, which translates to "surprising" in French, expresses the unlikelihood that Maria will choose an "American" life. Eutrope Gagnan is a *paysan* much like Maria's own father. The stable choice, Gagnan is a constant presence and help to the family. From a temporal standpoint, Gagnan is the present, the ever-advancing present of the frontier in liminal geographies. The surname Gagnan foreshadows the novel's dénouement. Gagnant signifies "winner" in French and the dependable option does win Maria's hand in the end. The third suitor, and most critical for the discussion of the representation of the Amerindian in Québécois literature is François Paradis. An evident ersatz for the coureur de bois figure, he is the dangerous choice, spending his winter in lumberjack camps in the Great North and with Amerindians. A pure adventurer and symbol of the

142 *Going Native: The Myth of Being Indian*

fur trade so central to the history of New France, the first name François is an allusion to the collective Québécois past: France. The choice of the surname Paradis, the cognate "Paradise" in French, hints at the unattainability of the seductive option of the three. It is through Paradis that the novel explores the theme of the Native. During Paradis' first visit to the Chapdelaine homestead, the young man recounts a story that engages in mythic representations of the Amerindian.

> No, I never had any difficulty with the Indians; I always got on very well with them. I know nearly all those on the Mistassini and this river, for they used to come to our place before my father died. You see he often went trapping in winter when he was not in the shanties, and one season when he was at the head of the Rivière aux Foins, quite alone, a tree that he was cutting for firewood slipped in falling, and it was the Indians who found him by chance next day, crushed and half-frozen though the weather was mild. He was in their game preserve, and they might very well have pretended not to see him and left him to die there; but they put him on their toboggan, brought him to their camp, and looked after him. Always after that they used to pay us a visit in the spring, and father had the pick of their best skins for less than the companies' buyers had to pay. When he died they treated me in the same way because I was his son and bore the same name, François Paradis. With more capital I could have made a good bit of money in this trade-a good bit of money. (Hémon 32)

In this passage, Paradis presents his credentials as an expert on the Amerindian, revealing a long familial history of positive relations with the Native. However, the tension between the Noble and Ignoble Savage lingers just below the surface, as does the danger that the forest represents. Paradis *père* is hunting on the Natives' land without permission, trying to exploit the natural resources of Amerindian territories held in common. Signaling the specter of the Ignoble Savage, Paradis *fils* speculates on the inhumane potential of the Native who could have left his father for dead. The violent and redemptive possibility of the mythic machine's image of the Amerindian is juxtaposed. The duality of the Noble and Ignoble Savage is doubled with that of the coureur de bois. There is a long history of the coureur de bois being associated with both the outlaw *and* the hero in the Québécois cultural imaginary. Historian Gilles Havard states that, "In Québec, the coureur de bois, like the maple leaf, snowshoes, and the sugar shack, is an idealized image, an object of historical significance (*lieu de mémoire*) that feeds the myth of Québécois identity" (9, my translation). Although this passage is Paradis *fils'* claim to "specialized knowledge" of the Amerindian, there is equally a mercenary bent. Both Paradis are focused on economic profit as a central aspect of their relations with the Native. The senior Paradis takes advantage of his rapport with the Amerindian community to remunerate their furs at below market value. "Specialized knowledge" of the Native allows

Going Native: The Myth of Being Indian 143

him to leverage his experience to profit from his interaction with his "friends". Indeed, the son has learned the lessons of the father, as the younger Paradis regrets not having enough "capital" to exploit the commercial potential of this "specialized knowledge" of the Native. In Garneau's "Le dernier Huron", the Amerindian was hailed as an image of the "anti-modern", invoked to critique industrialization. Hémon's backwoodsmen employ Native credentials to maximize economic opportunities in ways that would be anathema to the bucolic image in Garneau's poem. This duality, the capacity to be instrumentalized in an anti- and pro-capitalist discourse in the mythic mode, is central to the narrative technologies of myths of the Amerindian and their manifestations both in the French and Québécois cultural imaginaries. The younger Paradis does not take all the Natives' lessons to heart, however. In fact, he dies when trying to visit Maria during a blizzard, losing the battle of Man versus Nature. When others at the lumberjack camp urged him not to risk his life by making the voyage in such harsh conditions,

> he only laughed and told them that he was used to the woods and that a little difficulty was not going to frighten him, because he was bound to get to the upper side of the lake for the holidays, and that where the Indians were able to cross he could make the crossing too. Only—you know it very well, Mr. Chapdelaine—when the Indians take that journey it is in company, and with their dogs. François set off alone, on snow-shoes. … …He went astray. (Hémon 85)

Paradis' arc of Going Native is doomed to failure. Taking the (physical) path of the Native to traverse the landscape in treacherous weather, the individualistic bent of the young man leads to his undoing. The coureur de bois makes the mistake of going it alone in a blizzard, favoring the Self over the collective, something that even the misanthropic farmer, Mr. Chapdelaine, knows is folly. Paradis' hubris vis-à-vis Nature is based in part on his "specialized knowledge" of the Amerindian. However, as is reiterated throughout the Western literature *ad infinitum*, the adage of "pride cometh before the fall" is realized once again, because the lessons of the forest and of the Natives are not learned. In the world of Hémon's novel, Paradis' early end constitutes a cautionary tale, relegating the coureur de bois *and* the Amerindian to the past and the natural world, refusing a "modern image of the future" to either. Elsewhere in the text, Hémon depicts the Amerindian as an atavistic artifact in the mythic modes of the Noble Savage and the Vanishing Indian.

> Four hundred miles away, at the far headwaters of the rivers, those Indians who have held aloof from missionaries and traders are squatting round a fire of dry cypress before their lodges, and the world they see about them, as in the earlier days, is filled with dark mysterious powers: the giant Windigo

144   *Going Native: The Myth of Being Indian*

> pursuing the trespassing hunter; strange potions, carrying death or healing, which wise old men know how to distil from roots and leaves; incantations and every magic art. (Hémon 51)

Hémon distances the Natives in this passage from Euro-Canadian civilization, situating them at the antipodes of the modern world. This is an indication of the *authenticity* of this group who are different from other Natives, those in closer proximity to Whites. However, the passage puts the Euro-Canadian François Paradis in the scene. Obfuscating the Euro-Canadian presence in the *absence* of the White. Like "Le dernier Huron", Paradis is the only one capable of telling the *true* tale of the Native because he is uniquely equipped with "specialized knowledge" that adheres to his status as archetypal coureur de bois, as the "center of consciousness" of the Going Native narrative. Relegated to a "static" existence in "colonial time", the Natives in the excerpt are in a mythic space akin to Rousseau's state of nature. This mythic temporality and geography is reinforced by the appearance of the Windigo. The Windigo punishing the "trespassing hunter" recalls the story about Paradis' father who is saved by the Amerindians upon whose land he is, indeed, a "trespassing hunter". Rather than paying for his transgression, Paradis *père* is rewarded with hospitality and monetary gains. The "dark mysterious powers" attributed to the Amerindian elders are firmly entrenched in the Ecological Savage myth. These powers are attained through a preternatural understanding of the natural world, of its "roots and leaves". For all that, the passage is contradictory. The author attributes everything and its opposite to the mythic Native who can conjure "death and healing". The imagery Hémon utilizes resembles descriptions of another mythic European archetype rather than the Native, namely the much-maligned witch. With "dark mysterious powers", she concocts her "strange potions" and mutters "incantations", as she practices her "magic art". As will be reiterated in the following section, what emerges from an examination of the Québécois cultural imaginary's *crystallized* lexicon of mythic representations is its striking similarity to the French examples covered previously. Despite closer proximity and personal experience with the Amerindian, mythic messages continue to be a vehicle for (mis)understandings through the Noble, Ignoble, and Ecological Savage, the Vanishing Indian and Going Native.

As I stated above, the works that I cover in this chronicle are merely selections from a vast corpus that does not lend itself to the economy of a monograph. Some texts that I did not discuss at length, but that deserve mention as significant examples of the representation of the Amerindian in Francophone Québécois literature include the following texts. Continuing the "witch" theme, *La déesse brune* (The Brown Goddess) (1948) by Albert Gervais mythologizes a sexualized Innu sorcerer that is redolent of both Noble and Ignoble Savage mythologies (Morency 85–6). *Un dieu chasseur* (A Hunter God) (1976) by Jean-Yvès Soucy recounts a modern-day coureurs de bois who is initiated via the mythology

Going Native: The Myth of Being Indian   145

of Going Native yet does not internalize the Ecological Savage's purported symbiosis with Nature, rather both hunters give themselves over to excessive killing of non-human animals. The ironic final sentence of the novel is the author's acerbic commentary on the Going Native trope. For all his "initiation", the protagonist Mathieu only refers to his Native guide as "the Indian". In the dénouement, the Euro-Canadian finally thinks to ask the Native man his name (Soucy 241). Soucy insists on the lack of "specialized knowledge" obtained by the novel's main character, undermining the validity of the Going Native mythology. Daniel Pouliquin's *L'Obomsawin* (1987) is an exploration of the limits of recognition of the Other via a litany of stereotypes in the modes of the Ignoble, Noble, and Ecological Savages, as well as the Vanishing Indian and Going Native mythologies. Leaning heavily on sarcasm, cliché, and satirizing Euro-Canadian expectations of what "indians" should be, the text addresses authenticity and identity. The book's antihero Thomas Obomsawin, on trial for arson, reveals his lack of authentic Native credentials, despite having gained international fame as an *Indigenous* artist.

> "Obom, are you really an Amerindian? Everyone thinks so."
>
> "No. I do have some Indian blood on my mother's side. But I can tell you that I was raised like a savage, and that I still live like one. It's funny, these days, city folk just love it when you tell them you're an Indian. It's in style again. I let everyone think whatever they want about me. It seems to make them happy. (170, my translation)

The question of identity is answered via narrative of *passing for*. Never fully disavowing his Native identity, Obomsawin reflects back to Québécois culture its own mythic stereotypes about the Amerindian. He drinks and smokes to excess and is accused of the violent crime, in the Ignoble Savage mode. Additionally, he is a talented artist speaking to Noble Savage and New Age idealizations. In the end, it is revealed that many works that he has gained celebrity for were actually painted by Ojibway and Cree painters. When asked if he is tired of lying, Obomsawin responds, "No, I've spent my whole life believing I'm something I'm not and making others believe I am something I'm not. One time more or less, what difference does it really make?" (180, my translation). Pouliquin's novel pushes the mythic to caricature and beyond, challenging the preconceived notions at the core of the mythic machine's fabrication of the Native in the Québécois cultural imaginary. A brief remark on the presence of the Native in Québécois literature, before beginning the next section. The Amerindian does not figure as prominently in Québécois national literature in comparison to the centrality of the Native in American literature and popular culture. Many Indigenous critics have argued that the settler-colonial society defines its identity in contradistinction to and in cooptation of the Native. However, in the specific case of Québec, the more imminent cultural danger, particularly since the defeat

146   *Going Native: The Myth of Being Indian*

of the French on the Plains of Abraham in 1760, has been constructing a cultural identity in a contest wherein the Anglophone Canadian is the Other and not necessarily the Amerindian. This contextualization may help to better understand the relatively marginal role played by the Native in the literature and popular culture of Québec vis-à-vis the United States.

5.1   Berdache: Sexuality and Mythologies of Going Native in the Francophone Literature of Québec

This section explores some striking similarities and differences between the French texts discussed in the first section of this chapter and Québécois authors' techniques for representing the Amerindian in mythologies of Going Native. *Volkswagen Blues* (1984) by Jacques Poulin and *Le dernier été des Indiens* (1982) by Robert Lalonde are germane examples for a comparison with *Vendredi, ou les limbes du Pacifique* by Tournier and *Rouge Brésil* by Rufin, because they engage with the model of the voyage of self-actualization. In both novels, representations of ambiguous or androgynous Native sexuality play a key role in the articulation of Québécois versions of Going Native. Both *Vendredi* and *Volkswagen Blues* involve the psychological transcendence of the European protagonist. As opposed to Friday, the First Nations character, La Grande Sauterelle, a métis who functions as guide to the French-Canadian protagonist Jack Waterman is an androgynous character. I incorporate Morgensen's theorizing of berdache in my analysis of both La Grande Sauterelle in *Volkswagen Blues* and Kanak, the principal First Nations character in *Le dernier été des Indiens*. The plotlines of *Rouge Brésil* and *Le dernier été des Indiens* have parallel trajectories. Both instantiate a subcategory of Going Native: sexual liberation realized through contact with the Native.

In *Volkswagen Blues*, Jack Waterman, a Montréalais novelist is facing an identity crisis when he encounters a métis woman la Grande Sauterelle, the big grasshopper in French, so called because of her long legs. Pitsémine, la Grande Sauterelle's name in her mother tongue of Innu, plays a traditionally female Amerindian role, familiar in the history of the *discovery* and exploration of the Americas: she acts as guide, echoing examples like Malinche and Sacajawea. Waterman's voyage is one of self-actualization that mirrors historic exploratory expeditions. Waterman covers the same ground as Jacques Cartier and Lewis and Clark as he moves westward, looking for his long-lost brother Théo. Like Crusoe in *Vendredi*, Waterman is internally conflicted and seeks remedy in contact with indigeneity. *Volkswagen Blues* references violence in Settler-Indigenous histories yet retains a mythic discourse that instrumentalizes the Native via the myth of Going Native. Poulin suggests parallels between the protagonist's identity and the collective trauma of Settler-Indigenous relations. The text is transnational; the characters traverse border between Canada and the United States and interplay with both countries' fraught histories. Waterman seeks internal psychological *truth* while learning the history of Euro-Amerindian conflict, explained by La Grande Sauterelle. She leads by sleuthing clues about Théo's whereabouts *and* she initiates him to stories of the land in relation to settler-colonial histories. Both conflicts/journeys are characterized by the centrality of guilt. As Waterman confronts his personal guilt over the abandonment of his brother, that singular regret is echoed in the collective Settler guilt as revealed by La Grande Sauterelle. In this lies the dual function that Pitsémine fulfills in the narrative arc of Going Native: guide for the individual redemption and psychological healing of the protagonist Waterman as well as guide for a curative, collective reckoning with Canadian and American settler-colonialism.

As in *Vendredi* and *Rouge Brésil*, Poulin presents an Amerindian character that is somehow responsible for the self-actualization of a non-Native. *Volkswagen Blues* ends with the parting of Waterman and La Grande Sauterelle, which prompts the narrator to summarize the meaning of their encounter and experience together.

> [Waterman] waved his hand until the Volks disappeared. When he went back into the airport, he smiled, despite everything, at the thought that somewhere out there in the immensity of America, there was a secret place where the Indian gods and the other gods were gathered together and held counsel with the goal of watching over him and lighting his way. (Poulin 320, my translation)

While Poulin portrays Waterman's metamorphosis as redemptive, the final sentence suggests a different reading altogether. As in *Vendredi,* where the ending forces the reader to question the validity of the Going Native experience, Poulin's dénouement is comparably problematic. Native and other Gods holding counsel to watch over Waterman demonstrates that the protagonist has put far too much emphasis on the individualistic dimension of the novel's Going Native trope. The collective aspect of the Settler-Indigenous narrative arc is strangely absent in this finale. Indicating the appropriative impetus of Going Native, Waterman's initiation emphasizes "self"-actualization and not the reciprocal reckoning over the Innu Pitsémine and the Québécois Waterman's shared histories. Poulin's *recognition* of colonial conflict in Waterman's Going Native, does not present Amerindian lifeways as central. La Grande Sauterelle's role is as guide, just as the Native gods' role is to benevolently watch over the troubled Québécois subject. The Euro-Canadian is the "center of consciousness" in *Volkswagen Blues*. Once the unsuccessful journey of Going Native is complete, Pistémine is abandoned, affirming her status as mythic "indian" and "more or less incidental to the story" (Huhndorf, Introduction). This is doubly confirmed by the protagonist's myopy and inability to truly confront the larger sociocultural history of settler-colonialism. Echoing the metaphor of La Grande Sauterelle as ersatz of Malinche and Sacajawea, Poulin's Amerindian leads the European to spiritual discoveries. While Waterman's journey is geographical, it gains its significance

148   *Going Native: The Myth of Being Indian*

in relation to the internal existential quest and historical apprenticeship. It is through his "specialized knowledge" of the Amerindian that he realizes his own personal *truth*. As is the case with Tournier's Crusoe, the Going Native myth's conclusion is ambivalent. At the novel's close, the Euro-Canadian is not substantially changed. The exploitative nature of his relationship with Pitsémine echoes that between the Canadian Settler state and First Nations peoples. One way in which *Volkswagen Blues* does transcend the superficial and clichéd in its representation of the Amerindian, differing from the French examples examined previously, is in its attention to colonial violence and the consequences of that history for Amerindians and Euro-Canadians. Historical and mythic objects ranging from a hand-written note by Jacques Cartier to the myth of Eldorado are some of the *landmarks* that Waterman and La Grande Sauterelle explore together on a journey that takes them from the Gaspésie to San Francisco, locating the novel in the American tradition of the road novel à la Kerouac. Bloodshed is often at the center of the Settler-Indigenous history revealed in the novel.

> It's America. You start reading the history of America and there's violence everywhere. It seems that all America was built on violence. (141, my translation)

La Grande Sauterelle reveals the psychological consequences of colonial violence, not merely historical facts and figures. The geographical and metaphysical are linked in Poulin's depiction of the land and the Native through their shared heritage of (intergenerational) trauma. Metaphorically, Poulin transfers those nefarious consequences onto the object of the protagonist Waterman's long-lost brother Théo, who is vegetative and no longer recognizes brother. Théo's psychological devastation symbolizes the ravages of settler-colonialism. A key aspect of Going Native in *Volkswagen Blues* are the parallels the author draws between the individual and the collective. Presenting Théo's mental state as a direct result of colonial violence insists on the colonizer's collective guilt vis-à-vis genocidal expansionism. Théo is directly linked to the inherent illogic of Manifest Destiny.

> One last thing: my brother Theo and the pioneers. The connection between them might not be obvious, especially since the only things that I've found are meaningless stories to tell you about my brother – a big house, a yard, a river, a snowmobile and stuff like that. But I'm sure there is a connection and it's probably this: my brother Theo, like the pioneers, was absolutely *convinced that he was capable of doing whatever he wanted.* (Poulin 149, my translation, author's emphasis)

The author makes the connection between capitalism and its *comforts*, the large house and attached yard, leisure associated with a typically Canadian recreational vehicle, and the legacy of colonial violence explicit. Rather than simply appropriate the mythic Amerindian as catalyst for a journey of self-actualization, Poulin presents an alternative version of Going Native. La Grande Sauterelle instructs Waterman on Amerindian perspectives that differ substantially from the accepted histories and their "manifest manners", revising and often simply informing Waterman about incidents that have occurred since the contact period. This engagement with the imperial past *and* present reshapes both characters during their voyage. *Volkswagen Blues* differs significantly from Tournier and Rufin's Going Native mythologies. Poulin grapples with the aftermath and continuing tensions of settler-colonialism. This *recognition* of Settler-Indigenous relations does not transcend the mythic origins of Going Native, however. Although La Grande Sauterelle is superficially cast in the clichéd role of female Native guide to a male European explorer, she resists categorization as either cultural traitor or submissive sexual conquest, two designations often imputed to guides and Amerindian women respectively within the literary tradition of Native representation. La Grande Sauterelle contradicts many gender-role stereotypes. In the elaboration of the mythic Amerindian in the Québécois cultural imaginary, gender and sexuality are vectors of *truth*.

Throughout the history of the mythic representation of the Native, French authors have been intrigued by *and* fearful of Amerindian sexuality. Often in the Ignoble Savage mode, Native sexual practices are condemned as non-normative. Nudity and concurrent *shamelessness* have been severely critiqued by some writers while others, such as Jean De Léry, have been unable to fully conceal their fascination. In addition to early indictments of Amerindian sexuality, eighteenth- and nineteenth-century authors show a tendency to romanticize Native sexuality according to European norms. In contrast, Québécois authors Poulin and Lalonde challenge traditional representational motifs regarding Native sexuality. Reading *Volkswagen Blues* and *Le dernier été des Indiens* through the critical lens of berdache allows for a more nuanced understanding of the mythic appropriation that is iterated in the novels' articulation of European (sexual) fantasies of Going Native. Through a metaphorical plasticity often ascribed to the Amerindian, both authors explore gender roles and sexual stereotypes vis-à-vis Settler normativities.

La Grande Sauterelle belongs to both races (non-Native and First Nations); her father is Euro-Canadian and her mother is Innu. This hybridity instigates identity conflict as she struggles with the history of her ancestors. This tension is reflected in her two names: Pitsémine (Innu) and La Grande Sauterelle (French). Throughout the history of the representation of the Amerindian in the French tradition mixed-race characters are often portrayed as displaying the *worst* characteristics of both peoples; the French Western regularly employs the topos. La Grande Sauterelle represents a departure from that tradition because she is easily construed as superior on many levels to her Euro-Canadian counterpart. La Grande Sauterelle acts as guide geographically, leading Waterman to his brother,

150   *Going Native: The Myth of Being Indian*

but also epistemologically, revising his understanding of Settler-Indigenous relations and histories, thereby *enlightening* him. This directly opposes previous representations of the mixed-race Native as bane. The most interesting ambiguity associated with La Grande Sauterelle centers on sexuality and Poulin's bending of gender roles. La Grande Sauterelle is presented as androgynous. In a scene where they seek accommodations at YMCA, La Grande Sauterelle dons masculine garb and a baseball cap to *pass for* male and spend the night with Waterman. Obvious parallels exist between La Grande Sauterelle and Colombe. Both characters are represented as transvestite and androgynous. In both cases, their performance of crossdressing is contextualized as a necessary adaptation to accommodate Western normatives. Young girls are prohibited from embarking on French colonial adventures in Rufin's text and YMCA regulations dictate that only males can occupy the same sleeping quarters in Poulin's *Volkswagen Blues*. Therefore, crossdressing can be read as expediency; however, the representation of the sexuality of the characters is more complex. In addition to the example of transvestitism, La Grande Sauterelle is an avowed automotive mechanic. This echoes Colombe status as Native hunter, because as mechanic La Grande Sauterelle exhibits behaviors that are stereotypically culturally coded as male. When the eponymous Volkswagen begins to run poorly, it is La Grande Sauterelle who performs an emergency roadside tune-up, getting them on the road again. Poulin emphasizes the switched gender-roles by portraying Waterman as unable even to assist by handing over needed tools, because he does not even know their names. Read from a heteropatriarchal perspective, Poulin's portrayal of the European male explorer as passive and effeminate and the Amerindian female, typically marked as passive and sexually available in narratives informed by the legacy of colonial ideologies and the mythic machine, as agentive disturbs gender stereotypes. This role reversal is repeated in a scene recounting the unique example of sexual intercourse between them. While sexual tension is present throughout, the romantic plotline is secondary to the identity quest and historical overview of Settler-Indigenous relations. La Grande Sauterelle initiates the sole sexual encounter in the novel. Inversing typical sexual roles of dominance and aggression, La Grande Sauterelle does not reflect mythic (mis)representations of Amerindian women. Disseminating knowledge, leading the expedition, and sexually possessing the Euro-Canadian male, La Grande Sauterelle's sexual identity counters mythic circumscription of the Native commensurate with the instrumentalization of the colonial object berdache as discussed in the previous section in reference to Colombe's Native nudity and androgyny in *Rouge Brésil*. In Lalonde's *Le dernier été des Indiens*, the First Nations character Kanak plays a similar role.

Le dernier été des Indiens engages with several of the mythic paradigms we are now familiar with, such as the Noble, Ignoble, and Ecological Savages, and the myths of the Vanishing Indian and Going Native. However, it is the latter, the iteration of the Going Native myth that is most compelling. Lalonde presents

Going Native: The Myth of Being Indian   151

two main characters: a French-Canadian teen named Michel and an adolescent First Nations named Kanak. As in *Volkswagen Blues* and *Vendredi* the Amerindian character acts as guide in the transcendence of the European protagonist. In *Le dernier été des Indiens*, the relationship between the two young men is primarily sexual. While sexuality occupies a relatively central position within the process of Going Native in Tournier and Rufin's texts, it is *the* critical site of identity transformation and Going Native in Lalonde's novel. Michel is initiated into sexual pleasure and the discovery of his body by Kanak. While *Volkswagen Blues* and *Vendredi* dramatize the Going Native myth through collective meaning by metaphorical connections between the individual and Western culture. In Lalonde's text the stakes are more intimate. Because Michel's sexual desires place him outside the mainstream French-Canadian community, his story is not attached to larger collective entities or structures. This example of *queering* the Going Native myth is at once refreshing and problematic. Michel will enter the seminary at the end of summer, an unavoidable plotline that heightens the tension created by the two identity forces threatening to tear the young man apart: his Québécois family and his burgeoning (homo)-sexuality with the Iroquois (Haudenosaunee) Kanak. In some ways, a failed coming out story, *Le dernier été des Indiens* represents the struggles of a young man at grips with a culture that does not accept his sexuality *and* a religious future that requires its complete repression. What role does the Amerindian play in the struggle? What representational consequences arise from the playing out of this *queer* iteration of the Going Native myth? Typical of the narrative technologies of the mythology of Going Native, the objective is self-actualization, which entails the discovery of *truths* about oneself or the broader human condition that lead to better physical, mental, spiritual, or sexual life thereafter. In Michel's case, discovering his sexuality largely constitutes this actualization. In keeping with previous examples of the Going Native myth, contact with the Amerindian serves as catalyst for transformative identity experiences. In Lalonde's novel, within the main character Michel's binary cultural situation, homosexuality is associated with Amerindian space and the natural environment, metonymically linking Nature and Native in the mode of the Ecological Savage in convergence with the Going Native narrative. Kanak, Michel's Amerindian sexual guide evokes innocence and liberty.

> Angelic or demonic, whatever you wanta call him, but he isn't greedy and he isn't a coward. Not at all prone to massacre. Not given over to laziness either. Completely the opposite of his legend. I've never seen him destroy, pillage. He never complains. Just, sometimes, at night, he screams. It's like with the wolf: when things are too much, like a song. (Lalonde 63, my translation)

Dismissing the Noble and Ignoble Savage myths, Lalonde seeks to inform the reader about the Amerindian in a reciprocal tone. A reciprocal discourse transcends the mythic imperative of Western discourses on the Native. By imbuing

152 *Going Native: The Myth of Being Indian*

a narrative with reciprocal images, dehumanization of the Amerindian through myth are decentered. However, reciprocal passages do not preclude a text from also engaging in mythologizing. In this excerpt, Lalonde's demystification makes an abrupt about-face when the author introduces the wolf metaphor as a means of connecting Native and Nature. There are few animal metaphors more mythically charged in the Western literature than that of the wolf. The wolf has long been an inhabitant of spaces at the periphery of civilization, arousing irrational fears. The mythic parallels are evident. Barry Lopez explains that "The truth is we know little about the wolf. What we know a good deal more about is what we imagine the wolf to be" (3). This sounds eerily familiar. Not only does the wolf function as metaphorical bridge between Native and Nature, but the instrumentalization of this animalized image continues the theme of (homo) sexuality as synonym for freedom, identity, release, and *truth*. Orgasmic release is inserted into various scenes in reference to what Lalonde asserts as an essential difference between Amerindian and French-Canadian lifeways. In one poignant example, Michel is told to get on his knees by the parish priest to pray. Lalonde compares the servitude and humility of genuflection in the context of the Catholic mass with the same physical action leading to the much more spiritual and fulfilling experience of performing fellatio on Kanak (22). The song of the wolf echoes the metaphor of sexual release as a signifier of natural liberty. Lalonde naturalizes homosexuality, repudiating the imputation of abnormality.

> Yes, I was born that night with them [the Indians], in them, among their innocence. I didn't do anything evil. I don't see and I still don't feel evil. Everything that lives penetrates. Why make me believe in the dankness of the rosary, in the laziness of the Mass, in the bland, in the soft? Now I know that everything that comes for real comes with momentum, with strength, with teeth, with skin, with the evening air, red hot, with the night! I see them, I touch them, I'm still shaking, even after the painful convulsions, then less painful, then transporting. I didn't lose consciousness. I am completely conscious, finally, without books or novenas, without fear, without evil. I am in the world, deflowered, brand new. (Lalonde 20, my translation)

Catholic epistemology is represented as lifeless and flaccid, while the Native is tactile and hard. Employing the Christian mythology of rebirth, Michel's resurrection originates with intercourse (in all senses of the term) with the Amerindian. The innocence of the Amerindian, resonant with the narrative technology of the myth of the Noble Savage, transfers into Michel through the homosexual act, exculpating the protagonist. Guilt is only distanced for a time, however. The young Iroquois (Haudenosaunee) Kanak is a symbol of (sexual) freedom related to experiences in the natural environment. In this iteration, Going Native is as fleeting as the teen's love affair. *Le dernier été des Indiens* engages in and refutes mythic modes. The *salvation* that Michel confabulates with Kanak is redolent of

Going Native: The Myth of Being Indian 153

other mythic "indians" in French and Québécois cultural imaginaries. Unable to continue his relationship with Kanak, Michel is taken away to begin his new life as a seminarist. When the truck gets a flat, Michel contemplates running away to rejoin Kanak, an idealized escape that can never be realized, a commonplace in mythologies of Going Native, but instead he fiddles with the radio controls, happening upon a report about the death of the Premier of Québec, Maurice Duplessis. Of greater collective sociocultural significance, Duplessis' reign known as the Grande Noirceur ("Great Darkness" in French) is a period characterized by ecclesiastical authoritarianism and abuses. The death of Duplessis does not reunite Michel and Kanak, but it does signal the dawning of a new era, the progressist shift known as the Quiet Revolution, *la Révolution tranquille*. While Michel's Going Native is temporary and limited to sexual identity, this ambiguous iteration of Going Native situates the Amerindian as a site of veridiction, a mythic place where *truth* can be found in the Québécois cultural imaginary.

Both La Grande Sauterelle and Kanak's polysemous natures are resonant with the original mythic paradigms of the Noble and Ignoble Savage. These mythic devices reveal deeper truths about Amerindian representation and Québécois cultural concerns. Faced with difference, writers are unable to disentangle fictional or scientific representations of Amerindians from the myths that first defined these peoples for the West. The genealogy of the original Noble and Ignoble Savage myths demonstrates how persistent these simulations of the Native can be. Developing as a logical consequence of and in conjunction with the advent of the Noble Savage mythology, the myth of the Ecological Savage is equally a product of the earliest period of contacts. Subsequently, Noble Savage ideology evolved into a nostalgia and guilt-laden romantic image known as the myth of the Vanishing Indian. The last evolutionary turn of the Noble Savage, itself a direct consequence of the void created by the *disappearing* of the Native effectuated in the mythology of the Vanishing Indian, is the Eurocentric fantasy of Going Native. These models have shaped the French cultural imaginary of and (scientific) *knowledge* about Amerindians. Within the articulation of the Going Native myth in both French and Québécois contexts, sexuality coded as non-normative from a heteropatriarchal European (settler) colonial perspective (Native nudity, gender ambiguity, crossdressing, androgyny, and homosexuality), portrays Native identity vis-à-vis Québécois identity in specific ways. Berdache is an effective theoretical tool for unpacking the significance of La Grande Sauterelle's sexuality and performance of gender in *Volkswagen Blues*, Kanak's and Michel's interactions in *Le dernier été des Indiens*, and the role of representations of Native sexuality in myths of Going Native. In the twentieth century, first anthropologists and then non-Native LGBTQIA groups appropriated and instrumentalized constructed knowledges about Native sexuality centered around the term berdache. Berdache is prototypically used to identify, "a gender-transitive and homosexual subject, defined by male embodiment, who received social recognition in Native American societies" (Morgensen 55). This definition

154　*Going Native: The Myth of Being Indian*

applies to early iterations of berdache. Yet, the concept evolves and becomes a generalized manner to understand Native sexualities and roles associated with gender ambiguity. Morgensen reminds us that, "Over time, the object projected a uniformity of sex, gender, sexuality, and indigeneity that let it represent principles of human nature and culture" (55). Originally associated with specific practices and embodiments, berdache becomes semantically generalized to include any Native sexualities and lifeways viewed as non-normative. Berdache *queers* Native sexuality and other divergent practices. *Queering* is often related to the Ignoble Savage. However, it is through appropriation and Going Native that berdache takes meaning in modern non-Native contexts. In *Volkswagen Blues* and *Le dernier été des Indiens*, La Grande Sauterelle's gender ambiguity and crossdressing and Kanak's role as homosexual guide reference the same vision of the Native as that instrumentalized by non-Native LGBTQ understandings of berdache as a site of identity and veridiction in narratives of Going Native. It is through contact with the *queer* Native that French-Canadian characters achieve self-actualization and discover the *truth* about themselves. In French and Québécois fiction, berdache is critical to discourses that locate self-actualization in parallel with appropriative and constructed representations of Native sexuality. Morgensen affirms that non-Native groups, "organized in a political culture that validated journeys to personhood for white male citizens by translating *primitive* roots coded as Native American into white settler modernity" (45). The process of metaphorical transformation of the European descent sexualized narratives of Going Native in the novels I have been discussing by Rufin, Poulin, and Lalonde performs a similar operation in the domain of esthetics rather than that of modern *queer* politics through mythically inflected (mis)understandings of berdache. Even though French and Québécois writers attempt to valorize Native practices and lifeways in narratives of Going Native, such works fail to transcend mythic modes that circumscribe possibilities for reciprocal understanding of Natives as human subjects. Returning to the French cultural imaginary, in the final section I explore the ways in which French structural anthropology, specifically the father of that school, Claude Lévi-Strauss, and his student Pierre Clastres, engage in their own journeys of Going Native.

6　Going Native: Structural Anthropology's Quest for Universal Human *Truth*

Born in Brussels, Belgium in 1908, Claude Lévi-Strauss (1908–2009) is widely acknowledged as the father of structural anthropology and one of the most influential social scientists of the twentieth century. As with Durkheim and his sociological discourse considered in the preceding chapter, Lévi-Strauss instrumentalizes mythic (mis)understandings of the Native, inherited from the French cultural imaginary, in specific ways in his articulation of what anthropology studies, as a discipline is or should be. In my analysis of Durkheim, I

Going Native: The Myth of Being Indian   155

focused attention on *De la division du travail social* (1893), a seminal work that theorizes the basic tenets of the discipline of sociology by referencing the Amerindian, a text chosen primarily because of its influence as *the* foundational text of that discipline. It frames and shapes how later sociologists understand the object of their study by establishing a clear-cut distinction between *primitive* and *modern*. Claude Lévi-Strauss, who tends to downplay the role of Durkheim in the evolution of his own thinking, nonetheless produces similar mythically inflected definitions of the Self and the Other, classifications informed by the mythological genealogies of the Native discussed thus far but most readily associated with the mythic machine's Going Native mode.

Rather than interpret and analyze the author's dense theoretical works, such as the four volume *Mythologiques* or the seminal *Anthropologie structurale*, I have chosen to primarily examine *Tristes tropiques* (1955). It is his most popular book, read within the discipline, it is also widely read by non-anthropologists and the French public. For this reason, it can be argued that *Triste tropiques* has more purchase in the articulation of a French cultural imaginary of the Amerindian than his more theoretical works. No other text reveals the subjective side of the renowned anthropologist's personal life and character to such a degree. Wendy Doniger states that, "in *Tristes Tropiques* he founded a new genre of introspective, subjective, lyrical writing about fieldwork that rescued the field of anthropology from scientific posturings" (*Myth and Meaning: Cracking the Code of Culture*, x). Part *récit de voyage*, part fieldnotes, and part theoretical analysis of Indigenous tribes of the interior of Brazil, *Tristes tropiques* is germane to the purposes of this study precisely because of its subjectivity. To examine Lévi-Strauss' personal journey of Going Native, no better example can be explored than *Tristes tropiques*, where the author grapples with the meaning of his mission and of anthropology: not to discover and plunder riches, not to proselytize, but to uncover universal *truths* that the anthropologist can take home to Europe and transmit to readers for their edification. As Doniger contends, *Tristes tropiques* resists the designation of anthropology as science. The "rescue from scientific posturings" can best be understood as an engagement with mythologies of the Amerindian in a subjective voice, which nevertheless considered scientific discourse by readers of *Tristes tropiques*. Lévi-Strauss' status of director at the prestigious École Pratique des Hautes Études at the University of Paris at the time of the book's appearance ensure that the professor's writings are considered real *science*, even if delivered in a subjective tone. Certainly, his appointment, four years after the text was published, as the chair of social anthropology at the preeminent Collège de France, a post that he would hold until 1982, only added to the scientific "authorial authority" of the discourse of *Tristes Tropiques*, to return to Bourdieu's formulation. In *Tristes tropiques*, Lévi-Strauss engages in a self-reflexive probing that questions the scientific nature of anthropology. He claims that directing the ethnographical gaze at other societies creates a possibility for objectivity, "when dealing with different societies, everything changes:

156 *Going Native: The Myth of Being Indian*

the objectivity that was impossible in the first instance [the analysis of one's own culture], is graciously afforded to us" (*Tristes tropiques* 46, my translation). However, Lévi-Strauss obliquely admits that the *knowledge* obtained by the ethnographer is illusory. Toward the end of the text Lévi-Strauss includes a synopsis of a play he wrote during a period of ennui. The main character, an obvious stand-in for himself, is described as melancholy upon returning to civilization.

> Now that he has returned loaded down with treasures: an explorer that high society fights over to have on the guestlist at their dinner parties, he's the only one that knows that this fame that he's paid so dearly for is based upon a lie. Nothing that they are giving him credit for discovering is real; the journey is a hoax: all of it appears true to those who've only seen its shadow. (455, my translation)

Candid and morose, the passage intimates Lévi-Strauss' self-doubt regarding the reception of his work, equally disclosing the author's inner conviction of its unworthiness. Admitting to the reader and to himself, or so it seems, Lévi-Strauss reduces the elegant theoretical models that he has gleaned from his experiences in South America to a shadow play that hides more *truths* than it reveals. Lévi-Strauss does not only write about his own personal contemplations in *Tristes tropiques*. He also engages intertextually with many of the authors discussed throughout this study, such as Thevet, Montaigne, Rousseau, Durkheim, and Defoe. Lévi-Strauss' intertextual reflections are evidence of the existence of the genealogy of the mythologies of the Amerindian in the French cultural imaginary as traced in this volume. Chapter titles such as "*Bon sauvage*" and "*Robinson*" indicate how mythologies of the Native inform Lévi-Strauss' writing about and (mis)understanding of the Native. By periodically alluding to and quoting them directly, it is as if these texts *and their myths* accompany the anthropologist on his personal voyage of Going Native. Rousseau's articulations of the state of nature intermingle with Lévi-Strauss' own thinking.

> Rousseau undoubtedly was correct in his belief that it would have been better, for our happiness, if humanity had stayed "in that middle ground between the idleness of the *primitive* state and a frenetic activity dedicated to our selfishness"; that the latter wasn't the "best for humanity". ... ...Studying these savages leads to something other than a utopic state of nature, or the discovery of a perfect society in the heart of the forest; it helps us to build a theoretical model of human society that does not correspond to any observable reality, but thanks to that model we can manage to untangle "what is natural and what is artificial in the current nature of man and to be thoroughly familiar with what no longer exists, with what might have never existed, and with what will probably never exist, but about which it is nonetheless necessary that we have a solid understanding, if we are to comprehend our current state" (*Tristes tropiques* 469, my translation)

Going Native: The Myth of Being Indian   157

Framed and informed by Rousseau's abstractions on the state of nature in the Noble Savage mode, Lévi-Strauss suggests the purpose of anthropology. What both Rousseau and Lévi-Strauss echo is how myths about Amerindians can be theoretically instrumentalized to ameliorate modern European life. While that "specialized knowledge" has no basis in "observable reality", it paradoxically *does* contain universal *truth*. Lévi-Strauss correlates theoretical truths derived from Going Native and the *future* happiness of Europeans. Deciphering the social structures and systematic meanings and similarities of Native mythologies operates as catalyst in a discourse of Going Native, much in the same way that contact with the Native in the fictional texts discussed in this chapter does. It is through 'specialized knowledge" of the Native that the European can be realigned or repaired, that they can find "middle ground". The Amerindian is the source of information the European can utilize to construct an "image of the future", perhaps one that isn't quite so "modern". The origin and site of truth is located with the Caduveo, Bororo, Nambikwara, and Tupi-Kawahib tribes he encounters. Lévi-Strauss explains that, "As for me, I had gone to the ends of the earth looking for what Rousseau called "the tiny incremental developments of the beginning"" (*Tristes tropiques* 376, my translation). By citing Rousseau, Lévi-Strauss positions his discourse in genealogical connection with the mythic discourse of the Noble Savage. This genealogical link establishes anthropology as a philosophical abstraction that nonetheless makes claims of universal *truth*, in the authoritative discourse of social *science*. Lévi-Strauss discusses the alienation of the ethnographer from his own society, describing the study of exotic societies as an attempt to escape one's own (458–9). Lévi-Strauss reveals personal truths about his own relationship to his work, French society, and the societies where he conducts research. His individual alienation from French society is, nevertheless, useful for the very society the ethnographer abandons. According to Lévi-Strauss, the instrumentalization of *knowledge* about the Native can ameliorate Western society.

> By learning about [other societies], we gain a means to detach ourselves from our own. Not that our society is completely bad or the only bad one, but because it's the only one that we need to free ourselves from: we are only bad in comparison with other societies. We put ourselves in a position to pass on to the second stage which consists, without taking anything from any other society, in utilizing them all to uncover the foundational principles of social life that it then would be possible to apply to better our own morals, and not those of foreign societies. (470, my translation)

Echoing the depreciative view of French society that Rousseau espouses, Lévi-Strauss posits alienation as a primary condition of ethnographical work. Alienation can lead to personal liberty. Even if French society is not irredeemable, "it's the only one that we need to free ourselves from". The severing of the

158   *Going Native: The Myth of Being Indian*

anthropologist from his own society is a requirement for the "second stage" in the process. The second stage involves uncovering universal *truths* about other societies to then transform one's own. This formula is redolent of the equation of the narrative technologies of the mythic machine's Going Native mode. Appropriative and extractive, it does not challenge Europe's exploitative stance vis-à-vis human and non-human Others; it reconfirms it. From his journey of Going Native, he extrapolates a greater significance for the entirety of French society and the Western world while signaling the unilateral nature of the supposed *transformation* to come in a neocolonialist return to the origin of our tracing of the mythic "indian" in the French and Québécois cultural imaginaries. It is only Western society that can benefit from the "specialized knowledge" mined via anthropological investigation of Amerindians, because Lévi-Strauss' vision of *primitive authenticity* or archaism privileges isolated Native peoples as the only bearers of *true* Amerindian culture. Contact can only benefit the European who discovers *truths* about humanity permitting societal liberation and (collective) self-actualization. The similarities between the mythic Going Native journey's fictional, non-fictional, and scientific iterations are evident. All these discursive regimes coopt mythic (mis)understandings of the Native to propose a better "image of the future" in individual and collective contexts. Yet, for the Amerindian, contact entails destruction. This perspective illustrates the imbrication of the Vanishing Indian and Going Native. It is the *disappearance* of the Native that prompts discourses of Going Native wherein Europeans replace the *disappeared* Amerindian as original and rightful inheritor of American geographies, "specialized knowledge", and universal *truths*. Lévi-Strauss proposes to remedy the ills of Western society by a philosophical extraction of "treasures" from the Americas, which closely follows the ideological tendencies of the colonial project *ab initio*.

Lévi-Strauss' *discovery* of the Tupi-Kawahib of the Amazonian rainforest is a significant interlude in *Tristes tropiques*. From first contact to today, mythologies of the Amerindian circumscribe how the French understand the Native. Through the mythic lenses of the Noble, Ignoble, and Ecological Savage, the Vanishing Indian, and Going Native that French and Québécois writers frame and distort the Amerindian. Lévi-Strauss is enthusiastic upon finding the Tupi-Kawahib.

> It is highly likely that these Indians are the last descendants of the large Tupi populations of the middle and lower Amazon, related to the coastal groups who met, in their golden age, the explorers of the sixteenth and seventeenth centuries whose stories signal the first awakening of ethnographic awareness of modern times: and it was due to their unwitting example that the moral and political philosophies of the Renaissance went down the path that inevitably led to the French Revolution. To be the first, perhaps, to enter a Tupi village that is still intact, is to catch up with, over four hundred years later, Léry, Staden, Soares de Souza, Thevet, even Montaigne, who, in the *Essays*, in the

Going Native: The Myth of Being Indian 159

chapter "On Cannibals", meditated on a conversation with Tupi Indians he met in Rouen. What a tempting proposition! (399, my translation)

In this passage, Lévi-Strauss situates the mythologies of the Amerindian written during the earliest periods of contact as central to subsequent political transformations in French and European history. The Renaissance and French Revolution, those harbingers of Europe's "modern image" of itself are put in parallel with the inevitable *disappearance* of the Tupi, whose golden age is at least four hundred years in the past. According to Lévi-Strauss, it is the encounter with the New World that sparks the philosophical innovations that lead to both the French Revolution's radical political upheavals and the "first awakening of ethnographic awareness", placing the Native at the core of intellectual developments over four hundred years in a transcontinental, transhistorical evocation of the Going Native mythology. Lévi-Strauss ends the passage by passionately associating his journey with those of mythic mentors such as Montaigne (who never traveled to the Americas), as a proposition too tempting to pass up. However, as my analysis of *Tristes tropiques* confirms, the universal *truth* Lévi-Strauss seeks in his own voyage of discovery proves to be little more than illusory, echoing the tropes of centuries past, through the epistemological sieve of the topical concerns of his own time. This text exemplifies the inability of the French writer/ scientist to escape the narrative technologies of the mythic machine. Myth informs and delimits French visions of the Amerindian from the sixteenth to the twenty-first century, dehumanizing and objectifying the Native as simulations, as "indians". The *transferability* of myth across discursive regimes such as fiction, non-fiction, scientific discourse is a testament to the powerful pull of myth on the Western mind. Next, I examine a direct intellectual descendant of Claude Lévi-Strauss by exploring his student Pierre Clastres' work.

6.1 Pierre Clastres and the Cannibal Collective

Pierre Clastres is born in Paris in 1934. He dies at forty-three years of age in a car accident in Gabriac, in the department of Lozère in southern France, in the summer of 1977. After philosophical studies galvanized by the philosophies of Nietzsche and Heidegger, Clastres develops an interest in anthropology and goes on to study under Claude Lévi-Strauss at the Collège de France. Abandoning a fervent communist stance after the Hungarian Uprising, his political leanings are a central for understanding his ethnographical work. Clastres adopts anarchism, which heavily influences his articulation of political anthropology, a field with which he is typically associated (Kalyniuk 219). Clastres' career is cut short by his untimely death, but he is remembered for his divergences from Claude Lévi-Strauss, rather than as a disciple. The two complementary monographs that I address in this section are *Chronique des Indiens Guayaki* (1972) and *La Société contre L'État* (1974). In the first, Clastres presents ethnographic findings

160　*Going Native: The Myth of Being Indian*

based on fieldwork in Paraguay, attempting to compile a comprehensive portrait of Guayaki lifeways. The second, more theoretical piece, focuses on the author's main contribution to political anthropology, notably the eponymous concept of the society against the state. In *conversation* with Rousseau and Hobbes, Clastres' anarchist anthropology rejects the presumptive violence of the human condition, setting his theories of the nature of politics against Hobbes' famous formulation, "No arts; no letters; no society; and which is worst of all, continual fear, and danger of violent death; and the life of man, solitary, poor, nasty, brutish and short" (Hobbes, *Leviathan*, Chapter 12). Denying that the state is essential to effectuate a transition out of the violence of the state of nature, Clastres claims that in Guayaki and other *primitive* Amerindian societies, "the form of political power associated with the state was already understood in its essence, and that these peoples warded off its corrupting influence" by organizing their polity to structurally limit the rise of authoritarian power (Kalyniuk 218). Clastre states that "*Primitive* society is the place where separate power is refused, because the society itself, and not the chief, is the real locus of power" (*Society Against the State* 154). Clastres locates the Native as a site of veridiction for his own personal politics of anarchism, a viewpoint that advocates the abolishment of the state as an unnecessary, repressive apparatus, one that unacceptably limits freedom. However, Clastres does attack the preconceived notions of the discipline of anthropology, especially the paternalizing gaze cast from above by the ethnographic subject onto their *primitive* object informants.

> The necessary condition is to abandon—ascetically, as it were—the *exotic* conception of the archaic world, a conception which, in the last analysis, overwhelmingly characterizes allegedly scientific discourse regarding that world. This implies the decision to take *seriously*, at last, the men and women who live in *primitive* societies, from every viewpoint and in all their dimensions: the political dimension included, even and especially when the latter is experienced in archaic societies as the negation of its opposite number in the Western world... More simply: just as our culture finally recognized that *primitive* man is not a child but, individually, an adult, in the same manner it will mark a slight progress when it comes to acknowledge his collective maturity as well. (*Society Against the State* 15)

Echoing elements of my own argument concerning the mythically constructed nature of scientific discourses, Clastres calls for what Kalyniuk describes as a "Copernican Revolution in anthropology that would put an end to this sort of heavy-handed, Eurocentric theorising, and finally approach the indigenous world on its own terms" (219). While refreshing, it is debatable whether Clastres' critique of anthropology is evidence that he avoids those selfsame pitfalls in his own work. The author's insistence on reciprocity with the groups whose "treasures" anthropology mines, comes at a turning point for the discipline as

Going Native: The Myth of Being Indian   161

it begins to reform practices and ideologies, a task still being pursued today. Clastres engages in a similarly extractive narrative of Going Native in his elaboration of political anthropology. An anarchist, he not surprisingly emerges from his experience with the Amerindian having acquired "specialized knowledge" that supports that very political thought, what is known as an imposed etic bias in the social sciences, "etic" referring to the outsider position of the ethnographer vis-à-vis the community they investigate. Clastres states that *"Primitive* society is the place where separate power is refused, because the society itself, and not the chief, is the real locus of power" (*Society Against the State* 154). According to Clastres, *primitive* society has found an elegant answer to the political crisis of concern to the anarchist anthropologist, namely the eradication of authoritarianism. Clastres posits the Native as a site of veridiction for his own personal politics of anarchism, a viewpoint that advocates the abolishment of the state as unnecessary. Clastres' conception of the society against the state employs narrative technologies of the mythic machine's Going Native mode stemming from the author's inherited French cultural imaginary's distorted vision of the Amerindian. His analysis of *primitive* and *modern* politics is largely based on a comparison of the binary of the Western political leader and the Amerindian political leader's roles in their respective societies. One of the fundamental axes upon which Clastres' argument for this essentialist difference hinges is the author's conceptualization of generosity. Flipping Hegel's master/slave on its head to provide a sound anthropological standing for an anarchist view of history, Clastres represents the relationship of the *primitive* leader vis-à-vis the community as that of slave vis-à-vis master. The chief is not in an egalitarian relation with his constituents, rather a position of servitude. In keeping with the generosity principle of Amerindian power, the chief distributes material wealth, not the other way around. The position of leader in a *primitive* society is not a path to riches, rather the community rarely *distributes* anything to the leader, except greater access to women in a context of polygyny. The leader is not exempt from the common lot and must "cultivate his manioc and kill his own game like everybody else" (*Society Against the State* 40). In Clastres' analysis, it is the leader who works the hardest out of the whole society. The class-leveling, anti-authoritarianism that Clastres *reads* through the sieve of his own political education is grafted onto the relation of reciprocity that the Amerindian leader maintains with the people. This an example of the narrative technology of epistemological displacement. The restriction of authority that Clastres is looking for is not the lived experience of the Guayaki, because they have not, despite the author's persuasive prose, constructed their entire political outlook on something that does not exist in their culture: authoritarianism. In accordance with Occam's razor, wouldn't it make more sense if the authoritarianism, that bane of the anarchist anthropologist, serves as the binary opposite against which *Clastres* constructs a mythic narrative of Going Native, instrumentalizing what he *observes* as neatly responding precisely to what he seeks? Is it really that surprising that

162 *Going Native: The Myth of Being Indian*

the anarchist anthropologist finds the source of his own political viewpoints in the *primitive*? At this point, we are in familiar territory, indeed. After all, it is not a case of the Guayaki revealing their "radical rejection of authority", which Clastres defines as "an utter negation of power", but an anarchist anthropologist mistaking reciprocal relation as a conscious collective effort to ward off the evils of Western political manifestations of power by limiting the personal authority of the leader (*Society Against the State* 43). The society against the state is not a universal *truth*, but one of personal concern to the author and his own society. This echoes Lévi-Strauss' determination of French culture as the "only one that we need to free ourselves from". The epistemological displacement at the core of the mythic machine's Going Native is especially evident in the monograph's final sentence.

> It is said that the history of peoples who have a history is the history of class struggle. It might be said, with at least as much truthfulness, that the history of peoples without history is the history of their struggle against the State. (*Society Against the State* 218)

An imperious proclamation asserting that the deterministic political evolution of the Amerindian develops as a struggle against the very thing that anthropology has repeatedly insisted does not exist in this society: authoritarianism. The struggle Clastres ascribes to "peoples without history" is his own, and it is of his own (myth)-making. Mythmaking has a long history of damaging Native communities. Its consequences are not limited to the realms of the representational or the symbolic. In *Chronique des Indiens Guayaki*, Clastres explores mythic vectors that morph into violence in the context of (settler)-colonialism. Cannibalism is a privileged mythic machine of meanings in the French cultural imaginary, from earliest contacts until now, but it has also been part of the exploitation and genocide of the Native.

Clastres demonstrates both a mythic (mis)understanding of anthropophagy and an enlightened revisionist take on the practice. In the first flush of excitement of his ethnographical fieldwork, cannibalism is contemplated via the lens of the author's cultural heritage.

> When I arrived at the Guayaki camp, I was very nearly convinced that all these Indians were practicing anthropophagy because the reputation people gave them for it went far back, precisely to the period when the first Jesuit missionaries settled the region. I was expecting to find myself in the middle of—delicious excitement—a tribe of cannibals. To my disappointment, they weren't. (*Chroniques des Indiens Guayaki* 252, my translation)

Clastres evokes the mythic histories of the past, Jesuit accounts of anthropophagy, to explain his "delicious excitement" (the pun not being lost on his [or my]

Going Native: The Myth of Being Indian   163

readers) at the prospect of meeting the myth in real life, of being a witness to cannibalism. The author frames cannibalism in the voice of the French cultural imaginary as sensationalized exotic othering in the Ignoble Savage mode, but also with an eye to the spectacular à la Debord.

> War on the Natives was forbidden and was known to be illegal, except in the case where it was legitimized and even commendable: when it had to do with cannibal Indians. On them, a total and relentless war was waged. The equation was quickly solved: all one had to do was claim that a tribe practiced anthropophagy to justify sending out military expeditions against them. From that point, whenever they needed slaves, they went looking for them for the pious reason that they were dangerous to their neighbors, that they killed people with the aim of eating them. It was false, in nearly every instance, but so many tribes perished in the European plantations and mines, because they were simply keen to have carte blanche in the fiefdoms they'd carved out for themselves, all so they could increase their profits more easily. (*Chronique des Indiens Guayaki* 255, my translation)

For the Spanish, and in particular the Jesuits, the mythic mode of the Ignoble Savage is a narrative technology. The second term, technology, emphasizes the manipulation of the myth by the European to achieve specific objectives. In the case of the Going Native myth, the objective is often a reflection of the non-Native protagonist's own desiring for individual or collective avenues to self-actualization, redemption, or reform. In chapter three, I broke down the salient features of the mythology of the Vanishing Indian, what Gerald Vizenor calls "manifest manners", gesturing to the myth's complicity in the very real conquest of the Western United States. In *Chronique des Indiens Guayaki* we are confronted with an incontrovertible illustration of the narrative technology of myth. The Jesuits instrumentalize the mythic discourse of the Ignoble Savage in one of its most extreme forms, the cannibal. As discussed in the preceding chapter, Europeans have especially condemned the variant of the practice that they (mis)represent as anthropophagy-for-food (Lestringant 69). For the Europeans who profit from the enslavement and dispossession of the Amerindian, the apparatus of the collective cultural imaginary's distortions of the Amerindian is a superstructure vis-à-vis the base practice of (cultural) genocide. Myth is a weapon in the war waged against the Native, a narrative technology that isn't only aimed at the Amerindian through the barrel of the Ignoble Savage mode's cannibal iteration, but also in relation to non-normative sexual practices. Clastres goes on to inform the reader that the mythic machine's Ignoble Savage mode led to the "immediate exploitation and death" of the Native (256). Another mythic message that landowners and plantation overseers hungry for free labor employ in their arsenal of narrative technologies is to claim that an Amerindian group includes male homosexuals. Homosexuality functions in similar ways

164 *Going Native: The Myth of Being Indian*

as cannibalism, both lead to very real consequences for Native communities. The reality of sexualities that are taboo according to Western conceptions of normativity is contested by Clastres in *Chronique des Indiens Guayaki*. In a chapter entitled "The Bow and the Basket", Clastres regains his structuralist form and explains that gender roles in Guayaki society are constrained by a rigorous binary that is directly related to the use of the bow (exclusively handled by males) and the basket (exclusively handled by females). To immediately complicate matters, Clastres introduces two exceptions to the rule. Krembegi, who the ethnographer describes as openly homosexual, a man who lives "as a woman in the midst of women" and "conceive[s] of himself as a woman" (*Societies Against the State* 108–9). In contrast, Clastres presents Chachubatawachugi, a widower who does not possess a bow, only hunting for small game by hand. Furthermore, the anthropologist equates the bow as object and bow-hunting as practice as *the* Guayaki definition of masculinity. In Chachubatawachugi's case, he is shunned by women in the tribe and the subject of ridicule. To explain these two exceptions, which from a structuralist point of view somehow prove the *truth* of the binary opposition ethically imposed upon them, to which they are exceptions. Chachubatawachugi carries a basket, but does not enjoy it, appearing "anxious, nervous, and often discontent" (*Society Against the State* 110). Furthermore, Clastres deduces that Krembegi is "normal" and Chachubatawachugi is a "logical scandal" and an "element of disorder" (110). Clastres' analysis illustrates the inherent illogic not of the scandalous Chachubatawachugi, but of his own structuralist interpretation. The language of logic and disorder addresses how the behavior of an individual that does not neatly fit the structures proposed by the ethnographer but is quite natural according to the lived experience of the Guayaki. Discriminatory behavior is a complex issue that does not fit an etic dualist grid, as the anarchist anthropologist's categorization of *primitive* societies as anarchists. Anthropologist Clifford Geertz pinpoints the ways in which mythic (mis)understandings function in Clastres' articulation of the mythic "indian".

> It is true that Clastres's Rousseauian primitivism, the view that "savages" are radically different from us, more authentic than us, morally superior to us, and need only to be protected, presumably by us, from our greed and cruelty, is, some New Age enthusiasts aside, not much in favor these days. (Geertz)

What Geertz pans for its romanticism and antiquated epistemological displacements is the mythic orientation of Clastres' anarchist anthropology. Before concluding the discussion of the mythic discourse of Going Native in French structural anthropology, I will briefly mention that there is a particularly contentious relationship between Amerindians and the academic discipline of anthropology. One of the most cogent Indigenous critics of anthropology has been Vine Deloria Jr. (Standing Rock Sioux). Deloria Jr. both recognizes the negative aspects of the Indigenous-Anthropology interactions and maps his hopes for the future.

Going Native: The Myth of Being Indian   165

During the period of its formal existence, anthropology has taken the values and institutions of Western civilization, acted as if they represented normality, rationality, and sanity, and leveled severe criticism of tribal societies, finding them lacking in the rudiments of civilized behavior. The policies of political institutions and the attitudes of American society toward tribal peoples have been shaped largely by the descriptions forged by the social sciences. Instead of possessing cultures that were different, but nevertheless a valid expression of how our species can live on this planet, tribal cultures have been understood as *primitive* efforts to become scientific and industrial, and failing efforts at that. It is now time to reserve this perspective and use the values, behaviors, and institutions of tribal or *primitive* peoples to critique and investigate the industrial societies and their obvious shortcomings. (220)

Deloria Jr. identifies the unidirectional bias of the anthropological project vis-à-vis the Amerindian by exposing the inherent illogic of the mythic machine and its narrative technologies. As in my discussion of Jesuit utilization of mythic discourses surrounding cannibalism and homosexuality, Deloria Jr. recognizes the very real negative consequences that the social sciences have caused by perpetuating mythic (mis)understandings of the Amerindian. Refusing the evolutionist determinism that has characterized many social scientists' conclusions about the Native, Deloria Jr. calls for reciprocity in place of objectification. Deloria Jr.'s call for Native epistemologies to be leveraged to address current crises in the West demonstrates a generosity that would share knowledge commonly rather than take and misshape knowledge via myth in an extractive model. Anthropology has been much maligned in Indigenous communities, yet Deloria Jr. insists on the possibility of a "modern image of the future" wherein Indigenous and Western ways of knowing can collaborate.

7   Conclusion

In this chapter I have extended my examination of the representational tradition of French literature vis-à-vis the Amerindian to encompass not only twenty- and twenty-first-century Continental examples, but also the Francophone literature of Québec. In the first section, I explained the function of the Going Native myth in *Vendredi, ou les limbes du Pacifique* by Michel Tournier and *Rouge Brésil* by Jean-Christophe Rufin, demonstrating ways in which the Going Native myth influences the French cultural imaginary's vision of the Native. I demonstrated how the colonial object berdache can bolster interpretations of gender ambiguity and androgyny in representations of *Rouge Brésil*'s protagonist Colombe and how *queering* of the Native introduces an ambiguity that at once dehumanizes and attempts to coopt "non-normative" Amerindian sexual lifeways. After a brief historical sketch of the representation of the Amerindian in Québécois literature, the discussion of Native sexuality and its connection to the mythologies

166 *Going Native: The Myth of Being Indian*

of Going Native in French literature led to an examination of the role of *queering* Native sexuality and gender in the Québécois novels *Volkswagen Blues* by Jacques Poulin and *Le dernier été des Indiens* by Robert Lalonde. Sharing many characteristics of French narratives of Going Native, the Québécois authors attempt to integrate Native histories and viewpoints, although these revisionist discourses do not transcend the greater mythic machine's power. Lastly, the social sciences role in the articulation of universal *truths* regarding the Amerindian was investigated through readings of Claude Lévi-Strauss and his student Pierre Clastres. Both French structural anthropologists engage in epistemological displacement and construct "specialized knowledge" based on contact with the Native that does not reflect Amerindians' lived experiences. In the next chapter, the mythic "indian" in the French and Québécois cultural imaginaries will no longer be the "center of consciousness", rather the focus shifts to Indigenous voices and futures by exploring Francophone Amerindian writers and their contributions to Québécois and Native American literatures.

Works Cited

Bruyneel, Kevin. *The Third Space of Sovereignty: The Postcolonial Politics of U.S. –Indigenous Relations*. Minneapolis: University of Minnesota Press, 2007.

Clastres, Pierre. *Chronique des Indiens Guayaki: Ce que savent les Aché, chasseurs nomades du Paraguay*. Paris: Plon, 1972.

———. *La société contre l'État*. Paris: Éditions de Minuit, 2011.

———. *Society against the State: Essays in Political Anthropology*. Translated by Robert Hurley and Abe Stein. Princeton: Princeton UP, 2020. *Project Muse*. muse.jhu.edu/book/79033. 3 May 2023.

Deloria, Philip J. *Playing Indian*. New Haven, CT: Yale UP, 1998.

Deloria Jr., Vine. *Indians and Anthropologists: Vine Deloria Jr., and the Critique of Anthropology*. Edited by Thomas Biolsi and Larry J. Zimmerman. Tuscon: The University of Arizona Press, 2004.

Doniger, Wendy. Foreword. *Myth and Meaning: Cracking the Code of Culture*. By Claude Lévi-Strauss. 1978. New York: Schocken Books, 1995. pp. vii–xv.

Garneau, François-Xavier. "Le dernier Huron". *Allpoetry*. https://allpoetry.com/Le-Dernier-Huron-(1)#tr_8520455. 30 April 2023.

Geertz, Clifford. "Deep Hanging Out". *The New York Review of Books*, vol. 45, no. 16, 1998. http://hypergeertz.jku.at/GeertzTexts/Deep_Hanging.htm. 3 May 2023.

Handley, George. "The Postcolonial Ecology of the New World Baroque". *Postcolonial Ecologies: Literatures of the Environment*. Edited by Elizabeth Deloughrey and George Handley. Kindle version, Oxford UP, 2011.

Havard, Gilles. *Histoire des coureurs de bois: Amérique du Nord, 1600–1840*. Paris: Perrin, 2016.

Hobbes, Thomas. *Leviathan*. Kindle Version. London: Public Domain, 1651.

Huhndorf, Shari M. *Going Native: Indians in the American Cultural Imagination*. Kindle version. Ithaca, NY: Cornell University Press, 2015.

Kalyniuk, Gregory. "Pierre Clastres and the Amazonian War Machine". *Deleuze and Anarchism*. Edited by Chtelle Gray van Heerden and Aragorn Eloff. Edinburgh: Edinburgh University Press, 2019. *Jstor*, https://www.jstor.org/stable/10.3366/j.ctv2f4vf63.16.

Kimmerer, Robin Wall. *Braiding Sweetgrass: Indigenous Wisdom, Scientific Knowledge, and the Teachings of Plants*. Kindle version. Minneapolis: Milkweed Editions, 2013.

Krech III, Shepard. *The Ecological Indian: Myth and History*. New York: W.W. Norton & Company, 1999.

Lalonde, Robert. *Le dernier été des Indiens.* Paris: Éditions du Seuil, 1982.

Lestringant, Frank. *Cannibals: The Discovery and Representation of the Cannibal from Columbus to Jules Verne*. Los Angeles: University of California Press, 1997.

Lévi-Strauss, Claude. *Myth and Meaning: Carcking the Code of Culture*. New York: Schocken Books, 1995.

———. *Tristes tropiques*. Paris: Plon, 1955.

Lopez, Barry. *Of Wolves and Men*. Kindle version. New York: Open Road Integrated Media, 2013.

Morency, Jean. "Images de l'Amérindien dans le roman Québécois depuis 1945." *Tangence*, no. 85, Fall 2007, pp. 83–98. https://doi.org/10.7202/018610ar. 30 April 2023.

Morgensen, Scott Lauria. *Spaces between Us: Queer Settler Colonialism and Indigenous Decolonization*. Minneapolis: University of Minnesota Press, 2011.

National Gallery of Canada. https://www.gallery.ca/magazine/your-collection/at-the-ngc/the-last-of-the-hurons-by-antoine-plamondon?_gl=1*1aazfyd*_ga*ODE0MDkzNjg3LjE2ODI5MDAwNTE.*_ga_83BW334MD2*MTY4MjkwMDA1MC4xLjEuMTY4MjkwMzI2Mi4wLjAuMA. 30 April 2023.

Poliquin, Daniel. *L'Obomsawin*. Montréal: Bibliothèque Québécoise, 1999.

Poulin, Jacques. *Volkswagen Blues*. Canada: Babel, 1988.

Prats, Armando José. *Invisible Natives: Myth and Identity in the American Western*. Ithaca, NY: Cornell UP, 2002.

Racevskis, Roland. "Of Cannibals and Colonizers: Irony, Gender, and Ecology in 'Rouge Brésil'". *Journal for Early Modern Cultural Studies*, vol. 6, no. 2, Fall-Winter 2006, pp. 69–83. http://www.jstor.org/stable/40339574. 30 April 2023.

Roy, Fernande. "1845-François-Xavier Garneau: Histoire du Canada." *Monuments intellectuels de la Nouvelle-France et du Québec ancien: Aux origines d'une tradition culturelle*. Edited by Claude Corbo. Montréal: Presses de l'Université de Montréal, 2014. pp. 165–76.

Rufin, Jean-Christophe. *Rouge Brésil*. Paris: Éditions Gallimard, 2001.

Schweninger, Lee. *Listening to the Land: Native American Literary Responses to the Landscape*. Kindle version. Athens: The University of Georgia Press, 2008.

Soucy, Jean-Yvès. *Un dieu chasseau*. Montreal: Typo, 1997.

Tournier, Michel. *Vendredi, ou les limbes du Pacifique*. Paris: Éditions Gallimard, 1972.

5 Voices in Francophone Indigenous Literature

A History and Future of Native American Literature

1 Introduction

This chapter shifts from mythic (mis)representations of the Native to focus on Francophone Indigenous voices in Québécois literature. Maurizio Gatti was one of the only authors to dedicate academic research to this subject when he published *Littérature amérindienne du Québec: Écrits de langue française* in 2004. A growing group of scholars is now turning critical attention to this literature. It is a "rich and varied corpus that seeks to distinguish itself from the dominant literature" while simultaneously "aspiring to an autonomous status in the heart of Francophone literatures" (Gatti 21, my translation). Several writers covered in this chapter are unknown to the academy, specifically Native American and Indigenous Studies scholars. This volume attempts to partially remedy that. I begin with Yvès Thériault, who many categorize as Québécois, not Indigenous. I explain in the first section the choice to classify Thériault as Native. After Thériault, it is the revolutionary *Je suis une maudite Sauvagesse* by An Antane Kapesh (1976), that marks a point of origin. Considered by many as the first text published in an Indigenous language (Innu) in Canada, it is a bilingual political essay that is foundational in subsequent generations of Francophone Indigenous writers' articulation of identity. Kapesh lays the groundwork for future Native authors, such as the Innu poets Joséphine Bacon and Rita Mestokosho. An examination of their poetry leads to a clearer understanding of the influence of land, the non-human, and relation in Innu identity and art. Finally, I explore the work of the most celebrated Innu author, Naomi Fontaine, whose début novel was recently adapted into a full-length feature film directed by Myriam Verreault (2019). In Fontaine's work, the author engages in a pedagogy of generosity which shares vital information via a narrative of survivance *and* invites non-Indigenous readers to extend generosity by granting personhood to the non-human world, teaching that community is in the land, in "everything that exists". Francophone Indigenous writers work to "ensure the transmission and renewal of their culture", which prompts the forging of futurities that reappropriate the carceral reserve as a site of cultural revival, that reinhabit

DOI: 10.4324/9781032638751-6

Voices in Francophone Indigenous Literature   169

sacred ground, and realistically reflect on the lived experiences of First Nations peoples (Gatti 24, my translation). In the context of this monograph, I have been obliged to leave many authors out of the discussion, such as Bernard Assiniwi, Michel Nöel, Virginia Pésémapéo Bordeleau, Louis-Karl Picard Sioui, Jean Sioui, Natasha Kanapé Fontaine, Samian, Yvès Sioui Durand, Melissa Mollen Dupuis, and many more. It is my hope that Indigenous Studies will incorporate Francophone Indigenous voices more intentionally into their circle of critical reflection in the future.

2   Yvès Thériault: Situating an Indigenous Voice in Québécois Literature

Born in Québec City, Yvès Thériault (1915–83) has a long prolific career earning him the designation as "the first Quebecois author to live solely from the proceeds of his writing" (Perron 230). His First Nations father initiates him into Innu (Montagnais) culture as a child. Abandoning his studies following the eighth grade, Thériault goes on to be a trapper, cheesemonger, trucker, bartender, and tractor salesman, later working for the National Film Board of Canada and the Department of Indian Affairs as cultural director (1965–67) (Brostom and Draper 398). His oeuvre is generically diverse, from children's to erotic literature, from film and television to radio broadcasts, and from writing about urban immigrant experiences to remote locales exploring Native cultures. He receives the prestigious Prix Athanase-David in 1979 which commemorates the writer's lifetime achievement and contributions to Québécois literature. Thériault's fiction critiques Euro-Canadian encroachment on Indigenous lands and presciently tackles the climate crisis. Yet, Thériault's place in this corpus is contentious. Because of the Innu culture he inherits from his father and the expression of Innu identity in his work, Yvès Thériault belongs in a discussion of Francophone Indigenous literature. Thériault gains celebrity with the publication of his most popular novel *Agaguk* (1958), which engages with questions of identity, intercultural conflict, and human relations to the environment in Inuit communities of the Great North. However, my discussion focuses on a novel that reflects the author's Innu origins: *Ashini* (1960). *Ashini* explores exile as a theme of Indigenous experience. Rather than remaining on the reserve, where Innu culture is in crisis, the elderly hunter Ashini withdraws to the forests of the Ungava Peninsula, a refuge from and resistance to settler-colonial encroachment. Relation to the land and the non-human, including elements often considered inanimate, is a vital source of knowledge in Indigenous communities. Schweninger contends that for Amerindians, "there does indeed exist an indigenous relationship to, appreciation for, awareness of, or understanding of the land that is significantly different from non-Indian relationships" (Introduction). In addition to this profound connection, kinship ties are paramount in Native culture. These complimentary components of Innu identity are cast as conflictual in *Ashini*. Striving to

170 *Voices in Francophone Indigenous Literature*

"learn, hour by hour, the secret of solitude" (*Ashini* 4, my translation), the hunter explains Native ways of experiencing the land.

> You see, that's how man learned so many things from the ancient forests in times past. He wandered alone and didn't know where he was going. So, he took the time to kneel and observe life down at ground level. He climbed up the trees to observe the sky live. And if he heard the voice of the animals or the wind, the waters and the canopies, he listened to them until he knew them. (*Ashini* 5–6, my translation)

This passage unveils the "secret of solitude". While linked to voluntary exile, parallels are also drawn between the protagonist's current situation and ancestral lifeways, essentializing seclusion as typically Innu. Radical solitude is coupled with an atypical lack of knowledge of the land that echoes mythic (mis)understandings of the Native seen in previous chapters: Ashini's ancestors wander aimlessly not knowing where they are going. Both the Rousseauian radical solitude linked to the state of nature and the disorientation of the Innu ancestors here demonstrate how French and Québécois cultural imaginaries' mythic distortions persist. Locating caribou or seasonal resources, Innu moves with purpose in the landscape. All those who wander are not lost, except in the inherent illogic of the Ignoble Savage which casts the Native as lacking foresight and community connections, à la Rousseau. The mythic mode is replaced with another perspective, that of land-based knowledge creation, coded as Indigenous. Ashini takes all existence into account, foregrounding Amerindian inquisitiveness in the acquisition of this Native science. Environmentally reciprocal knowledge is a central feature of Indigenous knowledge systems. Inclusive of the whole cosmos, it relies on intimate contact with the land through mutual listening, an interdependent communication that travels in both directions, from the land to the people *and* from the people to the land. Whitt (Mississippi Choctaw) points to story as a key element in the construction of Indigenous knowledge in *conversation* with non-human entities.

> The integrative power of stories, the way they help us initiate and maintain relationships with others who may appear different from us, is especially needed to guide human interaction with the other-than-human world. Stories are related to convey the behavioral constraints that should guide us if we are to act responsibly, if we are to understand and respect the role of other entities and their unique contribution to the natural world we share. (Whitt 36)

Through the interrelatedness of story, Indigenous knowledge systems foster a more responsible, inclusive vision of the environment. As Whitt surmises, Indigenous stories have the power to bring together. This contrasts fundamentally with the neutrality upon which Western science is based. In this passage, mythic

Voices in Francophone Indigenous Literature 171

Rousseauian solitude with its concomitant roaming Amerindians is juxtaposed with Indigenous experiential learning in and with the land. The distinction is even more evident if one considers the original French, which distinguishes two radically different terms for knowing: *savoir* and *connaître*. When the ancient Innu are meandering through the landscape without *knowing* where they are going, the term is *savoir*. *Savoir* refers to factual knowledge, that can be verified; for example, Western scientific knowledge calls for *savoir*. The term *savoir* points to Western knowledge and the expression of the French and Québécois cultural imaginaries' deformations of the Amerindian in the Ignoble Savage mode. Thériault employs *connaître* in the last sentence, which describes all the antecedent knowledge gleaned from Innu *conversations* with the land. Knowledge built upon listening to the non-human denotes experience and familiarity, bonds of kinship or cooperation, the choice of *connaître* indicates relationality and intimacy linked to lived experience over time, to family and friends. The first part is coded Western in the mythic mode and the second part is coded Indigenous. *Savoir* and *connaître* signal the divergent cultural sources of knowledge and expression in Thériault's fiction. Mythic paradigms and Indigenous voices are recurrently juxtaposed in *Ashini*. In *Ashini*, sensorial mechanisms speak to the embodiment of learning in and with the land in the Innu geographies of the Ungava Peninsula. An immersive experience that subjectifies (makes subject) rather than objectifies (makes object) the natural world. The distinction between seeing the non-human as subject versus object is investigated by the French anthropologist Phillipe Descola. Former chair of Anthropology of Nature at the Collège de France, Descola is another pupil of Claude Lévi-Strauss. Descola contends that modern Western ontology is defined by a radical separation between culture and nature, one of the early proponents of which is René Descartes. Descartes' *Discours de la méthode* (1637) establishes the scientific method as a site of veridiction in Western knowledge production. It also hypothesizes that the human body and the soul are ontologically distinct, with the mind (soul) superior to matter (body). Relegating the non-human to object status, Cartesian metaphysics is a critical landmark in the inauguration of what Descola refers to as "naturalism". Naturalism is Descola's term for the unique way in which Western culture objectifies and reifies the category of nature. Far from universal, Descola problematizes the notion that nature and the non-human are ontologically separate, relying on ethnographic observations of Achuar attitudes toward the non-human. In the Achuar culture of the Amazon Basin, nature does not exist as a distinct category, rather the *human* subjectivity and soul are extended to all non-human things, including the inanimate. Recognition of the humanity of all things is common to many Indigenous societies.

When an Achuar or a Cree say that an artefact or an inorganic element of the environment have a "soul", they understand by that that these entities are endowed with their own intentionality which is of the same nature as

172   *Voices in Francophone Indigenous Literature*

the human's. This intentionality is not based on the molecular substratum wherein the entity exists, nor on the processes that over time brought it into being. Differences in form and behavior are recognized, but they are not sufficient criteria to exclude a blowgun or a mountain from being granted a shared interiority. (Descola, Ch. 8, my translation)

Descola labels this perspective on the non-human world animism. The kinship relationships that many Indigenous groups express regarding non-human animals is an example of this worldview, but this attitude often extends beyond the animal kingdom. In his most well-known book, *Par-delà nature et culture* (2005), Descola recounts how humanity is attributed to categories the West refuses to *recognize* as human. Intentionality is a key concept, because it does not exclude like Western naturalism which limits nature to either source of natural resources or outdoor museum not inclusive of the human, often to the detriment of Native claims to the land. Animism is evident in Indigenous literatures, art, and culture. In *Ashini*, Thériault invokes animist views of the environment. When the Innu learn to know (*connaître*) the voices of the wind, the trees, and non-human animals, this subjectifies the non-human in its animate *and* inanimate forms. This subjectification of the non-human accounts for the production of knowledge being experiential and situated geographically in Indigenous worldviews. In contrast, exploring far-flung "natural" vacation destinations, as in ecotourism, adheres to the inherent illogic of naturalism's radical separation of the human from the non-human by emphasizing the exotic and non-inhabited. Knowing (*connaître*) the land and maintaining enduring relationships with it is critical. In *Ashini*, decrying the injustice of Innu dispossession figures largely. Demonstrating a clear understanding of Settler-Indigenous relations between Québec and the Innu, Thériault calls for something that very few Euro-Canadians were thinking about in 1960. Following the death of Duplessis and the end of a reign of ultraconservatism, most Québécois view rapid economic development as a means to catch up with more dynamic Canadian provinces, especially Ontario, a booming post-war society of high mass consumption. Challenges to that headlong rush were few in public discourse in Québec when *Ashini* is released. In this context, the novel is even more striking for its steadfast defense of Amerindian land claims and acerbic critique of Western lifeways as disconnected from nature and reality and lacking meaning. While contemporary Indigenous Francophone writers discussed below, such as Naomi Fontaine, negotiate their Indigenous identity without insisting on a sweeping return to traditional lifeways or the abandonment of all aspects of Western technology, the question of Native identity in *Ashini* is presented as a binary. The *true* Native refuses modernity. The protagonist's voluntary exile serves as a model of Amerindian authenticity. Alternative in the text are few. Only one other Innu is mentioned who does not live on the reserve; Le Roc has also chosen the forest seeking solitude, hunting and trapping to survive. In opposition, the reserve destroys authenticity and

Voices in Francophone Indigenous Literature   173

health. When Ashini does return, he stops at the edge of the reserve, refusing to enter. He is there to commit suicide. In *Ashini*, *true* Amerindian identity requires seclusion, which is anathema to Indigenous lifeways. Education and cultural assimilation are condemned, as the (narrative) technologies of the settler-state. The adoption of Euro-Canadian practices and language is equated with death. Although he aspires for the "liberty of [his] people", Ashini wonders if the Innu people will be "eternal fake Whites", a prospect that seems as likely as it is tragic in the fictional universe of the novel (*Ashini* 55, 61 my translation). Nonetheless, the land and Innu reciprocal relations with it deserve further consideration. The resources of Ungava Peninsula are identified with the Innu people in an inclusive manner, reflective of the animist outlook already discussed. The historical realities of iron ore mining and the damming of rivers for hydroelectricity are counterpoints to the interdependence and relationality that describes the Innu's interaction with the non-human in the novel.

> They wouldn't come steal minerals or watersheds. They would let us have the fish in the rivers and the animals of the woods, the trees and even the smallest, prettiest flowers. There would be berries, tender herbs, and roots that heal and that enrich our well-being. The bird of the sky, the insect, the animal and the fish, the black pine and the timid lily of the valley, thyme and juniper, every pebble, every drop of water, every gust of wind, every pearl of dew would be ours along with the incontestable right to keep all of it until the end of time. As for me, I wanted nothing more than to stroll as I pleased on soil that was ours again. (*Ashini* 44–5, my translation)

In *Ashini*, the deterritorialization of the Native and their imprisonment on the reserve are of a piece. In addition to dispossession, the Innu suffer the spoliation of their land by Euro-Canadian economies of extraction. Iron mining and the hydroelectric dams are themes that also play an crucial role in the non-fiction text, *Je suis une maudite Sauvagesse* by An Antane Kapesh, that I turn to in the next section. The use of Native lands for the creation of wealth that does not return to the Innu in an equitable way is one side of an equation that also entails widespread pollution and the destruction of hunting grounds and non-human habitats. In one of the rare hopeful passages of *Ashini*, the hunter proposes a more holistic and sustainable conceptualization of riches, natural ones. Plants associated with the intimate reciprocal knowledge of the land would not be destroyed to enrich the avaricious, instead they would promote Innu health and well-being. Furthermore, inanimate entities are recognized as an integral part of life. Rock, water, and wind are subjectified along with plants and non-human animals in Ashini's comprehensive enumeration. The return of stolen Innu land is repeated throughout the novel, a rare example in Québécois popular culture of support for Innu claims. Other instances of environmental destruction are condemned when "Whites killed the granite, pushed back the forest, mutilated the mountains…to

174 *Voices in Francophone Indigenous Literature*

get at the iron or copper ore, to harness the rivers and conduct the electricity to the voracious monsters in the lands of the south" (*Ashini* 60, my translation). The Innu hunter mocks the arrogance of the settler-state, the infrastructure projects and economies of scale, contending that all that has been dug up would not equal one riverbed, claiming that Euro-Canadians are like children at play, pretending to be earth makers and gods (61). Thériault presents a confused message by minimizing the damage done by economies of extraction in order to insist on the over-arching vastness and power of the land, lamenting damage caused by industrial projects and greedy hunting practices. The Indigenously contextualized natural world in Thériault's novel goes beyond mythic (mis)understanding and voices the concerns of the Innu. The novel's dénouement reveals Thériault's perspectives and techniques. Throughout *Ashini*, the Innu hunter makes long treks to the edge of the reserve of Betsiamites to leave messages written in blood on birch bark on a signpost. Communications meant for the Great White Chief in Ottawa (the Canadian Prime Minister) that remain unread. Thériault foreshadows Ashini's suicide through the creation of these messages; the blood used to write them is obtained by Ashini slitting his wrists. A the end of the text, Ashini calls out to be heard.

> They hadn't heard my voice, the voice of a solitary man crying out in the desert. But they would hear other voices, the horrified voices of the just, for once more powerful, for once standing together and demanding legal equality. When I got to the signpost, the area was deserted. More deserted, it seemed to me, than it had ever been. What were the defeated Montagnais dreaming about in their soft beds? Under how many roofs, did they perform acts of continuation in the Indian village of Betsiamites that night, acts whose autumn fruits would be, without realizing it right away, the first arrivals of a new, a free Montagnais people. Will they know that they owe me for their new blood, even as a dim memory in the mind of a rowdy schoolboy or girl? Will my name fill them with feelings of sweetness and pride? (144, my translation)

Ashini constructs a "modern image of the future" for the Innu, insisting on a futurity that includes justice and a voice in the shape that their lives will take. Perhaps foreshadowing the self-determination movement and its less-than-hoped for post-recognition realties, nonetheless Thériault evokes a path forward in the same *conversational* mode that characterizes the reciprocal interactions between the Innu and the environment. However, the reproductive aspirations for the Innu are not without ambiguity. The bloodline that has been central in the text will endure. From the beginning, Ashini is described as the last *true* Innu in a narrative arc similar to that of James Fenimore Cooper's *The Last of the Mohicans* (1826). "Ashini, the last blood of a great line, who came from the south et made a world for himself in the forest of Ungava" (2, my translation). This is a

Voices in Francophone Indigenous Literature 175

framing device that informs the reader how to apprehend the character Ashini. The vitality of the Innu couples in the reserve is in direct contradiction with the characterization of that space as carceral, corrupting, and genocidal throughout the novel. However, the futurity presented in the passage casts doubt on the *authenticity* of subsequent generations of Innu. Ashini's existential questioning is linked to the loss of traditional *knowledge*; when Thériault writes "They hadn't heard my voice" it is not merely in reference to unread messages written for the Great White Chief (the Canadian Prime Minister) but also the lack of transmission of Ashini's story to the Innu on the reserve. This explains why he ponders the possibility of an intergenerational memorial trace of his presence in the thoughts of rambunctious children in an imagined future, because although the bloodline persists intact, yet it appears that the line of story has been broken.

> At the top of the white wooden pole, I hung the loop of the underarm harness that I'd made myself. Hanging like that, my feet could barely touch the ground if I tried, and I swung back and forth in the morning wind. Then, with my knife, I slit the artery in my right wrist and, quickly did the same to the left. In a rapid flow, in the pale morning light, all the life ran out of my body. I didn't know it then, as I was dying little by little, hanging on my new cross, that not one of my messages had made it to the Great White Chief. And that they would write on the official death certificate, a final shame: *Ashini, Montagnais, aged 63, suicide in a moment of alienation.* (145, my translation)

Taking his own life via self-immolation that makes obvious reference to the crucifixion of Jesus Christ; the final moments of Ashini's life are awash with meaning and symbolism. The justification for Thériault's choice of "new cross" is literal and metaphorical, due to the fact that it is the signpost designating the border of the reserve that reads: INDIAN RESERVE OF BETSIAMITES. The reserve sign resembles the lateral arm of a cross, anchoring the passage in religious Euro-Canadian ideologies of sacrifice and renewal. The "new, free Montagnais people" are only possible with a (Christian) sacrifice. Fulfilling a mythological arc that casts Ashini in the Vanishing Indian mode, the death of the solitary, elderly hunter has been announced from the outset. The end of the novel employs a similar technique as earlier excerpts: the juxtaposition of an Indigenous coded discourse, expressing Native ontologies and futurity, and a Euro-Canadian inflected narrative, manifesting a messianic myth of the Vanishing Indian. The dénouement also points to Thériault's dual identity. The elaboration of an albeit ambiguous Indigenous futurity is in contentious contiguity with the Vanishing Indian mythology and a Judeo-Christian passion play that reflect Québécois cultural visions and heritage. Sometimes transcending mythologies of the Amerindian, *Ashini* also contains narrative technologies that are a part of the mythic genealogy traced in this study. It remains to be explained how

176   *Voices in Francophone Indigenous Literature*

the cultural renewal of the Innu community is connected to Ashini's personal sacrifice or how it surpasses the shameful suicide that it is labeled in the settler-colonial archive's official documentation. Thériault suggests that the book *Ashini* is in fact a text written in the dead messiah's blood from the opening pages of the novel, but it remains obscure until the protagonist's suicide is revealed. The only chance for redemption and Innu futurity hinges on the transfer of knowledge to the Innu on the reserve.

> He remained impenetrable, because it is bad manners to show surprise. The social etiquette of our people demands this impassivity, this stillness. I am telling you this, so you will know everything about us. Now that I am far away and unreachable, where will you learn how things should be and how they shouldn't be? If not in this book of blood. You are probably a White who thinks he's clever and who has never learned the only science that matters, the science of living. (15, my translation)

In the end, the story of Ashini is transmitted to the Innu people *and* to the Euro-Canadian readers of the popular novelist Yvès Thériault. Who has found the blood script containing the knowledge of the Innu hunter? Is it a "White" who lacks the fundamentals of "the science of living"? The decisive act in the salvation of the Innu is the transmission of Ashini's story, without it the Vanishing Indian myth with all its "manifest manners" succeeds in *disappearing* the Native. The plotline wherein the novel assures the continued survival/cultural revival of the Innu is evidence of the author laying claim to his First Nations identity. The choice of writing a text that proclaims the rights of the Innu to land, liberty, and legal equality is intentional, which the author consciously makes to inform his readership about the genius of a people. It is Thériault himself who delivers the critical stories that are needed to ensure that the "new, free Montagnais people" are not disconnected from their culture, land, or past. Taking into account the mythic mode of the Vanishing Indian's conspicuous place in the novel, it is clear that an ambiguous duality juxtaposing Western and Indigenous ways of knowing is the final message of *Ashini*. Thériault's narrative techniques and technologies reflect a diverse heritage that includes multiple traditions and worldviews in *conversation*. Rather than refuse mutual interaction with the Other, or focus uniquely on the Other as enemy, Indigenous writers discussed in the following pages engage in a pedagogy of generosity like Thériault. Writing opens up a space wherein knowledge can be transmitted across barriers in a relational, reciprocal *conversation*. Indigenous cultures are built on story, first oral, then written. In the twentieth and twenty-first centuries Indigenous communities globally have written their stories, many for the first time, others in translation, but this pedagogical generosity, this willingness to share in an intentional, collaborative way is a critical aspect of Indigenous

Voices in Francophone Indigenous Literature   177

voices in *la Belle Province*. Throughout this study, I have referred to the mythic paradigms employed by the French and Québécois as narrative technologies, demonstrating how the mythic lens abets (settler)-colonialism, another weapon in the arsenal. Although the mythic machine commits acts of (symbolic) violence, story is not limited to destructive capacities. Story is creative and regenerative; it can be utilized as a narrative technology to collectively construct a "modern image of the future". Leslie Marmon Silko (Laguna Pueblo) recounts how language began as a warning system to help each other stay alive when faced with danger.

> Considerable details and vivid descriptions were essential to the telling; the most important actions in a story might be repeated to make sure the listeners remembered what to do to survive in a similar situation. I like to imagine that the listeners took solace but also pleasure in hearing these stories told by survivors—amazing stories with happy endings. These stories gave them the heart to face danger with the hope that if they did exactly what the survivor had done then they too might survive. So they paid close attention to the survivor's story, and thus stories rich in detail and description became the most pleasurable because they gave the listeners the most information. The association of knowledge with power begins here. (Introduction)

According to Silko's recounting of the origins of language, Native futurities represent a return to the original function of story: to help rather than to hurt, to warn and to guide, to survive together. The power of the Indigenous voice globally is now being employed as a regenerative narrative technology. That invocation of renaissance is not solely meant for the Native community, but is freely given to the world, including the colonizer, in an act of pedagogical generosity. This story power is what Gerald Vizenor (Chippewa) refers to as survivance. Survivance is in opposition to seeing contemporary Indigenous peoples as survivors to be pitied for their "tragic victimry", which perpetuates the mythic machine's distortions. Survivance foregrounds perpetual actions of living as agency and resistance, a movement that has nothing to do with Western notions of progress but is circular and reciprocal. Survivance, regenerative story, and pedagogies of generosity are "part of an ancient continuous story composed of innumerable bundles of other stories" that are circulated in "an exchange of stories" whose purpose is not profit, but to share information for survival. For the storyteller, there is power in a tale that adopts a pedagogy of generosity instead of narrative technologies that are complicit with economies of extraction. In the following section, I consider a historic text, one of the first ever published in an Indigenous language in Canada, specifically Innu-aimun, the language of the Innu people, also translated into French: An Antane Kapesh's *Eukuan Nin Matshi-Manitu Innushkueu/Je suis une maudite sauvagesse* (1976).

178   *Voices in Francophone Indigenous Literature*

3   Speaking the Truth: A Bilingual Conversation with An Antane Kapesh's *Je suis une maudite Sauvagesse*

The creation story of *Je suis une maudite Sauvagesse* is remarkable. The translator, José Mailhot (1943–2021) has a long, personal experience with the Innu over a lengthy career as an ethnographer and linguist working to help Innu speakers train others to teach Innu-aimun to new generations, collaborating to compile a multi-lingual online dictionary of the language (https://dictionary.innu-aimun.ca/Words). In *Shushei au pays des Innus* (2021) Mailhot details the creation story of what many consider the first Indigenous language text published in Canada. Since the book's appearance, there has been considerable speculation that Kapesh did not in fact write the text, but dictated it to Mailhot, or even that the translator Mailhot wrote it herself (Chapter 1). These rumors reflect a refusal to accept that an Indigenous woman could be granted an author. Mailhot dispels these fabrications, confirming Kapesh's profession as "writer" and her limited role as a "specialist of the Innu language" (Chapter 1).

> After six days, I noticed that her right hand was very swollen and that she could hardly move her fingers or hold the pen. When she saw panic on my face, she did her best to reassure me: "That's completely normal, it's the first book that I've ever written, it's something that I'm not used to" (Mailhot Chapter 1, my translation)

Mailhot painstakingly details the physical process of the work of writing and its effects on Kapesh's body, even describing the pen and color of ink Kapesh used, as a response to those who doubt. I include this chronicle investigate to explore why, nearly fifty years later, opposition continues to the concept that An Antane Kapesh could have possibly written such a "political testimony" (Papillon 58). The refusal to accept the Amerindian authorship of the book is a testament to the revolutionary and radical shift that Kapesh accomplishes through the act of speaking back to settler-colonialism through the power of story. To publicly denounce the inequalities and violence of Québec vis-à-vis the Innu through a published essay in both Innu-aimun and French is profoundly different than mythic (mis)understandings of the Native. Kapesh speaks to and for her people, but also to Euro-Canadians, condemning them for the destruction of Innu families and culture. The political act of a First Nations woman writing is significant, in no small measure because of its bilingualism. Mailhot discusses the difficulty of type-setting the Innu-aimun language without a standardized orthography. The momentousness of the decision to print *Je suis une maudite Sauvagesse* in French *and* an Indigenous language is a radical one with far-reaching consequences. As will be highlighted in greater depth in my discussion of the Innu poets Joséphine Bacon and Rita Mestokosho in the next section, the

Voices in Francophone Indigenous Literature 179

inclusion of Innu-aimun in Kapesh's foundational Francophone Indigenous text influences subsequent generations of Amerindian artists to share their language with their readers. Returning to the text's authorship, Naomi Fontaine, an Innu writer whose work is the subject of the final section of this chapter, affirms the *authenticity* of Kapesh's writing.

> I read [her] words without ever having a doubt cross my mind about the truthfulness of what she was saying. She told me a History that I had never heard. My own. A violent, brutal, and impossible account. She taught me that I had a past that was attached to the flame burning inside, consuming me. My desire to stand up straight, far from prejudices, far from lies, so far away from self-hatred. I believed every word she said. (Fontaine *Préface* 4, my translation)

For Fontaine, Kapesh's political essay is a revelation of something very intimate and personal. She *recognizes* the veracity of Kapesh's words viscerally. Furthermore, the work allows her to connect with intergenerational trauma, echoing Fontaine's own struggle against injustice. In addition to the transmission of vital information, the book is a roadmap, a guide to the land, an essential feature of Innu knowledge and story. Fontaine signals Kapesh's pride in her identity in the face of racism and the carceral geography of the reserve, locating the source of that pride in "what few now possess, knowledge of the land" (*Préface* 4, my translation). Fontaine not only pinpoints a crucial element of Native knowledge, but also a divergence between Kapesh and later generations disconnected from the land. As demonstrated below, Fontaine's fiction reinvigorates connections with community and the land, addressing what the lesson to be learned individually and collectively in order to blaze a trail forward for the Innu. Fontaine confides that, "when I read [Kapesh's] writing, I can open up my heart to my own path" (*Préface* 5, my translation). Kapesh critiques the violence of settler-colonialism, insisting upon a synergistic connection between Innu culture and relationship to the land. Employing anaphora, Kapesh opens *Sauvagesse* by forging an indissociable link between these concepts that are not only fundamental to Amerindian knowledge *and* (narrative) technologies employed by the colonizer.

> When the Whiteman wanted to exploit and destroy our land, he didn't ask anyone's permission, he didn't ask the Indians if they agreed. When the Whiteman wanted to exploit and destroy our land, he didn't make the Indians sign a document saying that they accepted that he exploit and destroy all our land so that he would be the only one to make a living from it from then on. When the Whiteman wanted the Indians to live like the Whites, he didn't ask them their point of view and he didn't make then sign something saying that they agreed to renounce their culture for the rest of their days. (21, my translation)

180   *Voices in Francophone Indigenous Literature*

In this passage, Kapesh defines environmental degradation as *the* objective of settler-colonial encroachment. In a world dominated by neoliberal ideologies, economic imperatives are presented as self-evident and naturalized as *true*. However, Kapesh begins here, because the author is pinpointing the initial error of the European, which is the objectification and instrumentalization of non-human and human Others. The self-evidence most apparent to Kapesh: the irrationality of a perspective that denies the tenets of Innu ontology, which insist on the intrinsic value of all things, not only the myopic and narrow category of European (male), as worthy of respect. The first chapter of *Sauvagesse* emphasizes incredulity and exasperation at the arrogance of the European's refusal to speak to the Native, to address the Innu on their own terms, to reach collective agreement. This lack of *conversation* signals another cultural divide that Kapesh maintains as a fundamental fact of Settler-Indigenous relations. Kapesh employs repetition to accentuate important points. The anaphora in the essay's opening mirrors Native narrative technologies of survivance. Silko explains how repetition functions in story.

> I imagine that at first humans exchanged stories to acquire knowledge as a survival strategy, to learn to anticipate the many threats and dangers in their world. Considerable details and vivid descriptions were essential to the telling; the most important actions in a story might be repeated to make sure the listeners remembered what to do to survive in a similar situation. (Introduction)

The function of repetition is to highlight the most critical information in a story, to ensure that attention is drawn appropriately to the best method to make it through a dangerous situation together. Kapesh repeats the two themes of environmental destruction and lack of reciprocity as the most significant knowledge she transmits. Kapesh speaks from a place of trauma, collective and intergenerational, but also immediate and individual. The author's own personal interactions with residential schools, government officials, and the police are foregrounded throughout the text. *Sauvagesse* symphonically arranges stories to concentrate thinking on the harmony that connects the individual to community, in good times and bad. Anaphora demands deliberation and invites interactive "exchange of stories" to find solutions for the Innu. As a narrative technology of survivance, Kapesh does not employ anaphora to underscore the "tragic victimry" of the Native, but to promote solidarity in resistance to settler-colonial violence. Furthermore, the lesson is not restricted to the Innu, which is confirmed by the bilingualism of the text. The author's urgent call is not univocal and unidirectional, which typifies the mythic machine's simulations of the "indian". Kapesh insists on the bad "manifest manners" of not asking for permission, of not engaging with the Innu in *conversation*, because the "exchange of stories" is an epistemological *and* ethical value of Amerindian cultures. Therefore, the urgency of the anaphoric insistence on an environmentally and culturally sound strategy for dealing with the Other is a message meant for the European, as well. Presenting both Innu-aimun and French in *conversation* in the essay's typesetting indicates the centrality of exchange and the dual destination of its discourse, intended both for Innu and Québécois. This is the pedagogy of generosity in action. Kapesh's critique of the colonizer does not condemn in the mythic mode of the *Ignoble Invader* but seeks to share information: to teach the right path forward for the Innu *and* the non-Innu. As opposed to mythologizing the Other, Kapesh begins from a concrete place of consequences, consequences born bodily and spiritually as trauma. Rather than transmogrify through mythic messages, the writer locates the danger and shouts in an act of survivance that alerts *all* to the perils of objectification. Native story and survivance stand in stark opposition to the mythic machine's modes of distortion. Native narrative technologies communicate wisdom to all within a pedagogy of generosity. By locating the discursive duplicity of the Europeans in reference to the missing "document" (treaty), Kapesh demonstrates her willingness to meet the Québécois in a cultural "middle ground". In the preface, expressing reservations about writing as not original to her culture, Kapesh deems the information she has to share too crucial for collective survival to keep to herself, opting instead for an ethic of exchange, a pedagogy of generosity.

Inextricably bound to one another, land and culture are at the center of Innu knowledge and community. In Kapesh's analysis, the destruction of the land is of a piece with cultural genocide. The author identifies settler-colonial education as a site of danger that Innu and non-Innu alike should be warned about. The emergency that prompts a narrative technology of survivance in *Sauvagesse* is cultural death. Kapesh emphasizes the critical question of the Canadian residential school system. Recent archeological efforts have revealed that thousands of First Nations children died and were buried without recognition in residential schools across the federation. The horrific volume of lost life is doubled with that of lost culture, according to Kapesh. The residential system has a multifaceted effect on the Innu community, one which the writer delineates in all its complexity. The breaking of bonds intrinsic to the kidnapping and imprisonment of Native children is evidence of the consequences of the residential school system. One vital way the *pensionnat* (boarding school) attacks the bases of Innu culture is by disrupting connection to the land.

The Indians could no longer go north into the forest for ten months out of the year because their children were being kept as residents. They obviously wanted to see them and find out how they were being cared for, if they were being treated well or not. In my opinion, that is also the reason why Indians considered getting jobs at that time. (59, my translation)

182 *Voices in Francophone Indigenous Literature*

Kapesh cites two ramifications of the residential school system for the Innu: removal from the land and insertion into economies of extraction. Interring Innu children in boarding school leads directly to sedentarization of adults. The transmission of knowledge of the land is severely diminished and leveraging Native parents' love of their children curtails movement. According to Kapesh, both are intentional. In *Sauvagesse* Kapesh discusses a dispute over where reserve housing will be constructed in Matimekush. Kapesh refuses to move into town, remaining along the lakeside where she wants to build a "modern image of the future" for herself and her family. Elaborating on the machinations of government officials, Kapesh shows how they pit members of the community against one another to realize their project of removing the Innu from the lakeside forest and forcing them into town. In the end, Kapesh's persistence and political activism pays off, after ten long years, and she finally gets a house where she wants one, it should be noted: on her land, Innu land. The governmental pressure and political maneuvering to impose urban existence on the community is evidence of the intentional sedentarization and disconnection from the land that has driven Settler-Indigenous relations in many contexts. Recent scholarship in Indigenous studies has made a push toward a post-recognition interaction with settler polities. This move acknowledges the ways in which *recognition* entails entanglements with economies of extraction and lifeways that are anathema to core Native values. This is an appropriate juncture to recall a point that I raised in chapter two's discussion of La Condamine. Coulthard (Yellowknife Dene) argues convincingly how the Marxist notion of "*primitive* accumulation" is a useful theoretical lens for understanding the consequences of the separation of Indigenous communities from their land. Coulthard cautions that Marxist thinking is problematic on its own and should be "transformed *in conversation* with the critical thought and practices of Indigenous peoples" (17, emphasis in original). What Coulthard does retain from Marx is "the silent compulsion of economic relations" that "[set] the seal on the domination of the capitalist over the worker" (qtd. in Coulthard 18). The ontological difference between the storying of the Native and the myth-making of the European is based upon a temporal relation and an epistemological relation to reality. For the Amerindian, the concrete consequences of the site of danger are critical in the articulation of the European Other based on a regard that looks back to outcomes of interactions with that group. For the European, mythic modes are always already there in the cultural imaginary. They inform the interaction prior to any real *knowledge* being acquired experientially, rather they are temporally predictive. The mythic machine predetermines outcomes rather than accurately assessing events. The chasm between (mis)representing the residential school system as charitable and generative of opportunity and the cultural consequences of sedentarization and the weakening of connections between the community and the land demonstrate these complex differences between narrative technologies of myth and those of survivance. The "silence" that Marx signals is key to an indigenized reading of his anti-capitalist critique. As Kapesh repeats anaphorically throughout *Sauvagesse*: the Euro-Canadians did not tell us what the consequences of residential schools, economies of extraction, or language loss would be. In the mythic guise of helping prepare a "modern image of the future" for Innu children, the residential school system, according to Kapesh's analysis, broke the connection between the community and their children, between the community and the land, and forced them to enter the extractive economy as wage-laborers. Wage-labor erases the possibility for the Innu to live according to their own ontology in relation to the non-human world. Living in *conversation* with the non-human is replaced by the inherent illogic of extraction as the Innu are separated from the land and an economy of relation. Forced into settler-colonial capitalism, Kapesh pinpoints the difficult path forward for Innu children.

> Because they went to the Whiteman's school, now our children are in an in-between space (*entre-deux*): they are unable to earn a living in their Indian culture and they are not used to earning a living in the Whites' way either. …the Whiteman's education isn't worth anything for us Indians. (62–3, my translation)

Kapesh laments the difficulties her children encounter once they are "silently inserted" into Québécois society. She underscores the disorienting effect of the residential school system on young Innu. Effectively eliminating the very opportunities that the Canadian government promises, Quebecois educational initiatives stifle futurities and disconnect children from both their First Nations heritage and the inculcated Canadian culture to which they are constrained to assimilate. Intentional in her word choice, Kapesh zooms in on the site of danger as a misjudgment of value. Not valuing Native lifeways and knowledge systems, exploiting and destroying the land, disconnecting Innu children from their heritage, separating Innu parents from their children, and forcing the community to enter the market economy does not have a positive outcome for the Native. The consequences of colonialism inspire Kapesh to evaluate the promise of assimilation as illusory and to conclude that Euro-Canadian knowledge has no value for First Nations communities. Kapesh does not cast her critique in the mode of "tragic victimry"; she proposes alternative Amerindian-specific forms of education anchored in the land. Through anaphora and repetition, Kapesh insists that Innu children must "know the forest", proposing that Innu adults could teach children, in keeping with the centrality of spatially situated knowledge and story (63–4). Joëlle Papillon contends that Kapesh "privileges an intergenerational bond, one characterized by teaching, that allows the inscription of young Innu on the land, showing them the relationships that they should cultivate with other living beings" (60, my translation). Focused on Indigenous geographies

184   *Voices in Francophone Indigenous Literature*

and pedagogies of generosity, Kapesh fosters strategies that reflect their most cherished cultural values. Kapesh honors the importance of language as another pillar of Innu identity.

> Now that we live like whites, in my opinion, we don't speak the real Montagnais language anymore. We live in white houses and use all the elements of white culture; that is the reason why we are quickly losing our Native language. When we lived an Indian lifestyle on the lands of the interior, the language that we spoke was different. Our real Indian language is the one we use in the hinterland. The way I see it is, the true Indian language that we have lost isn't going to come out of the Education Commission's school or the white university either. (63, my translation)

Kapesh locates significant linguistic shifts she attributes to the move to the reserve and the Québécois education system. Assimilation is blamed for the loss of a pure form of Innu-aimun. Once again, space is essential to Kapesh's understanding of the problem. The physical space of the house is an important aspect of how Amerindians live in and view the world. The Euro-Canadian style housing on the reserve modifies lifeways, altering thought and speech with its "elements of white culture". Espousing a narrower vision of linguistic *authenticity* than later generations of Francophone Indigenous writers, Kapesh limits "real Indian language" to non-Euro-Canadian geographies and cultural milieux. Language, like knowledge and its transmission, are situated in a geographic context. Space is critical. Vine Deloria Jr. (Standing Rock Sioux), echoes Kapesh's insights. He insists that place is paramount to Native ontologies, spiritualities, and futurities, explaining that the relation to place in Amerindian cultures "is this unbroken connection that we have with the spirit world that will allow us to survive as a people" (*God is Red* xvii). While the separation from the land transforms linguistic practice, especially among Innu children, according to Kapesh, there is a path forward. "I believe that it is very important we make enormous efforts, setting out in search of our Native culture and language and that we preserve them" (66, my translation). Kapesh calls for an Indigenous-centered revival of language teaching starting at a young age, *before* instruction in settler-colonial languages begins. Additionally, Kapesh demands that the process be removed from the Canadian educational structure, power be put back in the hands of First Nations communities, and that Innu teachers oversee the instruction. Mailhot, the translator of *Sauvagesse*, in *conversation* with Kapesh and other Innu writers, including the poet Joséphine Bacon discussed below, create a network of Innu language teachers.

Kapesh represents a turning point in Québec-First Nations relations and the history of Indigenous writers in Canada. With the publication of her bilingual "political testimony", Kapesh opens the door for Francophone Indigenous voices to be heard on their own terms. Kapesh's intercalation of Innu-aimun in contiguity, juxtaposition, and *conversation* with French is a model that ensuing

Voices in Francophone Indigenous Literature   185

generations of Francophone Indigenous authors will follow. Directly speaking to the injustice and cultural erasure of settler-colonial policies, Kapesh nonetheless does so in a voice of care. Demonstrating a pedagogy of generosity, Kapesh calls on her Euro-Canadian readers to see things differently and to see the Innu as a people worthy of respect and consideration as equal partners, with something valuable to contribute to a conversation about our collective survival in an uncertain future beset by the excesses of economies of extraction and the specter of environmental collapse. Lastly, the distorted images of the mythic machine's (mis) representations of the Native are discredited in *Je suis une maudite Sauvagesse*.

> Today when you see them talking about us Indians, in the newspapers, I believe there is nothing true in it. And when you see when they put us on the television and in the movies, there isn't anything real about it. (122, my translation)

Kapesh does not pay heed to the mythic modes of the Ignoble Savage or the Vanishing Indian which abound in Québécois popular culture, "manifestations of the influence of a shared cultural imaginary that disfigures Native via (symbolic) violence with its *crystallized* narrative technologies. She quickly dismisses those tropes as illusory, as simulations of the "indian". In a rhetoric similar in some regards to that of the Negritude movement led by the Martinican poet and philosopher Aimé Césaire, Kapesh (re)writes the history of the Ignoble Savage as a symbol of authentic Amerindian identity and survivance.

> I am a damned Savage. I am very proud today when I hear someone call me a Savage. When I hear a Whiteman pronounce that word, I understand that he is telling me over and over again that I am a real Indian and that I'm the first one that lived in the forest. Well, everything that lives in the forest is connected to a better life. May the Whiteman always call me a Savage. (163, my translation)

In Kapesh's reclamation of the Savage label, she continues to teach. Testifying to the (mis)understandings of the Euro-Canadians who hurl the term as an insult, Kapesh instructs the reader on the true meaning of the pejorative. The author inverts the categories and explains that her authentic Innu identity is a source of pride. The geographically situated Native ways of knowing through and with the land are "connected to a better life" and will never make her or her people "poor", despite settler-colonial devaluing of their culture and language. In *Je suis une maudite Sauvagesse*, Kapesh speaks to Indigenous and Québécois readers alike, transmitting the dignity and wisdom of the Innu community via a pedagogy of generosity. In the next section, I explore two Innu poets, Joséphine Bacon and Rita Mestokosho, in the context of the history of Francophone Indigenous voices in Québécois literature.

186 *Voices in Francophone Indigenous Literature*

4 The Power of Poetry: Land, Language, and Futurity in Joséphine Bacon's *Un thé dans la toundra/ Nipishapui nete mushauat* and Rita Mestokosho's *Atik^u Utei: Le cœur du caribou*

An Antane Kapesh's *Je suis une maudite Sauvagesse* (1976) has a deep impact on the history of Francophone Indigenous writing in Québec. First, the act of speaking (and publishing) truth to power, insisting on the value of the Indigenous voice in a settler-colonial is an inspiration and roadmap for later writers. Second, the typesetting of the Innu-aimun language in *conversation* with French is influential, copied by several Francophone Indigenous writers, especially in the genre of poetry. The typical structural divisions of the poetic text, verses and stanzas, a relative lack of long passages of condense prose, lends itself more readily to a bilingualism that is fundamental to the chronicle of Francophone Indigenous literature in *La Belle Province*. Both poets that I discuss adopt Kapesh's emphasis on Indigenous language in *conversation* with the settler-colonial. Joséphine Bacon and Rita Mestokosho argue for the equality of Innu-aimun in their work. In this section, I demonstrate the ways in which their poetry situates knowledge and spirituality firmly in the land, highlighting how they call for respect of nature and offer wisdom about our collective survival. In addition, I argue that the notion of family and community, which figures centrally in their poetry, is expanded beyond narrow *national* definitions of Indigeneity, to encompass a *transnational* perspective.

Joséphine Bacon (1947–) is originally from the Innu community of Betsiamites (Pessamit) in the Côte-Nord region of Québec. Her work as a translator and interpreter of Innu-aimun and French inspires her to share the "richness of Innu culture" with the Francophone world through publishing and documentary filmmaking, becoming the first laureate of the Aboriginal Filmmaking Program of the National Film Office of Canada in 1996 (Gatti 246). Since that award, she has made several films that teach about and valorize "Innu communities, elders, land, language, and concerns" (Gatti 246, my translation). In addition to filmmaking, Bacon has collaborated with actress and singer Chloé Sainte-Marie to create Innu-aimun lyrics as part of the growing folk-Innu genre's popularity. However, it is Bacon's poetry that is the form of Indigenous voice that I will examine here, her 2013 collection: *Un thé dans la toundra* /*Nipishapui nete mushauat* (A Tea in the Tundra). *Un thé dans la toundra* is a finalist for both the Governor General's Award and the Grand Prix du livre de Montréal. Bacon garners the Indigenous Voices Award for lifetime achievement in publishing in French in 2019.

Rita Mestokosho is born in 1966 in a First Nations village called Ekuanitshit (Mingan) on the northern banks of the Saint-Lawrence river and she still lives there today. She is the first Innu woman to publish a poetry collection in Québec. *Eshi uapataman Nukum* appears in 1995. After studying political science at the

Voices in Francophone Indigenous Literature 187

Université du Québec-Chicoutimi, Mestokosho returns to Ekuanitshit, becoming active in teaching Innu-aimun, culture, and drama to Innu youth. Mestokosho participates regularly in pan-Indigenous activism and organizations globally. She navigates identity in her work, negotiating traditional and modern lifeways (Gatti 263–4). Mestokosho juxtaposes Innu-aimun and French, as well. Centering her work on questions of land and community, Mestokosho critiques cultural assimilation and Native dispossession (Premat "Mémoire et survivance" 93). The poet's engagement with Indigenous communities beyond the confines of Ekuanitshit reveals a *transnationalism* that is a central element of the collection that my analysis concentrates on: *Atik" Utei:Le cœur du caribou* (2022).

Bilingualism is a critical lens through which to read Joséphine Bacon and Rita Mestokosho, both publishing in Kapesh's wake. Bilingualism responds to a settler-colonial reality that has attempted to exclude and erase Native languages and cultures. The juxtaposition of the Innu-aimun and French languages in Bacon's *Un thé dans la toundra* and Mestokosho's *Le cœur du caribou* is visually distinct in each poet's text. While both are faithful to the example set by Kapesh, Mestokosho takes bilingualism a step farther than Kapesh and Bacon. In *Sauvagesse*, the formatting of the bilingual edition presents the languages in keeping with the hierarchy established in the essay's title. The title foregrounds Innu-Aimun, placing *Eukuan Nin Matshi-Manitu Innushkueu* before *Je suis une maudite Sauvagesse*. In the structure of the text then, chapters are first typeset in Innu-aimun followed by French. Long stretches of prose in Innu-aimun are opposed to entire chapters in French. While the prioritization of Innu-aimun that is indicated by the title and the book's structure are critical to the politics and message of Kapesh's text, it does not facilitate language learning in *conversation* in the same way that Mestokosho's *Le cœur du caribou* does. In contrast to the ordering of *Sauvagesse,* the title of Bacon's *Un thé dans la toundra* is reversed linguistically, the French being followed by the translation in Innu-aimun: *Un thé dans la toundra/Nipishapui nete mushauat*. This French first, Innu-aimun second pattern is echoed in the collection's typesetting of the collection itself. This structural arrangement of the bilingualism of the text is intentional and is informed by Bacon's personal and professional commitments to share Innu language and culture with the world. Bacon's anxiety over language is evident in the following poem, "I've Worn Out My Life On The Pavement".

I've worn out my life on the pavement	Ninanutan nitinnium ka pitshikat-meshkanat
Words come to me	Aimuna nipeten
In a language that isn't my own	Namaieu innu-aimun
At night, Innu-aimun	Tepishkati nitinnu-puamun
Opens me up to space	

188 *Voices in Francophone Indigenous Literature*

I am free	Apu auen tipenimit
On the land of Papakassik^u	Papakassik^u utassit
I am free	Apu auen tipenimit
In the waters of Missinak^u	Missinak^u unipimit
I am free	Apu auen tipenimit
In the skies where Uhuapeu traces a	Uhuapeu niminik^u
vision	nikan-tshissenitamunnu
I am free there where	Apu auen tipenimit
Preserves the flame of my people	Uapishtanapeu kanuenitam^u
	nitishkuteminu

I am free
There where I look like you (49, my
   translation).

Apu auen tipenimit
Uesh ma tshinashpitatin (50).

The discomfort the poet experiences when her thoughts arise in French, a language the "isn't [her] own", is associated with the barely veiled reference to Western economies of extraction in the opening verse. The fatigue and incremental degradation of market economies and their leveraging of labor as a means of survival is equated with a profound sense of alienation in the urban geographies in the poem. In *Un thé dans la toundra*, the form of movement that is privileged most often is walking. In settler-colonial North America "pavement" clearly evokes another form of mobility: the personal automobile. In the context of the collection, the word is jarring due within the themes and geographies that dominate most of the pieces. The opening line equates the Euro-Canadian's motorized, urbanized society with death, a space where the poet has "worn out [her] life". Claustrophobic and carceral, the "pavement" and its concomitant Euro-Canadian lifestyle are decried here and elsewhere in Bacon's oeuvre. In contrast, the tundra is emancipatory. This emancipatory transition is only accessible through the Innu-aimun language, however. Hinting at the emergence of her Indigenous language while dreaming, Bacon confides that, "At night, Innu-aimun, Opens me up to space". This symbiotic relationship between land, language, and culture is a recurrent theme in Francophone Indigenous literature. The collection, *Un thé dans la toundra*, is a love letter to the tundra. Bacon uses the intimate form of you, '*tu*' to address that space. Inclusive to all the cosmos and non-human, Bacon's conception of the tundra is ontological and spiritual. The pieces of the collection serve as a pedagogical tool. Through the introduction of terms in French with the Innu-aimun on the opposite page, but also the introduction of ideas that are at first uniquely in French but are then replaced with the Innu-aimun equivalent without translation, the poet teaches the reader critical terms in her Indigenous language. Innu-aimun is presented here in "I've worn out my life on the pavement" as the gateway to understanding Innu culture. That extends to poetry. To illustrate the pedagogical technique, previous pieces repeat that it is a sacred "mushroom" that "preserves the flame". After having seen this equivalency in multiple other poems, when Bacon uses "Uapishtanapeu" with "Preserves the flame of my people", the astute reader understands and learns that Uapishtanapeu is the sacred mushroom that the writer has been referring to throughout the collection. The Innu-aimun language leads to the land which subsequently leads to liberation. Bacon opposes the elements of land, language, and liberty to the constraints and costs of a Euro-Canadian way of life. Furthermore, the author's anxiety about language addresses a key question with which many Francophone Indigenous writers struggle: the navigation of dual cultural traditions and the preservation of their Indigeneity. The poem identifies that question and responds by demonstrating that even in urban geographies, access to Innu sacred places is possible through the Innu-aimun language and culture. The emphasis on the urban as carceral reaffirms the poet's identification with the tundra as sacred space and skeleton key to liberation. Rita Mestokosho structures the bilingualism of her poems in *Le cœur du caribou* differently. In this collection, several of Mestokosho's poems are in both Innu-aimun and French. While any poems are monolingual (French), in the bilingual pieces, the poet employs the same prioritization as Kapesh in *Sauvagesse*, placing Innu-aimun before French. However, the typesetting of *Le cœur du caribou* is unique. To return to Kapesh, her text introduces an entire chapter in Innu-aimun, followed by its translation in French. In Bacon's *Un thé dans la toundra*, the French verses on one page are mirrored in Innu-aimun on the opposite leaf. In *Le cœur du caribou*, Mestokosho's poems contain intercalated verses first in Innu-aimun, then in French. These alternating lines are separated into stanzas indicated by line breaks. Accordingly, the stanzas include all verses rendered both in Innu-aimun and French. This structure is intentional; its effect is to encourage the reader to become familiar with the Innu-aimun language. When a monolingual French-speaker reads the bilingual pieces, as they are seeking out the lines in French, the eye is drawn to the intercalated verses in Innu-aimun. This favors a more sustained exposure to Innu-aimun. In Kapesh and Bacon, it is up to the reader to make an additional effort to engage with the Indigenous language. In Mestokosho's bilingual pieces, the reader is invited to read the poem in *conversation* with both. Mestokosho also employs the technique used by Bacon: introducing key concepts in Innu-aimun directly followed by their equivalent in French, until the reader is sufficiently familiarized with the term, then only presenting them in Innu-aimun. Bilingualism in Bacon and Mestokosho participates in a pedagogy of generosity addressed to the Innu community *and* to the French-speaker.

Coming from a culture with a rich oral history, writing, like the French language, emerges as a source of tension in Bacon and Mestokosho's writing. Both poets emphasize oral communication in their poetry. In the first section of *Le cœur du caribou*, Nomad Liberty, in a piece titled "Assi Umashinaikana/ The Library of the Earth", Mestokosho integrates the concepts of writing and nomadism.

190   *Voices in Francophone Indigenous Literature*

My people wrote by walking
my people wrote on the line of memory
that way, their baggage was less heavy
he had a library of the earth with him
My people wrote millions of books
scattered over the land
encyclopedias of rivers dictionaries of mountains
geographies of forests
every line that my people wrote
kept its memory awake
its spirit lively and its heart light (35, my translation).

The nomadic movement of walking and the oral tradition of the Innu are introduced in "The Library of the Earth" as a form of writing. This definition of writing challenges Europe's insistence on a lack of writing as a marker of inferiority vis-à-vis Western scriptural traditions. Mestokosho insists that the lack of writing is an advantage, making the trek of life easier, an image to which the author returns in the ultimate verse. The narrative technology of repetition allows the Innu to write knowledge on "the line of memory". The library that is formed is one that takes shape in *conversation* with the land. Mestokosho enumerates reference books that imply comprehensive knowledge to signal the depth of Innu understanding of the environment and the human experience. These "encyclopedias of rivers dictionaries of mountains, geographies of forests" compose the library that each Innu carries with them. As the poem ends, Mestokosho concludes that the land-based knowledge that is maintained through a strong oral tradition within the Innu community results in "[keeping] its memory awake, its spirit lively, and its heart light". The consequences of a land-based knowledge system that forms in *conversation* with the non-human world and is sustained through active communication within the community to ensure the transmission of essential information from one generation to the next leads to a connection to past and place. Europe's expansion into non-European geographies has broken that connection, something to which Mestokosho points the reader's attention with the implication that non-Natives' memory is asleep. Robin Wall Kimmerer (Potawatomi) points to possible ways of understanding why memory anchored in the land in Indigenous communities is "asleep" in European memory.

After all these generations since Columbus, some of the wisest of Native elders still puzzle over the people who came to our shores. They look at the toll on the land and say, "The problem with these new people is that they don't have both feet on the shore. One is still on the boat. They don't seem to know whether they're staying or not." This same observation is heard from some contemporary scholars who see in the social pathologies and relentlessly materialist culture the fruit of homelessness, a rootless past. (207)

Voices in Francophone Indigenous Literature   191

The place-based knowledge and "memory" that Mestokosho describes as "scattered over the land", in contradistinction to the written knowledge of the West, is a lens through which one can interrogate European attitudes to American geographies in the context of settler-colonialism. Kimmerer underlines the disconnect between the settler and the soil as a fundamental fact with concrete consequences. Kimmerer explains the emergence of the economies of extraction in the Americas as a "fruit of homelessness". The Amerindian relation to the land is rooted, not "rootless" and is tied to the past. Throughout Bacon and Mestokosho's oeuvre are countless examples of knowledge coming from conversation, ancestors, and collective wisdom. Oral knowledge formation and storage is not only valid but capacious in Indigenous cultures. The in-between attributed to the European with "one foot on the boat", is a question that I return to at the end of this section. In "The Library of the Earth", Mestokosho insists on Native ways of knowing's capacity as replete. The connotation in the ultimate verse is that Western knowledge, despite its association with writing, is that the non-Native ways of knowing that proclaim their inherent superiority do not lead to a "light heart", rather they are a heavy burden to bear, one that interferes with intimate connection to the land. In Joséphine Bacon's poem "No need to know how to write", the poet covers similar ground.

No need to know how to write
Or how to work out problems
  anymore
It's enough for me to know
  (*connaître*) the directions
	Anutshish apu apashtaian
	  mashinaikana
	Apu apashtaian atshitashunan
	Nimeshkanam takuan
	Anite tshe ituteian

To gather the mushroom That preserves the flame Immortal	Ninanatuapamau pushakan Uin tshika kanuenitamu ishkuassenu Apu nita tshika ut ashtuet
I bring my talking stick And go and talk to the stars I sit to rest my feet I know how to be alone to hear The auroras borealis I sway In the blue of the blue Of a night that puts to sleep My grandfather bear	Nititutatan nashashkauteun Nitaimiauat utshekatakuat Nitapin nitashteieshkushin Niminunuau uashtuashkuan Nimitak uashkut Nipekueu nimushuma mashkua
The horizon will be there Waiting for me	Tshishik^u nitashuapamikun Uin nika peshuk shipit

192   *Voices in Francophone Indigenous Literature*

And will lead me to the river	Nanikutini tshishkutshuan
To the current	
Deceiving sometimes	

I finally arrive	Nitakushin tapue
At the land that is hoping for	Assit
My coming (29, my translation).	Ka pakushenimit(30).

As in Mestokosho's "The Library of the Earth", Bacon deals with the tension between traditional Innu oral tradition and European writing. In a similar move, Bacon dismisses settler education, particularly writing and arithmetic. The site of veridiction in the poem is the land. Beginning with the four directions, everything that follows is framed with the French verb "*connaître*". As discussed above, "*connaître*" refers to an intimate, personal knowledge, one that is experiential rather than factual. Kimmerer contends that the natural penchant in Amerindian ontologies is to look for ties that bind, rather than a Cartesian division and dissection of the non-human. Western knowledge systems are "rigorous in separating the observer from the observed, and the observed from the observer" (Kimmerer 42). This radical distinction between the human and non-human, between knowledge and its object, is characterized by the French verb "*savoir*", implicitly paralleled with the Québécois school system. Kimmerer's insight pinpoints the divergence between the opening two lines' refutation of the structures of government education and the movement to a more experiential knowledge. Looking back to Bacon's "I've worn my life out on the pavement", the poet employs a similar structure wherein cultural elements associated with Euro-Canadian culture are identified and refuted before entering a new space with an Indigenous perspective. Resituating the eternal memory associated with the written word, Bacon ascribes that responsibility to the mushroom, the Uapishtanapeu, which preserves the flame of the Innu people. This juxtaposition accentuates the anchoring of Amerindian knowledge in the non-human world. The reciprocity that Innu ontology cultivates with the non-human is echoed in multiple ways in "No need to know how to write". Bacon describes a conversation between the Innu and the tundra. In the collection, *Un thé dans la toundra*, two elements that represent the comprehensiveness of the Innu outlook and inclusion of the non-human are and the aurora borealis. Integral to the tundra landscape, as a site of repetition because of their attachment to the precise geographies of Innu territory, but also how they delimit the cosmos, with the lichen on the ground below and the aurora borealis floating high above. The incorporation of a Haudenosaunee talking stick indicates a conversation based on mutual respect, reciprocity, and democratic equality. The interlocutors in this communal dialog are the stars, the auroras borealis, the constellation "Grandfather bear", and the poet. In the Innu worldview, the human is not the only entity that it is

Voices in Francophone Indigenous Literature   193

necessary to listen to. The introduction of the Haudenosaunee walking stick is intentional. Indeed, one would not need a talking stick if one did not intend on being silent and listening, in turn. Bacon insists that Native knowledge includes the ability to *hear* the non-human Other. Kimmerer reminds us that Indigenous languages often employ the narrative technology of using "the same words to address the living world as we use for our family. Because they are our family" (55). This inclusive practice contrasts starkly with the exclusionary inclusion of the Native into the European family in a relation of hierarchy known as paternalism, wherein the Amerindian is held in contempt as infant. Instead, what Kimmerer calls a "grammar of animacy", is expressed not only in the reference to the constellation "Grandfather bear" but in the poet's foresight to bring along the talking stick, with the plan to listen that gesture suggests. The anticipatory in "No need to know how to write" is not attached to the author's agentive position alone, rather it is extended to the land, as well. In Innu country, the land hopes for the people to come as much as the Innu cannot wait to arrive. Mestokosho's prologue to *Le cœur du caribou* expresses a similar viewpoint.

> [The] forest's call sharpens instinct. The rivers are our blue highways. We speak with the birches to build our canoes et go toward the home of the man of the North, there where the auroras borealis remain a holy secret. We speak to each tree that we pass on our nomad road. The earth carries us in its wintry silence. Even the smallest rock has a story. A great part of our humanity lives under every leaf. We have been children of the Earth and we will always be. Yes, she is sacred, Nutshimit, our home. Nikaui Assi, our Mother Earth, carries so many memories inside of her: our dreams, our songs, our prayers, our steps, our stories. She is old, the soul of the Earth. He is old, Papakassik", the spirit of the Caribou. It is sacred, the life of an Innu. The heart of humanity is humble. Innu means "human being" (9–10, my translation)

The non-human and human are in *conversation* in this passage in much the same manner as they are in Bacon's "No need to know how to write". This democratic dialog is essential for Innu survival. Speaking with the birch to ensure a properly built canoe is a critical aspect of the construction. Talking to each tree is accompanied by the active agency of the land carrying the people. The thematic of conversation continues with the statement that "Even the smallest rock has a story". The implication is not purely perspectival, but a call to action. The exchange of the talking stick means that one must listen to learn. By adopting a "grammar of animacy", one that extends humanity to the non-human, one can uncover a truth not available to knowledge systems that deny the connection between the two. To self-locate as the pinnacle of creation and ontologically distinct from all else on earth is an arrogance that does not belong to the Innu cultural imaginary, which affirms that, "The heart of humanity is humble". Mestokosho contends there is a wealth of knowledge, "a great part of our humanity" that hides beneath

194   *Voices in Francophone Indigenous Literature*

all the leaves of the forest. This declaration is in concert with the poem "The Library of the Earth", wherein "encyclopedias, dictionaries, geographies", a "million books" are "scattered over the land". The "grammar of animacy" which insists upon the familial relation between the Innu and the natural environment is echoed in Mestokosho's discussion of Mother Earth and her intimate relationship and communication with the Innu community. A repository of knowledge, a "Library of the Earth", Mother Earth is capacious enough to hold all Innu dreams, songs, prayers, travels, and stories. Mother Earth serving as a receptacle is only possible through shared communication with Nutshimit, the land. Kimmerer explains the centrality of land in Indigenous ontologies.

> Children, language, lands: almost everything was stripped away, stolen when you weren't looking because you were trying to stay alive. In the face of such loss, one thing our people could not surrender was the meaning of land. In the settler mind, land was property, real estate, capital, or natural resources. But to our people, it was everything: identity, the connection to our ancestors, the home of our nonhuman kinfolk, our pharmacy, our library, the source of all that sustained us. Our lands were where our responsibility to the world was enacted, sacred ground. It belonged to itself, it was a gift, not a commodity, so it could never be bought or sold. (17)

Echoing many of the principal themes of the poetry of both Bacon and Mestokosho, as well as Kapesh's political essay, with repetition indicating a site of danger, vital information, essential to our collective survival. The "meaning of land" is so critical to Amerindian ontologies that none of the violence of genocide, removal, confinement, allotment, termination, or the "cunning of recognition" could alter this fundamental relation to the non-human world in Indigenous communities. The history that Kimmerer recounts is of loss, but also of power. The elaboration of an ethic that foregrounds the connection to the land is a narrative of survivance. It establishes an unbreakable bond between Native and environment, which transcends the transactional values of the economies of extraction and the inherent illogic of the commodification of home. By putting Kimmerer's insights into *conversation* with Mestokosho and Bacon's poetics, we arrive at the most crucial consequence of the familial relation to the non-human: responsibility. One of the recurrent problems that both poets address is the threat of environmental collapse associated with the climate change crisis brought on by the excesses of late-liberal capitalism. If the enunciation of an ethic that grants personhood to the non-human world is a narrative of survivance, then employing knowledge learned for the land to map a path forward for the planet is to articulate an Indigenous futurity that would maintain the connection to the land intact. As I mentioned in the first section, story is regenerative and productive. It can be utilized as a narrative technology to create a collective "modern image of the future". In keeping with the moral principle of the pedagogy of generosity,

Voices in Francophone Indigenous Literature   195

which offers up sacred, place-based knowledge to the Indigenous community *and* the non-Indigenous community alike, the narrative of survivance as wisdom for taking responsibility for and taking care of the environment can be a citing of danger and a call to listen, a futurity for all. In Mestokosho's "The Language of the Earth", the author draws parallels between the connection to the land and the creative energy that forges the power of poetry.

> Nete ishpish utatshakusha mishta-atamit assit
> A soul as deep as earth
> katak^u ututeu katshi pamishkat
> coming back from a long voyage
> kashekau-aimun ka inniuimakak ut assit
> poetry is born of this earth language
> tshui tipatshimushtatin apishish
> i want to tell you a little
> tshekuan ne assi nete Nutshimit
> story of Nutshimit
> tauat anite aueshishat e inniuht
> animals live there
> miam tshikanishat etenitakushiht
> like our brothers (15, my translation).

In this brief piece, Mestokosho not only makes a connection that we have grown quite accustomed to in the discussion of the history of the Indigenous voice in the Francophone literature of Québec, that between the land and the community, but the poet also locates the power of story. As Whitt contends, "the integrative power of stories, the way they help us initiate and maintain relationships with others who may appear different from us, is especially needed to guide human interaction with the other-than-human world" (36). Whitt calls attention to the potential of story to bring people and people and non-humans together. Whitt confirms the urgency of narratives of survivance at a time when climate crisis threatens the balance of human and non-human interdependency. The power of narratives of survivance originates in a language that teaches the listener to respect the non-human, incorporating a "grammar of animacy". The Language of the Earth" is the second poem in the first section of *Le cœur du caribou.* It functions as a framing device guiding the reader to a certain interpretation. It performs an invitation to join the conversation, to be a part of the family, with the non-human, to get to know (*connaître*) Nutshimit in the hope of constructing a "modern image of the future" together. The door through which vital information is accessible is through the power of story, precisely the power of poetry. Poetry that transmits the narrative of survivance is inclusive in Mestokosho's *Atik^u Utei: Le cœur du caribou,* the reader is asked to listen to the "little story" the poet tells. In Kimmerer's analogy, the

196   *Voices in Francophone Indigenous Literature*

poet reaches out a hand to invite the immigrant settler to take their other foot off the boat, to put both feet firmly on this sacred ground.

The pedagogy of generosity at the center of Native narratives of survivance is an expression of the profound connection between the Indigenous and the non-human, but is also destined for the Québécois community (and beyond). The teaching of a relation of respect and responsibility toward the environment and Others is part of sharing Innu language and culture through writing. The choice to present these teachings in *conversation* with the language of the empire, the colonizer, the residential school, the priest, the government official, is an intentional one that invites the Québécois to listen. This spirit of inclusivity and that of the Haudenosaunee talking stick is exemplified by the poetry collection *Aimititau!/Parlons-nous!* (Let's Talk!) (2008) which includes contributions from both Bacon and Mestokosho with several other Indigenous and non-Indigenous voices in *conversation* with one another. Mestokosho's "The Language of the Earth" invites the reader to listen to vital poems of survivance that are calls to attention. Narratives of survivance locate and cite danger and its consequences in the Francophone Indigenous literature of Québec. Bacon's "Your alarm jostle's life" cites a danger that hangs over us all.

Feathers move away in the gray sky	Mikunat upauat
And land on a threatened earth	Patshishinuat assit ka ui pikunkanit
You hope for the teaching of the ancestors	Tshipakusheniten tshetshi kau Tshishkutamashkau tshimushumat
To survive in that wisdom (77, my translation).	Tshethsi minu-shaputuetein tshitinniunit (78).

In the final stanza, the poet focuses the reader's attention on the distancing mobility of birds in the sky. This movement is indicative of a warning, rather than the emancipatory semantics often attached to movement throughout the rest of the collection *Un thé dans la toundra*. Unable to move to a place other than a "threatened earth", the birds have nowhere to which they can escape environmental collapse. A pedagogy of generosity implies a common path forward, a collective narrative of survivance, a fraternal futurity. Bacon's message in this ultimate stanza of "Your alarm jostle's life" returns to the initial line of the poem by indicating to the reader what alarm should be listened to in order to survive the danger faced. A multitude of sources of knowledge are presented in this strophe. The incorporation of animal-life, the land, ancestors which represent the Innu specifically and humanity more generally, and that crucial ingredient of hope that fuels the articulation of futurity and survivance. Attentiveness to and awareness of the land in intimate *conversation* is distinct from knowledge about the earth that cannot fully capture the consequences nor compel the necessary care. It is the wisdom of the ancestors, constructed in *conversation* with the land, in observance of the family of non-human animals, that creates the conditions of

Voices in Francophone Indigenous Literature 197

possibility for a knowledge that can "preserve the flame", that can be employed as a narrative technology of survivance. The disinterested distance, the separation of the "observer and the observed", the objectification of the non-human are all complicit in a knowledge system that abets efforts to "exploit and destroy". In the final poem of her collection *Le cœur du caribou*, "Tshin an ume", Mestoko-sho shares insights for survival in a conversational mode.

> To you (toi)
> who doesn't know (connaître) the song of the seasons
> receive the breeze
> of its unique music
>
> to you
> who doesn't know the name of the wind
> it's no doubt the wind of the North
> that brings agonies to mind
> and makes the regrets disappear
>
> to you
> who doesn't know the mountain
> even though you live so close to her
> know that she is sacred for us Innus
> and the Anangus
> my brothers from Australia
>
> to you who doesn't know the river
> you navigate your dreams there
> by drowning the spirit of what's real
>
> to you
> who doesn't know the age of the earth
> see its skin is wrinkled by the salt of the sea
> its lines imprinted by humanity's footprints
> its nighttime dances
> its sun songs
>
> that's the spirit of the word
> that guides the feather
>
> color of our union
>
> atik^u utei
> keeps its promise (118, my translation).

198   *Voices in Francophone Indigenous Literature*

Using the informal, intimate form of you (*tu*), Mestokosho invites the reader to receive information contained in the song of the seasons. Music goes beyond language and speaks to us on multiple levels simultaneously. No specialized academic training is required to understand music. Mestokosho's reference to music is an affirmation of the accessibility of the message of futurity contained in the collection and confirmed in the closing piece. Citing the Indigenous scholar Greg Cajete (Tewa), Kimmerer explains that, "in indigenous ways of knowing, we understand a thing only when we understand it with all four aspects of our being: mind, body, emotion, spirit" (46). This is why Mestokosho frames her invitation to listen to a very important story filled with pertinent information for survival by alluding to the music of the seasons. Through the allusion to music, the poet encourages the reader to learn what they do not yet know in keeping with Indigenous knowledge systems. She calls on the reader to ingest the message with their "mind, body, emotion, spirit". In addition to the specific decision to employ the familiar form of you, Mestokosho employs a version of the verb to know that I have discussed at length. When the poet welcomes the reader to listen with "all four aspects of their being", it is reinforced by the use of "*connaître*" which implies on the experiential, the sensory, the seasonal (indicating the fact that this knowledge can only be acquired over time), the site specific. "*Connaître*" implies knowledge of people and places. They are one and the same in the poem "Tshin an ume". Mestokosho appeals to the reader to listen and pay attention so that they can learn an urgent lesson. Further establishing the reader's lack of awareness of the secrets of the non-human world, the poet claims that the reader does not know the name of the wind or the mountain. Incredulous, Mestokosho points to the proximity of the mountain, which should, in Indigenous ways of knowing confer knowledge, but does not for the reader. All the elements in the first three stanzas of the poem, taken cumulatively, substantiate a reading that the poem is addressed primarily to a non-Indigenous audience. This is further validated by the exclusion of the reader from the communal "us Innus" and from the Aboriginal Anangu of the Ayers Rock region of central Australia, with whom the author indicates a transindigenous affiliation. A transindigenous or transnational move, Mestokosho is known for her activism for and collaborations with Indigenous peoples globally. Bacon demonstrates a similar transnationalist gesture by using the Haudenosaunee talking stick in the personal context of speaking to the non-human world with the help of that sacred object in her poem, "No need to know how to write". This inclusivity is typical of many contemporary Francophone Indigenous writers of Québec and of the transnational turn in Indigenous culture. Huhndorf (Yup'ik) states that, "Common histories of colonization and shared relationships to the land that predate the arrival of settlers provide a foundation for such global political alliances" (13). These parallel experiences have often led to an "exchange of stories" that strengthens bonds between disparate communities. Transnationalism expands in *conversation* with the transition to a post-recognition politics in Indigenous

Voices in Francophone Indigenous Literature 199

communities. Coulthard (Yellowknife Dene) advocates a shift away from recognition as understood by the settler-state.

> [From] the largely rights-based/recognition orientation that has emerged as a hegemonic over the last four decades, to a resurgent politics of recognition that seeks to practice decolonial, gender-emancipatory, and economically nonexploitative alternate structures of law and authority grounded on a critical refashioning of the best of Indigenous legal and political traditions. (217)

Transnationalism finds inspiration in the same place that Coulthard locates the path forward for Indigenous peoples. Decolonial and gender egalitarian, Coulthard's post-recognition vision is that of a structural redefinition of the recognition paradigm, one that accepts difference rather than promote sameness. In Mestokosho and Bacon's poetry, transnationalism is the recognition of the same challenges in confrontation with settler-colonialism's exclusionary *and* inclusionary discourses. Huhndorf predicts that "transnationalism has come to occupy ever more expansive ground in Native cultural practices in recent decades and will likely continue to do so in the years ahead" (177). Mestokosho's call to *recognize* the Innu and the Anangu as family, as Same and not as Other, is a call to a transnationalism that is critical for understanding the recent history of Francophone Indigenous voices in Québécois literature. To return Mestokosho's final piece in the *Le cœur du caribou* collection, apart from the semantic fields that pinpoint the destination of the poem as non-Indigenous, the poem situates itself structurally as a narrative of survivance.

In my discussion of Kapesh's *Sauvagesse*, I pointed out how repetition, specifically anaphora, calls the reader's attention to vital information in a story of survivance. "Tshin an ume" employs the same narrative technology, insist on the seriousness of the poem's message. As Silko contends, Native narratives would often utilize repetition "to make sure the listeners remembered what to do to survive in a similar situation" (Introduction). For Mestokosho, anaphora serves to recall the personal invitation to the non-Indigenous reader to listen to the vital story that her poem has to tell by repeating the intimate, epistolary "to you". Furthermore, anaphora that insists upon the urgency of the call to action is equally concerned with the reader's lack of awareness. As the author suggests in the prologue, "The heart of humanity is humble". The anaphoric recall of the ignorance of the reader is a device that seeks to humble the reader in hopes of increasing their receptivity to vital information. In the fourth stanza, Mestokosho summons the reader to consider that their perspective on the non-human is flawed. The "dreams" that the non-Indigenous engage in with the river is a reference to the mythification associated with the radical Western othering of Nature in Phillipe Descola's categorization of Europe as ontologically adherent to naturalism, rather than animism. Naturalism, despite its naturalized categories, falls woefully short of accounting for the complexity of non-human entities according to

200 *Voices in Francophone Indigenous Literature*

an Indigenous worldview that grants personhood to the non-human world. This is the lacuna that Mestokosho signals with the claim that Western ways of knowing only succeed in "drowning the spirit of what's real", which is to say denying it mutual spirit and life at all. In the fifth stanza, Mestokosho subjectifies Mother Earth further by referring to her surface as a face, as skin, as a page written on by the movements of nomads. Naming the reader's unawareness of the age of the earth is a call to respect. In Indigenous communities, while the young are certainly prized and cared for, the relationship to elders is one that prioritizes care and reverence. Economies of extraction are guilty of abandoning elders once they have outlived their profitability in accordance with the mandates of late-liberal capitalism. Reminding the reader of the venerable age of the earth is to demand respect for one's elders, rather than the forgetfulness that characterizes Western ways of (mis)understanding. The connection between humanity and the earth is bolstered by the integration of human dances and songs within the very body of the land. This comes full circle to call the reader's attention back to the music of the seasons that inspire the people's singing and dancing. In the final two stanzas, Mestokosho completes another circle, that of the entire collection. The spirit that needs to be experienced and learned, to be believed, is that which fuels the emergence of the word. In French, as with the English word knowledge, there are two separate terms for word. "*Mot*" refers to the written or spoken word, whereas "*parole*" is only the spoken word. In the couplet "that's the spirit of the word, that guides the feather" it is necessary to unpack the vocabulary choices that the author makes in French to comprehend the meaning of the text's message more fully. The term that Mestokosho opts for in this couplet is "*parole*", the spoken word. This intentional vocabulary insists upon the oral tradition of the Innu people. The tension at the core of the author's grappling with writing as a mode of communication associated with the colonizer finds its resolution here. The subjectified spirit of the "*parole*", is the force that drives the intentionality of the feather, "*plume*" in French. The use of "*plume*" makes a direct connection between the oral tradition of the Innu and the writing culture of the West, because a "*plume*" is also a writing tool, one that incorporates non-human animals as participatory in the scriptural act. Organic, the "*plume*" reinserts the act of writing in the universe of the Innu, an element of the land and its animal abundance. The next line, which is separate from two couplets as a solitary verse that refers directly back to the act of writing, specifically employing the "*plume*". The "color of our union" is a reference to the color of the ink used to unleash the power of the "*parole*", the power of the poem. This reading is verified when one considers the poem's final couplet: "atik[u] utei, keeps its promise". Atik[u] utei, "the heart of the caribou" is the title of the collection itself, the act of writing, the poems that the reader has just read. The kept promise is the promise to fulfill the ethical choice of a pedagogy of generosity, one that shares vital information in a narrative of survivance with Indigenous and non-Indigenous alike. It is clear Mestokosho exemplifies the spirit of the pedagogy of generosity, which is two-fold. The generosity of sharing wisdom with the non-Indigenous is coupled with the primary message of the imparted lesson: adopt the generosity of the Innu which grants personhood to the non-human world. Leaving behind the naturalist mythologizing of the human as superior to all other entities *and* the radical othering of nature as products of the mythic machine in the same way that the genealogy of mythic modes and their distortions of the Native traced over the first four chapters of this study are, is the generosity that the current crisis calls for. In her poem "Tonight Tundra", Bacon proclaims that, "I teach my identity, In a classroom", highlighting her personal commitment to sharing Innu truth with the world via a pedagogy of generosity (69, my translation). Gatti explains that Mestokosho "considers her work with young people the basis for building the future" (263–4, my translation). Both poets embody a pedagogy of generosity in their poetry by insisting on citing danger and crafting narratives of survivance that they voluntarily share with Indigenous and non-Indigenous, as evidenced by the bilingualism of their texts, but also by the specificity of their words. Mestokosho explains the meaning of Atik^u Utei more explicitly in the collection's prologue.

We are deep in the heart of the caribou, in a world of change. Words are important when we tell the truth. I see the heavy portages that are taking shape before us. We are going to walk with joys, tribulations, teachings, carrying our grandchildren in our outstretched arms. (9, my translation)

While the heart of the caribou may represent a world in transition, one that presents opportunities for happiness and struggle, Mestokosho, like many Indigenous authors, insists on continual striving. Creating a Native futurity, a "modern image of the future", and a narrative of survivance, Indigenous voices of the Francophone literature of Québec construct a path forward through story. Kimmerer, continuing her reflection on the "homelessness" of Europeans in the Americas, asks the following questions.

What happens when we truly become native to a place, when we finally make a home? Where are the stories that lead the way? (207)

To respond, I would argue that the poets Joséphine Bacon and Rita Mestokosho, are both well on their way to guiding readers home. The French Nobel Laureate J.M.G. Le Clézio mentions the poet Mestokosho directly in his acceptance address in Stockholm in 2008, raising awareness internationally about the importance of her work. In Le Clézio's preface to a trilingual edition of *Eshi Uapataman Nukum* published in Sweden in 2010, the French-Mauritian writer positions her poetry within the paradigms of the pedagogy of generosity and contends that hers is a voice that should be heeded by all.

Rita's poetry is full of that feminine power that ancient peoples are steeped in...the voice of shamans, the voice of storytellers. Something calm and

202 *Voices in Francophone Indigenous Literature*

incorruptible that opens onto the future. Her poems don't make any claims or demands. Thanks to this love and sharing, Rita's poetry is addressed to us all, no matter where we are in the world, no matter our origins or our history. (qtd. in Premat "Retrouver les voix autochtones" 119, my translation)

5 Reinhabiting the Reserve, Pedagogies of Generosity, and Forging Futurities in Naomi Fontaine

The Innu novelist, Naomi Fontaine was born in Uashat, reserve No. 27 located northwest of the town of Sept-Îles, in the Côte-Nord region of eastern Quebec. She graduated from the Université de Laval and teaches French. Her first novel, *Kuessipan* (2011) is a text comprised of short sketches that present different characters illustrating daily Innu lives both on the reserve and in relation to one another and to Nutshimit, the land. It quickly became a *"succès de librairie"*, garnering widespread admiration in *La Belle Province* and beyond. The author is awarded an honorable mention in the prestigious Prix des cinq continents de la francophonie, which rewards texts from all over the French-speaking world outside of the Hexagon. In addition, the novel is adapted into a scenario for a filmic version, directed by Myriam Verreault and released in 2019 which was nominated for and received many prizes and awards. Her second novel, *Manikanetish* (2017), a finalist for the Governor General's Award, is an autobiographical text that recounts the author's life as schoolteacher on a reserve. It engages the reader with the transmission of Innu culture and lifeways, while also addressing the issues facing today's First Nations youth. *Manikanetish* proclaims a discourse of futurity that is forward-facing. The writer's first essay is entitled *Shuni: ce que tu dois savoir, Julie* (2019). Structurally similar to the author's first two novels, it is composed of short vignettes. *Shuni*, the Innu-aimun approximation of the name "Julie", is written to a Euro-Canadian childhood friend returning to the reserve as an adult to perform missionary work with the Innu community. The book functions as a deeply personal conversation, but also as a roadmap for Settler-Indigenous relations from an Amerindian perspective. As such, it participates in a pedagogy of generosity which I have identified as a unifying feature of Francophone Indigenous voices in the literature of Québec. In this final section, I examine how an Innu novelist incorporates the land, Innu-aimun language, community, and teaching into her oeuvre in familiar *and* unique ways. I end my discussion of Fontaine's work with a brief analysis of the cinematic adaptation of her first novel *Kuessipan*, concentrating on a scene near the film's dénouement that delivers a powerful message of Indigenous futurity.

To begin with is the land. A theme that has repeated itself in all the discussions in this chapter bringing us back to that point of departure. In Fontaine's work, there is a tenuous relationship with the land. In one of the vignettes in her novel *Kuessipan*, Fontaine recounts the experiences of a forty-year-old woman who

Voices in Francophone Indigenous Literature 203

leaves the reserve in search of peace. Going into the hinterland, she seeks (re) connection with her culture and ancestors.

> Rowing, walking, carrying, camping, eating, sleeping, breaking camp, rowing—that was her life. The life she had chosen now, that she had borrowed from her ancestors; an heiress by choice. The path had been broken by thousands of other travelers. All she had to do was follow them and believe in the promise of an easier day. She gathered the purity of water in her hands, free, with survival her only constraint. Surrounded by tall spruce and stunted deciduous trees, she saw rabbit tracks and spotted the silent partridge. She thanked the four other women for having helped her to persevere. She thanked the heavens for its sweetness on these May evenings. To her very last step, she thanked the Creator for having guided her. (*Kuessipan* 66–7)

This moment of completing the "work" of life on the land is critical. It is a trajectory that reinvigorates relations with elders and the land, what Premat refers to as a "resacralization of natural spaces" (*Mémoire et survivance* 98, my translation). Fontaine intimates that the pursuit of the character's cultural heritage is motivated by the desire to engage with the land and with ancestors. Often repeated in Francophone Indigenous writing, the land holds the memory of the ancestors. This is why interaction with the land is regenerative and educational. The woman does not come to the frenetic enumeration of actions listed in the first sentence of the passage, very easily. Knowledge is only possible in relation to the land, ancestors, and community. In this sketch, the convergence of these three elements leads to gratitude that circles back to them. Directed by ancestors, the woman is merely following the trail blazed by "thousands of other travelers". In Fontaine's work, the land is a catalyst that connects the past, the present, and the future in the "circle of life" (*Manikanetish* 95). Ancestors are accessible through the land. This vision of the Innu's relation to Nutshimit (the land) is mirrored throughout the author's texts. In the essay *Shuni*, Fontaine explains that, "The foundational mythologies of nomads can only be written in the places they've been. Memory has been our survival" (*Shuni* 80, my translation). This statement calls to mind Mestokosho's poem "The Library of the Earth" discussed in the previous section. In Mestokosho's formulation, nomadic movements scattered "millions of books" all over the land. The unbreakable bond between the Innu and the land is inscribed in these geographies. Fontaine draws powerful parallels between the knowledge of the ancestors, represented by the term "memory" (past), the act of engaging with the land (present), and an Indigenous future, suggested by the word *survival*. Christophe Premat argues that in the novel *Kuessipan*, Fontaine is seeking to "reappropriate an image of [Innu] identity; literature becomes a site of investment in an imaginary. There are no real individual characters, rather the description of a collective ethos which is presented via the immersion of the Innu being in their environment" (Premat "Mémoire et survivance" 101, my

204   *Voices in Francophone Indigenous Literature*

translation). The construction of a collective imaginary for the Innu community is one that only occurs in *conversation* with the land. However, there are often difficulties with the transition from an urban environment to the forest or the tundra. In addition to geographies, patterns of behavior are depicted in conflict. The tension between Native and Euro-Canadian lifeways is articulated in Fontaine's work in a much different way than in Kapesh's *Sauvagesse*. Whereas Kapesh denounces Euro-Canadian cultural encroachment as a wholly destructive force, Fontaine is much less categorical.

> A few days later, she started wanting to be home again, in her house, in her bed with her man, nice and warm, clean and fresh, drinking a cup of coffee with cream and sugar in the morning. She didn't want to live like a nomad any more; she didn't want to carry everything on her back for one more second. She wasn't one of those women from the past who had no sense of time or effort, who climbed every mountain as if it were the first. How could she fight nature—starting with her own nature? (*Kuessipan* 66)

The state of gratitude expressed in the passage above is not arrived at without overcoming trials and tribulations. The habits of Euro-Canadian lifestyle are not rebuked, but resituated in subtle ways. Rather than being a landmine, non-traditional lifeways are not condemned, but dealt with as realities that effect everyone. The creature comforts of coffee are not to be shunned but overcome. Marie-Ève Vaillancourt remarks that, for younger generations of Innu, their experience is "no longer mainly, or exclusively, shaped by a very concrete contact with the land, but is confronted daily with the consequences and effects of an imposed sedentarism" (27, my translation). Fontaine validates the non-Indigenous and the sedentary of the quotidian lived practice in *conversation* with, not to the exclusion of, Indigenous lifeways. The supreme effort that the woman in the vignette needs to arrive at her destination comes from her fellow travelers, the four women whom she thanks, but also from an ancestor. The passage asks the essential question of the woman's true nature. The question of the Innu woman's nature is answered when, frustrated and ready to give up, she looks into a mirror and recognizes her mother's face. The identification with her mother is a clear indication that the woman's nature is Innu. Describing the mother's eyes that are also the woman in the sketch's eyes, Fontaine tells the reader that, "They spoke of challenge, struggle, quest—but not defeat" (*Kuessipan* 66). Through experience with the land, the woman connects with her past, which propels her forward. Yet, the author indicates that there is an intrinsic duality, one whose axis is cultural, a battle between Innu and Euro-Canadian practices. Moreover, in Fontaine's work, the author confides that there is a rupture between the Innu of the present and the land, Nutshimit. In the essay *Shuni*, the narrator's cousins mock her for her wonder and awe at a starry sky, calling her a "city girl". The narrator does and does not believe them, "There, at the center of the world,

Voices in Francophone Indigenous Literature 205

I knew that they weren't wrong. But I also felt that they were mistaken" (*Shuni* 16). In these two passages from *Kuessipan*, the conjunction of land, ancestors, knowledge, and futurity is acknowledged in the living body of the contemporary Innu. Fontaine recognizes a generational break that must be repaired, positing agency as the ultimate purview of the individual Native. Fontaine does not accept the mythic machine's temporalities, which would imprison the Amerindian in a perpetual past, denying a "modern image of the future". In *Shuni*, Fontaine argues against the facile designation of her people as *primitive*. Fontaine takes issue with a hackneyed explanation for (neo)colonialism, a myopic reading of history that situates modernity as being solely European, claiming such a viewpoint is a "rather narrow idea of what modernity is" (38, my translation). The author contends that Indigenous people have always been eager to adapt and adopt new technologies whenever they have had the opportunity to do so in a discourse that would counter an imposed traditionalism that is typical of the mythic machine's distortion of the Amerindian since the period of early contacts. Moreover, the appropriation of modernity by the thinkers of the Enlightenment is condemned, insisting that modernity is something that "exists, in different ways, in every society" and that it "belongs to the entire world", not uniquely to the European.

> You see, Julie, modernity had already made its way to our forests. You can believe me or not, but democracy instead of monarchy, equality between men and women, human freedom had already existed here, for a longtime. (39, my translation)

The positively coded elements that Fontaine lists are cultural ideals that originate in Native geographies and cultures, as well as in European progressivism. This inclusiveness is redolent of the Francophone Indigenous writers that I have discussed in the final two sections of this chapter, including many others. Rather than adopt the hierarchical lens that would position one people above another, Fontaine simply advocates for the existence of these aspects of a supposed modernity that Julie needs to know. The author's challenging introduction of this enumeration of Amerindian cultural heritage insists on the value of Indigenous knowledge and cultures in the face of the prejudice and dehistoricization typical of Settler-Indigenous relations. As we have seen in previous chapters, when Europeans recognize the items that Fontaine lists as inherent to Native lifeways, they are inevitably distorted via the mythic machine's Noble Savage or Going Native modes. They are never accepted as integral to Amerindian identity in the way that racial superiority purportedly is adherent to Europeanness. Putting the notions of modernity and democracy in parallel, Fontaine understands that injustice is nevertheless inherent to that form of political system, stating that "You have to see democracy as a circle. That being said, democracy does not mean equality" (*Manikanetish* 128, my translation). This statement comes from

206 *Voices in Francophone Indigenous Literature*

the author's second novel, *Manikanetish*, which centers on education. It is an assignment prompt for the narrator's class that indicates what Fontaine considers vital information, a message of survival. Inclusivity is key to the pedagogy of generosity. It is not reserved solely for those that look, speak, or think like the Self, but is resolutely given as a gift to all. The teacher in *Manikanetish* responds to her own question, answering that, "If everyone, women, men, the poor, the rich, the right, the left, Innu and Québécois, have an equal place in the circle, that's when we can say it is a successful democracy" (128, my translation). This line of reasoning echoes Kapesh's critique of Western democracy. Kapesh associates Canadian democracy with corruption and governmental manipulation in Innu-Québécois relations. Specifically, Kapesh gives the example of provincial pressure on the community to move closer to town rather than continue living lakeside. Officials intimidate and misinform, holding multiple votes until they get the desired result, which is the opposite of what is best for the community (144). Inequal power dynamics infiltrate the geographies of Fontaine's fictional and non-fictional Innu universe; consequently, Fontaine interrogates the concept of freedom in multiple ways. Individual or collective, freedom is an objective that the author maps in her work.

> Someone asked me what the most beautiful word in French is. Here it is: freedom. It's a word that doesn't exist in my language though. Freedom is a concept that is intrinsic to everything that exists in our vision of the world. We come from a space without enclosures, without borders. Free beings from childhood, starting as soon as the child becomes autonomous. Even animals, we never captured them to make them into livestock. Freedom is a state that never needed to be named. The only way to see freedom in Innu-aimun is in reference to the end of an imprisonment: Apikunakanu. (*Shuni* 12, my translation)

Language is a critical component of Francophone Indigenous literature, often fraught with tension. Fontaine assumes the French language as part of her identity more than other author's explored in this chapter. However, in this passage there is an echo of Michel de Montaigne's version of the mythic machine's privative mode from chapter one. On one hand, Montaigne lists vocabulary items that define Native culture in the Noble Savage mode, terms exclusively based the semantic field of immorality: "treachery, lying, cheating, avarice, envy, backbiting". On the other hand, Fontaine posits the lack of the positive term "freedom" as a cultural advantage. Indeed, the incommensurability of the Western and Native worldviews is on full display in this passage, where the author pinpoints how personal and communal liberty is (not) conceived of in First Nations lifeways. While Western thinking naturalizes exclusionary concepts like racial hierarchy, patriarchy, and economic inequality, Innu culture naturalizes freedom as synonymous with existence. So integral to Indigenous lifeways that it "never needed to be named", because it had been the status quo of all things from time immemorial. This is reinforced by the double reference to imprisonment, that of animals in chattel farming and that of people on reserves, which is thrown back at Fontaine's Euro-Canadian interlocutor as something from their tradition, not hers. It is especially telling that in a discussion of freedom, a concept that is reserved solely for the category of human in Western philosophical tradition, the Innu writer includes elements that are critical to Amerindian thinking on the subject: the land, non-human animals, as well as an inclusionary reference to "everything that exists". Isabella Huberman refers to this perspective as "a conception of the world anchored in the collective. and in the gathering together of all beings, animate and inanimate" (114, my translation). Resisting the exceptionalist Cartesian paradigm associated with Western naturalism, Fontaine reminds her Euro-Canadian interlocutor that there is agency and intentionality in all things, including in the frontier-less, fence-less space that the Innu call home, Nutshimit.

> Years later, the authorities took down the fence that they'd erected. But it was too late. We were born imprisoned, and that imprisonment became our salvation. Us nomads, travelers, who had the entirety of the North as our territory, we ended up believing that that fence protected us. From contempt, from being swindled, from the hatred of those who'd erected it. The most solid barriers are those that persist in the mind... You see, my friend, that's how the impossible sometimes happens. In a fenced-in reserve, a place closed off to strangers, we recreated the community. Strong, united. Able to welcome in visitors. It's fascinating to me. What battle they must have had to wage? What strength must have been inside them? So that, years and decades later, this transformation came about. (*Shuni* 10–1, my translation)

The geography of the reserve is given special attention in Naomi Fontaine's writing. Papillon contends that *Kuessipan* focuses on characters' relationships with the spaces of Nutshimit and the reserve, rather than foregrounding the communal bond (Papillon 63). While largely true of *Kuessipan*, Fontaine introduces a different reading of the reserve, echoing the carceral imagery seen in many Indigenous portrayals, while insisting on the centrality of other members of the group, in the essay *Shuni*. Reclaiming the penitentiary confinement of the reserve, the Innu seek refuge there to cultivate relation, a critical concept in many Indigenous groups. Huberman identifies the cooperative nature of identity in Innu cultures in Fontaine's writing, describing the "preeminence of relationships and connections in the constitution of subjectivity, which differs from the persistent vision of the subject in the Western imaginary which sees the being as something that creates itself and is self-sufficient" (113, my translation). For the Innu on the reserve, community is a crucial component in identity construction and continuance; it is tantamount to survival. Fontaine deconstructs the

208 *Voices in Francophone Indigenous Literature*

term "resilient" elsewhere in *Shuni*, decrying the passivity of a term that is used to describe "the strength to survive the savage colonization that First Nations peoples were victims of" (53, my translation). In this passage, Fontaine presents a narrative of survivance that reappropriates what was meant to destroy, transforming the carceral confinement of the reserve into a source of solidarity, community identity, and creative collaboration in the construction of a future. Gerald Vizenor (Chippewa) states that "Native Americans were cursed by racialism and separatism on federal reservations in a constitutional democracy, and the stories of that time necessitate new words" (*Native Liberty* Chapter 1). Fontaine's recasting of the evolution of the reserve from carceral to communal are just the new words that Vizenor calls for. Reserve-as-refuge can be situated through the concept of inhabiting, the lived experience of a place, no matter how dystopian. The urgency to make the reserve home in a hostile world is a result of "this anti-nature space, which seems on the brink of implosion, necessarily becoming the new inhabited space" (Vaillancourt 28, my translation). The Innu forcibly forge the ancestral communal bond within the penitentiary order of the reserve, in response to the violence of Settler-Indigenous relations. This determination of space, which forces some to seek refuge from violence on one hand, whereas it opens up the land and marginalized populations to exploitation on the other, is in stark contrast with the inclusivity and hospitality of First Nations cultures, specifically the pedagogy of generosity, which simultaneously invites all to join the circle *and* to enlarge their ontological horizons to encompass all things. Related to that narrative of survivance is the articulation of an Indigenous futurity, one that serves to reappropriate the laden space of the reserve.

> In my language, to name the reserve, we say innu-assi, the land of the Innu. Belonging settles inside the places and the people that inhabit them. The day when there is no longer a reserve, and I do believe that that day will come, we will dream, we will make babies, we will dance the makushan, freely in the innu-assi. (*Shuni* 66, my translation)

Naming is a powerful act of defining with myriad ramifications. It has been discussed at multiple points throughout this study in the context of European colonialism. For the West, naming has played a role in dispossession and making geographies of the Americas a part of economies of extraction. In Innu there is a different ideology at work in naming practices. Rather than ownership, Innu naming foregrounds the presence of the people, their inhabiting of a place whose purpose is to "destroy their culture" in the words of An Antane Kapesh. As seen above, this reappropriation speaks to the ingenuity of the Innu people in the face of tragedy. This is an example of survivance, because rather than internalize or echo settler-colonial messages of "tragic victimry", the reserve in Fontaine's writing is a place that manifests resistance. It is what Vizenor calls a tribal story "told at the end of federal exclaves and reservations", one that challenges

Voices in Francophone Indigenous Literature 209

prevailing simulations and hierarchies to recenter the Native on the land (*Manifest Manners* 68). It is not surprising that the people come first in the Innu-aimun formulation of reserve: *Innu-assi*. For Fontaine, the reserve paradoxically solders bonds and rebuilds bridges strained or broken by settler-colonialism *by* institutionalizing the carceral space of the reserve itself. Elsewhere, Fontaine points to the legal structures that deny true ownership of reserve lots to Indigenous residents, reserving ownership for the settler-state. The long history of violence associated with imprisonment on the reserve is not perceived in the same way by all. The passage does not speak for the entire Innu community. What Fontaine envisions in this passage is forward-looking. The author predicts the end of the reserve, not as inhabited space, not as the land of the Innu, but as a settler-colonial structure, one that defines the space as reserve and settler-state property. What Fontaine foresees is a return to the ontologies that she mentions in a previous citation, to that land "without enclosures, without borders". This is echoed in the actions she envisions: dancing, dreaming, procreation, which will all be undertaken "freely". The return of the land signals a return to Native ontologies, to that world wherein the word "freedom" did not exist, because it "never needed to be named", as it was the normal state for "everything that exists". Fontaine's revisionist take on the meaning of reserve geographies, reappropriated and transformed into productive of communal bonds, is essential to the Indigenous futurity that the author imagines when the Innu-assi becomes Nutshimit once again. Indeed Fontaine's writing is centered on both teaching (pedagogy of generosity) and futurity, both of which function as narratives of survivance. Education is a fraught topic in Settler-Indigenous relations. The residential school system and the recent discoveries of the extent of abuses and deaths that occurred under the aegis of the settler-state's assimilatory policies are coupled with tensions related to linguistic and cultural erasure inherent to a Euro-Canadian curriculum.

> How the Indians, who never wanted to be white, were kidnapped, the children scattered, taken elsewhere during the hard months of the school year to give, so they were told, some meaning to their intelligence. This family feud will never be settled; how can the son ask the father for forgiveness? A cinder on the heart, one more wrinkle on the brow. (*Kuessipan* 44)

The intergenerational trauma signaled by Fontaine refers to the residential school system. While explicit for First Nations, Indigenous Studies scholars and critics engaged with research in settler-colonial practices in North America, the allusions to the residential school system are opaquer for the non-informed reader. A characteristic trait of her writing, Fontaine often speaks through silences and lacunae. Huberman contends that, "Silence reveals itself by a reticence in her writing: the presence of large blank spaces, the ambiguity of words and the starkness of short austere sentences that only say the minimum (120, my translation).

210   *Voices in Francophone Indigenous Literature*

Suggesting and hinting, employing the implicit, rather than tearing off the bandage to expose the wound underneath, Fontaine's style mirrors the traumatic ground that her writing covers. To encapsulate the intergenerational break caused by the residential school, one that attempted to teach Native children to depreciate and renounce their culture, in such a terse way, is evidence of the trauma at the heart of the "feud" that tears families apart. Education in the settler-colonial system is at once negative and positive, which represents a considerable evolution since Kapesh's *Sauvagesse*. Kapesh unrepentantly denounces the Euro-Canadian education system as premediated cultural genocide. Fontaine's relationship with institutional structures is more ambiguous. Fontaine argues that the reasoning given for the violent confinement of First Nations children is to "give some meaning to their intelligence". This statement merits further consideration, especially given the fact that Fontaine herself is professionally dedicated to teaching French, the subject of her second novel *Manikanetish*. Much like the author's reappropriation of reserve spaces, the educational system's cultural eradication is inverted in her oeuvre. A Université de Laval graduate, Fontaine returns to Uashat and teaches French.

> It was unthinkable that I would resign myself to only teaching grammar, all those incongruous rules and the cedilla that makes a letter soften. I would teach them the world and how to see it. And how to love it. And how to defeat that immobile, outdated fence: the reserve, that we call a community to soften the heart. (*Manikanetish* 13, my translation)

This scene takes place before the first class begins. A young teacher named Yammie readies the classroom and reflects on what her goals are for the academic year. Rather than limit herself to the required material, the novel ends after a successful class performance of Pierre Corneille's *Le Cid* at the end of the school year, the narrator having acquired a broader view of her role as teacher in the Innu community. The teacher in *Manikanetish*, a clear autobiographical reference to the author herself, intimates her vision of the pedagogy of generosity in an Indigenous community. The young pupils are more than mere students, they are children of the community, and as such of supreme importance. Instilling Indigenous knowledge is a critical aspect of the narrator's plan for the schoolyear. To 'teach them the world and how to see it', is indicative of the pedagogy of generosity, an ethos that infuses all three texts under discussion in this section. As Bacon writes, "I teach my identity, In a classroom" (69, my translation). In Fontaine revisionism of the space of the reserve, the positive discourse and Indigenous futurity that it entails is a lesson to the Innu community *and* the Québécois community. Teaching the Innu community to look differently at the reserve is to prepare a path forward to effectuate the transformation of that settler-colonial space into one of futurity where original "freedom" is revived. This message, as well as the commitment to instruct Innu children to overcome

Voices in Francophone Indigenous Literature   211

barriers that delineate the reserve. The pedagogy of generosity provides vital information. The act of teaching is intentional, and according to Huberman, is motivated by love.

> The transmission of knowledge passes through a relation of love and connection... Far from a simple transfer of information from a teacher to a student, the founding principals of education are spiritual, which leads to personal and compassionate interactions. The transmission of knowledge is *felt* rather than being purely cognitive; the learning process takes place via a multitude of cognitive and emotional functions. (Huberman 119, my translation)

Huberman affirms that the pedagogy of generosity exceeds the bounds of the typical teacher-student relationship. The spiritual and emotional is evident in *Manikanetish*. Throughout the schoolyear, Yammie helps her students navigate tragic events that occur outside the classroom and that extend her relationship with them into the emotional and spiritual places that Huberman identifies, engaging in interactions that are frequently "personal and compassionate". By underlining the essential nature of an Indigenous approach to teaching, Huberman recalls Greg Cajete's (Tewa) insight, that in Indigenous communities knowledge passes through all four states of being: mind, body, emotion, spirit (qtd. in Kimmerer 46). It is necessary for the narrator to involve herself in such an intimate way because the students of Uashat face many challenges. Suicide, teen pregnancy, and the death of a parent are some of the troubles that the young teacher confronts with her students, demonstrating love and a pedagogy of generosity. Huberman's accentuation of the emotional and spiritual aspects of knowledge transferal in Amerindian culture is echoed in how the Nutshimit (the land) plays a significant role in the development of a more personal connection between the narrator and her pupils. The land is critical to the transmission of knowledge. When Yammie decides to take her students on a fieldtrip into the forest, both teacher and student learn something. The narrator describes it as the first time she had ever personally experienced Nutshimit, though she had "often heard people talk about it" (*Manikanetish* 104, my translation).

> We were someplace else, someplace better, very far from books and desks. Very far from social media and gossip on reserve. Very far from suffering and family tragedies. Farther still than any place I'd ever set foot before. And yet we were so close. So close to who we are. (*Manikanetish* 106, my translation)

The connection with the land is a catalyst that ignites a rekindling of community. One of the recurrent themes of *Manikanetish* is the narrator's struggles with self-confidence in the classroom. During the fieldtrip, the geography of Nutshimit leads the teacher to feel accepted and safe in the community, something the narrator was in search of all along. The students even drop the formal

212 *Voices in Francophone Indigenous Literature*

madame in favor of her first name, Yammie. In *Sauvagesse*, Kapesh insists that there should be "Indians who teach [the child] in the forest, so that he knows the forest" (64, my translation). Kapesh's advice that Innu teachers should take Innu children into the forest and teach them manifests in Fontaine's *Manikanet-ish* as an example of a pedagogy of generosity and a narrative of survivance. The skeleton key to profound knowledge of the self, the land is the best class-room. *Manikanetish* speaks to a visceral reality in the author's private life, the profession of teaching, specifically in the context of teaching children from the Innu community on her home reserve of Uashat. A pedagogy of generosity is teaching through the land and through the community, teaching the Indigenous *and* non-Indigenous reader to expand personhood to "everything that exists". Radical inclusivity is a hallmark of a pedagogy of generosity. In her third book-length project, Naomi Fontaine writes an essay titled *Shuni: Ce que tu dois savoir, Julie*, the subtitle can be translated as "What you have to know, Julie". Written to a childhood friend, the daughter of a missionary now return-ing to the reserve as a missionary herself, *Shuni* reveals the centrality of the pedagogy of generosity in Fontaine's writing. To dedicate an entire non-fiction text to a non-Indigenous person who is coming to the community in a role that has historically been fraught in Settler-Indigenous relations, is clear evidence of the author's commitment to an ethic of inclusion. The essay functions as a guidebook for Julie to best understand the Innu. Fontaine shares of herself and her community in *conversation* with the non-Indigenous interlocutor.

> Everything that went through me, that I left behind, that made me grow up, that I love. Without advice, without judging. Because I believe that before helping someone, before trying to transform their unfathomable pain into joy, their unspoken tragedies into happiness, before talking to them about Jesus, you should start by getting to know them. Their stories, their identity, their ideals, what they dream about at night. The daily lives of the people she has chosen to help. I would add that I respect those who take distant roads in order to work in the heart of our communities, those like Julie. I admire their courage and their empathy. I know that the intentions are good. But I also know that that is not enough. (*Shuni* 7, my translation)

Fontaine situates this passage very near the opening of the text. It serves as a framing device, providing clues to the reader and Julie, the recipient of the text. It lays groundwork for what follows by identifying the urgency of the essay, the questions it seeks to answer. Rather than a wholesale indictment of non-Indigenous culture, *Shuni* is offered in "respect" and with a fair dose of "ad-miration" for the Euro-Canadian woman to whom it is written. The essay is a roadmap for those who "take distant roads" to do charitable work in Native com-munities. The urgent direction that it provides is to take a profound interest in the daily lives of the Innu people. Without knowing someone, Fontaine argues,

Voices in Francophone Indigenous Literature   213

it is inconceivable that one could assist them in alleviating their agonies or over-coming obstacles. To get to know the Innu, Fontaine offers a broad inventory of her own lived experience. This type of far-reaching dispensation is redolent of a pedagogy of generosity because it models that attribute and encourages its extension to others. When the author recognizes the good will of those who would offer their time and energy to Native communities, she also signals a site of danger, an urgency that must be addressed. Without mutual understanding and reciprocity, "good intentions" can have disastrous consequences. What is shared over the approximately ninety following pages is a comprehensive supply of vital information meant for the success of the Euro-Canadian's mission in Innu country. As discussed above, Fontaine views the revolution whereby the reserve becomes a bastion of community and solidarity as indicative of Innu identity, as a narrative of survivance, referencing the Innu's astonishing ability to invite others into the circle, despite the difficult history of Settler-Indigenous relations. This type of relentless invitation is characteristic of a pedagogy of generosity. *Shuni* reveals an insider's view of the Innu community but later concludes that this collective perspective is problematic.

> I don't condemn your fear or your ignorance. What bothers me are the boxes. Those little, tiny boxes into which outsiders think they are qualified to clas-sify us. The good Indian, the spiritual Indian, the civilized Indian, the savage Indian, the down-trodden Indian. To undo a prejudice, you have to start by admitting that it exists. I hate those preconceived notions that make it so we are all the same... Writing to you in the name of this "we", reminds me that this "we" only exists in speeches. Where I'm from, you will see the Innu identity of the group, but you'll never really get to know us until that totality disappears, making way for each one of us [each individual Innu]. (*Shuni* 41, my translation)

In this passage, Fontaine engages directly with the subject of this study. The mythic machine's distortions, (mis)understandings, and (mis)representations in the form of the Noble and Ignoble Savage, the Ecological Savage, the Van-ishing Indian, and the Going Native mythologies, categorizing in ways that do not take the internal reality of the Amerindian Other into account. These nar-rative technologies abet (settler)-colonial encroachment and violence, racism and discrimination, the murder and rape of Indigenous women, the deaths of First Nations children in residential schools, removal and confinement, allot-ment and blood quantum, and other offenses. Fontaine locates the site of danger very clearly, pinpointing where the mythic machine's myopia resides, it is the mythic penchant that erases individual realities, the "daily lives" of the Amerin-dian Other, that must be warned about. While the West deals freely in sweeping generalities and dangerous mythic messages that are adopted in a variety of dis-cursive regimes, adapting and evolving into scientific *truth*, Indigenous cultures

214   *Voices in Francophone Indigenous Literature*

promote inclusivity, relationality, mutual respect, and listening. The Haudeno-saunee talking stick discussed in the preceding section is a pertinent example of how Indigenous cultures cultivate community in *conversation*, not univocal and unidirectional mythmaking. Fontaine deconstructs the mythic machine by con-demning how it distorts the individual into the collective. It does not consider the complex experiences of the Other as equal to non-Indigenous experiences. This is a failure to communicate in mutuality and is not commensurate with Na-tive lifeways. As Fontaine says so simply and elegantly: "To undo a prejudice you have to start by admitting that it exists". That has been the aim of this study, to reveal the existence of this peculiar variety of prejudice, the mythic lens as a means of apprehending and representing the Other, one that certainly must be undone. To conclude, I will examine a scene in the cinematic version of Naomi Fontaine's début novel, *Kuessipan*, released in 2019, directed by Myriam Ver-reault, and starring Sharon Fontaine-Ishpatao as Mikuan and Yamie Grégoire as Shaniss.

In a writing contest, the protagonist Mikuan finishes the reading of her piece by paraphrasing the citation discussed above wherein the author states that there is no word for freedom in her language, Innu-aimun. Standing before a large audience, the camera focuses on Mikuan's face as she reads, panning back to her parents and her best friend Shaniss holding her new-born, all look on sup-portively, registering the truth of the words they are hearing. Mikuan tries to find a word in her language that might be close to freedom.

> Perhaps Nutshimit. Nutshimit is the land, the land of our ancestors. Nutshimit is peace. The silence of the stream following its path, hidden under a meter of snow. Nutshimit is not a place. It's the vastness. The reserve is a place. I hate this word. But since it exists, we must name it. I think it's possible, without our realizing, that the place where we live rubs off on us. To believe those who tell us who we are. To embrace a life of limited ambition. And meekly accept that we are born without promise. Pride is not a repressed emotion. or feathers worn in our hair or beads sewn on my jacket. Pride is something you build.

As the last sentence is read, the shot fades in on a caribou skin drum being rhyth-mically struck. Mikuan continues reading.

To stand up straight, you must believe in your legitimacy.

As the sentence is trailing toward the full stop, the camera backs away and reveals the face of an elderly Innu man beating on the drum.

And thus, perhaps, you can begin to conceive what freedom is.

The camera pans left to reveal Mikuan's best friend Shaniss bouncing her newborn in her arms as she dances in a circle with other Innu women and girls. Still following Shaniss and her baby, Mikuan switches to Innu-Aimun.

You who understand what I am saying, I want you to know that my pride is us.

Voices in Francophone Indigenous Literature 215

The camera briefly follows Mikuan's young sister before turning to reveal that Mikuan's mother Louise is dancing in the circle.

Like you, I am Innu.

The camera moves away from Mikuan's mother and lingers on young girls who watch the dancers, learning how the dance is done. One girl holds birthday balloons, the camera backs away revealing a birthday banner and community members sitting on tables behind the dancefloor. The camera switches focus to a closeup of Mikuan's grandmother Nukum who looks pensively into space, leaning her head on her hand like Rodin's *The Thinker*. The camera leaves Nukum and shows a toddler with a pacifier in his mouth, a baby bottle half full of milk in one hand, trailing a blue baby blanket on the concrete floor of the community center, another toddler approaches. Suddenly, the mood shifts. The camera focuses on Mikuan's younger sister laughing joyously, hugging other children. More girls, teenagers, are shown embracing in circles and laughing boisterously. The camera switches back to Nukum who is now in the dance circle and laughing as enthusiastically as the children. Mikuan and Shaniss, sitting on folding chairs watching the dance circle, burst into laughter. More circles of embracing, laughing people are formed. A middle-aged man in a baseball cap joins in the dance and embraces several little girls. A circle of elders, men and women, is shown embracing in uproarious laughter. Mikuan's voice is heard reading again, in French now.

For if my feet are drawn down new paths,

The camera returns to the auditorium, leaving the dancers at the reserve's community center behind, abruptly showing a closeup of Shaniss and her newborn. Shaniss listens in rapt attention as Mikuan goes on.

If my eyes tirelessly scan the horizon,

The camera moves to Mikuan at the podium looking out at the crowd.

I will always know where my heart is rooted. That, perhaps, is part of what freedom is.

After an awkward, uncertain pause.

Thank you.

The camera moves behind Mikuan, she is a pyramid in the center of the frame, but the focus is on the crowd, with familiar faces, such as Mikuan's parents, but mostly Euro-Canadians. The crowd erupts in ardent applause and Mikuan walks away from the podium.

This scene reveals many of the features of Francophone Indigenous voices in Québécois literature. The centering of the idea of freedom in the land, Nutshimit, echoes the prioritization of the land in all the authors' works that we have explored. In addition, it foregrounds community and stepping outside into non-Indigenous geographies. The scene begins in an auditorium filled mostly with non-Indigenous. Mikuan is the only First Nations writer in the contest. Before returning to the auditorium, most of the scene takes place in a community center on reserve. The birthday party that includes a traditional Innu dance,

216 *Voices in Francophone Indigenous Literature*

with a caribou skin drum keeping the rhythm, is redolent of the passage quoted above wherein Fontaine reappropriates the carceral space of the reserve as constructive of collectivity. The camera moves from focusing on Mikuan's younger sister, to Mikuan's mother, and then to Mikuan's grandmother. Throughout the dance portion of the scene, intergenerational relationships are emphasized, with chronological movement through life stages beginning with the baby in Shaniss' arms, moving to toddler, teenage, adult, and elderly. Papillon notes that to understand Fontaine's *Kuessipan*, it is crucial to recognize that "the community is inscribed in a network of intergenerational relations that extends forwards and backwards in time" (64, my translation). The scene also calls to mind the citation discussed above that imagines the end of the reserve and the joyousness and procreation that will ensue when that miracle finally comes to pass. The insistence on Shaniss' baby situates the scene as one based on forging a futurity for the Innu people. This reading is reinforced by the realistic, yet optimistic outlook espoused throughout the film. The eruption of hilarity and laughter is a contagious moment in a film that has otherwise been laden with seriousness and tragedy. This scene clearly portrays the happy day when the reserve is no more and now is transformed from Innu-assi into Nutshimit. All the texts that we have examined in this chapter are narratives of survivance, insisting on building a "modern image of the future", one that denounces the simulations of the "indian", the mythic machine's distortions and (mis)representations. Gerald Vizenor (Chippewa) contends that the tragic mode, one that has all too often been employed to portray the reserve as a carceral geography associated with (cultural) death, should be met with Native laughter (*Manifest Manners* 83). To engage in a pedagogy of generosity is to share vital information, sites of danger, to share strategies for survival. A key element of the pedagogy of generosity is that generosity is a fundamental component of the imparting of vital information to the Indigenous community *and* the non-Indigenous community. In addition to the sharing of essential knowledge, an urgent aspect of the knowledge itself is the generosity, not only to include the Amerindian in the human community as an equal member of the "circle" of democracy, but also to include the non-human into the community as a member with the intentionality adherent to the full range of human experience. Narratives of survivance are not merely stories that bolster communal bonds, they expand them outward.

Works Cited

Bacon, Joséphine. *Un thé dans la toundra/Nipishapui nete mushuat*. Kindle edition, Mémoire d'Encrier, 2013.

Brostom, Jennifer Allison and James P. Draper. "Yvès Thériault". *Contemporary Literary Criticism Vol. 79. Internet Archive*. Edited by Jennifer Allison Brostom and James P. Draper. Gale Research, 1994. https://archive.org/details/isbn_9780810349872/page/398/mode/2up. 4 May 2023.

Voices in Francophone Indigenous Literature   217

Coulthard, Glen Sean. *Red Skin, White Masks: Rejecting the Colonial Politics of Recognition*. Kindle edition. Minneapolis: University of Minnesota Press, 2014.

Descola, Philippe. *Par-delà nature et culture*. Kindle version. Paris: Éditions Gallimard, 2015.

Deloria, Vine Jr. *God Is Red: A Native View of Religion, 30th Anniversary Edition*. Golden: Fulcrum Publishing, 2003.

Fontaine, Naomi. *Kuessipan*. Translated by David Homel. Kindle version. Montréal: Arsenal Pulp Press, 2013.

————. *Manikanetish*. Montréal: Mémoire d'encrier, 2017.

————. "Préface". *Eukuan Nin Matshi-Manitu Innushkueu/Je suis une maudite sauvagesse*, by An Antane Kapesh. Translated by José Mailhot. Edited by Naomi Fontaine. Kindle edition. Montréal: Mémoire d'Encrier, 2019. pp. 4–9.

————. *Shuni*. Kindle version. Montréal: Mémoire d'encrier, 2019.

Gatti, Maurizio. *Littérature amérindienne du Québec: Écrits de langue française*. Montréal: Bibliothèque québécoise, 2009.

Huberman, Isabella. "Les possibles de l'amour décolonial: relations, transmissions et silences dans *Kuessipan* de Naomi Fontaine." *Voix plurielles*, vol. 13, no. 2, 2016, pp. 111–26. doi:10.26522/vp.v13i2.1441. 10 May 2023.

Huhndorf, Shari M. *Mapping the Americas: The Transnational Politics of Contemporary Native Culture*. Ithaca, NY: Cornell UP, 2009.

Kapesh, An Antane. *Eukuan Nin Matshi-Manitu Innushkueu/Je suis une maudite sauvagesse*. Translated by José Mailhot. Edited by Naomi Fontaine. Kindle edition. Montréal: Mémoire d'Encrier, 2019.

Kuessipan. Directed by Myriam Verreault. Performances by Sharon Fontaine-Ishpatao and Yamie Grégoire. Max Films Media, 2019.

Kimmerer, Robin Wall. *Braiding Sweetgrass: Indigenous Wisdom, Scientific Knowledge, and the Teachings of Plants*. Kindle version. Minneapolis: Milkweed Editions, 2013.

Mailhot, José. *Shushei au pays des Innus*. Kindle edition. Montréal: Mémoire d'Encrier, 2021.

Mestokosho, Rita. *Atik^u Utei/Le cœur du caribou*. Kindle edition. Montréal: Mémoire d'Encrier, 2022.

Papillon, Joëlle. "Apprendre et guéirr: Les rapports intergénérationnels chez An Antane Kapesh, Virginia Pésémapéo Bordeleau et Naomi Fontaine." *Recherches amérindiennes au Québec*, vol. 46, no. 2–3, 2016, pp. 57–65. https://doi.org/10.7202/1040434ar.

Perron, Paul. *Narratology and Text: Subjectivity and Identity in New France and Québécois Literature*. University of Toronto Press, 2003. *JSTOR*, https://doi.org/10.3138/9781442677562. 5 May 2023.

Premat, Christophe. "Retrouver les voix autochtones: L'hommage de Jean-Marie Gustave Le Clézio à Rita Mestokosho." *Les Cahiers J-M G Le Clézio*, vol. 7, 2014, pp. 119–26.

Schweninger, Lee. *Listening to the Land: Native American Literary Responses to the Landscape*. Kindle version. Athens: The University of Georgia Press, 2008.

Silko, Leslie Marmon. *Storyteller*. Kindle version. New York: Penguin Books, 2012.

Thériault, Yvès. *Ashini*. Longueil: Le Dernier Havre, 2006.

Vaillancourt, Marie-Ève. "Un heritage à habiter: Lecture géopoétique de *Kuessipan/À toi* et de *Puamun, le rêve*, de Naomi Fontaine." *Recherches amérindiennes au Québec*, vol. 47, no. 1, 2017. https://doi.org/10.7202/1042896ar. 10 May 2023.

218 *Voices in Francophone Indigenous Literature*

Vizenor, Gerald. *Manifest Manners: Narratives on Postindian Survivance*. Lincoln: University of Nebraska Press, 1999.

———. *Native Liberty: Natural Reason and Cultural Survivance*. Kindle version. Lincoln: University of Nebraska Press, 2009.

Whitt, Laurelyn. *Science, Colonialism, and Indigenous Peoples: The Cultural Politics of Law and Knowledge*. Cambridge: Cambridge UP, 2009.

Index

Abenaki 13, 32, 37
Achuar 171
Aimard, Gustave 80, 96, 98, 99–100, 102–106
Alès, Catherine 58
Alfred, Taiaiake 1–2
Algonquin 31
anaphora 179–180, 183, 199
anarchism 159–161
Anderson, Benedict 49–51, 72, 84
androgyny 9, 115–116, 135–137, 150, 153, 165
animism 130, 172, 199
Anishnaabe 131
anthropology 9–10, 22, 41, 50, 92, 114, 120, 154–155, 157, 159–162, 164–166, 171
anthropophagy (cannibalism) 47, 53–56, 58–59, 62, 65, 95, 116, 133, 162–165
Araucanian 106, 126
Armouchiquois 7, 13, 30–36, 42, 45, 47
Assiniwi, Bernard 169

Bacon, Joséphine 168, 178, 184–189, 191–194, 196, 198, 201, 210
berdache 9, 80, 114–115, 119, 135–137, 146, 149–150, 153–154, 165
Berkhofer Jr., Robert F. 16, 36, 39
Bhabha, Homi 9, 55, 100, 110
bilingualism 178, 180, 186–187, 189, 201
Billington, Ray Allen 83, 87, 93
Blanchard, Pascal 92–93
Bourdieu, Pierre 10, 15, 17, 29, 48, 84–86, 155
Boussenard, Louis 80, 94–95
Brostom, Jennifer Allison 169

Bruyneel, Kevin 110, 126, 134
Buffon, George-Louis Leclerc 2, 5, 7–8, 15, 37, 46, 49, 63–77, 116
Byrd, Jodi 4

cannibalism (anthropophagy) 47, 53–56, 58–59, 62, 65, 95, 116, 133, 162–165
Carib 16–20
Cartier, Jacques 30–31, 146, 148
Césaire, Aimé 185
Champlain, Samuel de 7, 13, 29–36, 42–43, 45, 47, 69, 137
Chevalier, Henri-Émile 80, 96, 101–102, 104–106, 137
Chinook 104–106
circumscription 24, 29, 45, 100, 150
Clastres, Pierre 120, 154, 159–164, 166
colonial culture 92–93, 95
Columbus, Christopher 91, 94, 125, 190
compartmentalization 26–27, 108
conversation 4, 170–171, 176, 181–183, 189–190, 193, 196, 198
Cooper, James Fenimore 80, 83–84, 174
Coulthard, Glen Sean 1, 33, 52, 182, 199
coureur de bois 80–81, 94, 142–143
Crosby, Alfred 94
crossdressing 136–137, 150, 153–154
crystallization 9, 79, 90, 138
Cuvier, Georges 15

D'Auriac, Jules Berlioz 98
Darwin, Charles 15, 63
De Léry, Jean 133, 137
De Lutri, Joseph R. 38
Debord, Guy 163
Defoe, Daniel 10, 119–121, 123, 156

220 *Index*

Deloria Jr., Vine 3, 49, 52, 112–113, 164, 184
Deloria, Philip J. 2, 23, 82, 131, 140–141
Descartes, René 68, 70–71, 171
Descola, Phillipe 171–172, 199
Dickason, Olive P. 30–31, 128
disappearance 4–5, 97–98, 100, 103, 106, 111, 141, 158–159
discovery 10, 17, 146, 158
Doniger, Wendy 155
Douglas, Bronwen 47, 50
Draper, James P. 169
Duchet, Michèle 14, 48, 53
Duplessis, Maurice 153, 172
Dupuis, Melissa Mollen 169
Durand, Yvès Sioui 169
Durkheim, Émile 2, 5, 9, 37, 79–80, 107–116, 154–156

Eldorado 8, 46, 53, 58–62, 77, 148
embodiment 8, 46, 57, 114, 135, 153, 171
Enlightenment 8, 13, 26, 36, 43, 45–47, 49, 56, 61–62, 70, 72, 75, 121, 123, 126, 205

Fanon, Frantz 19, 89
Ferry, Gabriel 96–98
Fontaine, Naomi 11, 65, 168, 172, 179, 202–216
Fontaine, Natasha Kanapé 169
Foucault, Michel 27–28, 68, 72, 75–76
Freud, Sigmund 121, 128
frontier 4, 41, 79–89, 96, 98, 102–103, 106, 141, 207

Gamber, John 92
Garneau, François-Xavier 138–143
Gatti, Maurizio 168–169, 186–187, 201
Geertz, Clifford 164
gender 5, 9, 65, 79, 107, 113–116, 125–126, 135–137, 149–150, 153–154, 165–166, 199
Gervais, Albert 144
golden age 61, 141, 158–159
Guanches 94
Guayaki 159–165

Handley, George 130, 133–134
Haudenosaunee (Iroquois) 31, 101, 115, 138, 151–152, 192–193, 196, 198

Havard, Gilles 142
Hegel, Georg Wilhelm Friedrich 49, 161
Heidegger, Martin 159
Hémon, Louis 141–144
Hobbes, Thomas 160
Howard, Richard 25
Huberman, Isabella 207, 209, 211
Hugo, Victor 45, 47
Huhndorf, Shari M. 5, 9, 81, 118, 123, 126, 130–133, 147
Huron (Wendat) 5, 101, 138–144
Hurtado, Albert 65–66

imagined community 49–50, 67, 82, 89, 102
Inca 39, 60
indolence 51–53, 59
innocence 17, 24, 29, 40–42, 61, 140, 151–152
insensitivity 104–106
Inuit 11, 64, 68–72, 169
inversion 38
Iroquois (Haudenosaunee) 31, 101, 115, 138, 151–152, 192–193, 196, 198

Jesuit 53–57, 69, 162–165

Kalyniuk, Gregory 159–160
Kapesh, An Antane 11, 168, 173, 177–189, 195, 199, 204, 206, 208, 210, 212
Kerouac, Jack 148
Kimmerer, Robin Wall 131–132, 190–195, 198, 201
Krech III, Shepard 133–134
Kroeber, Karl 92, 118

La Condamine, Charle-Marie de 8, 45, 48–53, 57, 72, 75, 77, 116, 182
Lalonde, Robert 10, 119, 146, 149–152, 154
Lescarbot, Marc 34
Lestringant, Frank 54, 163
Lévi-Strauss, Claude 5, 9, 18, 22, 37, 120, 154–159, 162, 166, 171
Lévy-Bruhl, Lucien 37
Lewis and Clark 146
Lopez, Barry 152

Magellan 28
Mailhot, José 178, 184
Malinche 146–147

Manifest Destiny 81, 106, 148
martyrology 98–100, 106, 139
Marx, Karl 52, 182–183
McNab, David T. 31
Memmi, Albert 91–92
Mestokosho, Rita 168, 178, 185–203
métis 146
Micmac 31–34
mission civilisatrice 54, 63, 93, 97, 100, 103, 122
Montaigne, Michel de 3, 7, 13, 35–43, 60–62, 125, 156, 158–159, 206
Morency, Jean 144
Morgensen, Scott Lauria 9, 56–57, 80–83, 114–116, 119, 135–136, 146, 153–154

nationalism 4, 9, 84, 89
natural abundance 18, 41, 53, 72
natural history 5, 8, 46, 65–72, 75–77
naturalism 171–172, 199, 207
naturalization 8–9, 23, 27–28, 42, 50–52, 57, 79, 81, 88, 91, 107–110, 116, 135–136, 152, 180, 199, 206
Negritude 185
New Age 124, 130, 145, 164
Nietzsche, Friedrich 159
Noël, Michel 169
nudity 57, 64, 125, 136–137, 149–150, 153

Oreillons 8, 45–8, 53–60, 62, 75, 77

Papillon, Joëlle 183, 207, 216
Patagonian giants 7, 13, 24–29, 32, 42, 47, 72–76
perfectibility 15, 21, 72
Perron, Paul 169
Plamondon, Antoine 138
polygenism 47, 59–60
Poulin, Jacques 10, 119, 146–150, 154
Pouyllau, Michel 58
Povinelli, Elizabeth 17, 55–56
Prats, Armando José 97–99, 102–103
Pratt, Mary Louise 9, 51–52, 93
Premat, Christophe 187, 202–203
primitive 1, 5, 9, 17, 20–21, 87, 107–110, 114, 116, 121–122, 130, 132, 134, 136, 154–165, 205
primitive accumulation 52, 182
progress 52, 71–74, 99–102, 106–116, 177

queer 5–6, 9–11, 56–58, 77–81, 114–116, 135–137, 151, 154, 165–166
Quiet Revolution 153

Racevskis, Roland 132, 137
recognition, limits of 17, 56, 64–65, 194
reserve 168–169, 172–176, 179, 182–184, 203, 207–216
residential school system 180–183, 196, 209–210, 213
retrograde 107, 110–111, 115–116
Richman, Michèle 37
Rousseau, Jean-Jacques 3, 7, 13–24, 35–37, 40–42, 53, 72, 83, 111, 125, 156–157, 160, 164, 170–171
Rowe, John 47
Roy, Fernande 138
Rufin, Jean-Christophe 10, 119–120, 124–127, 132–137, 146, 149–151, 154, 165

Sacajawea 146–147
Saïd, Edward 15, 24, 88
Samian 169
Schweninger, Lee 1, 130–131, 134, 169
Seth, Vanita 88, 118
settler-colonialism 1–2, 4–9, 33, 36, 46, 55–57, 62, 65, 81–83, 96, 99, 106, 114–116, 134–135, 145–154, 162, 169, 172–188, 191–199, 202, 205, 208–213
Silko, Leslie Marmon 177, 180, 199
simulation 6, 23–24, 92, 101, 127, 131, 135, 135, 153, 159, 180, 185, 209, 216
Sioui, Georges E. 5
Slotkin, Richard 85
sociology 5, 9, 79, 107–116, 155
Soucy, Jean-Yvès 144–145
Souriquois 31–33
Soyinka, Wole 26–28, 108–109

terra nullius 1, 33, 34, 54, 134
Thériault, Yvès 10, 168–176
Thevet, André 7, 13, 24–29, 30, 32, 42, 45, 47, 63, 119, 125, 156, 158
Tierra del Fuego 53, 72–75
Todorov, Tzvetan 25–26, 36–37
Tournier, Michel 10, 119–132, 146, 148–151, 165

222 *Index*

transferability 8, 13, 22, 33, 43, 45, 47, 50, 75, 109–110, 159
transindigenous 7, 198
transnational 7, 51, 80, 138, 146, 186–187, 198–199
Tupinamba 7, 13, 25, 38–41, 69, 119–120, 125–126, 133
Turner, Frederick Jackson 81
Turnovsky, Geoffrey 48

Vaillancourt, Marie-Ève 204, 208
Verne, Jules 94
Verreault, Myriam 168, 202

Villegagnon, Nicolas Durand de 26, 119, 125–127, 132–133, 136
Vizenor, Gerald 4, 6, 9, 12, 13, 23–24, 91–92, 96, 100–101, 124, 127, 130, 163, 177, 208, 216
Voltaire 8, 45–50, 53–62, 75, 77, 138

Wendat (Huron) 5, 101, 138–144
Whitt, Laurelyn 6, 10, 76, 112–113, 118, 170, 195
Windigo 131–132, 143–144
Wolfe, Patrick 57

Printed in the United States
by Baker & Taylor Publisher Services